Indian Renaissance

Indian Renaissance

The Modi Decade

edited by
Aishwarya Pandit

Published by Westland Non-Fiction, an imprint of Westland Books, a division of Nasadiya Technologies Private Limited, in 2024

No. 269/2B, First Floor, 'Irai Arul', Vimalraj Street, Nethaji Nagar, Alapakkam Main Road, Maduravoyal, Chennai 600095

Westland, the Westland logo, Westland Non-Fiction and the Westland Non-Fiction logo are the trademarks of Nasadiya Technologies Private Limited, or its affiliates.

Selection and introduction copyright © Aishwarya Pandit, 2024
The copyright for the essays vests with the individual authors.

ISBN: 9789360454968

10 9 8 7 6 5 4 3 2 1

The views and opinions expressed in this work are the authors' own and the facts are as reported by them, and the publisher is in no way liable for the same.

All rights reserved

Typeset by Jojy Philip, New Delhi

Printed at Thomson Press (India) Ltd

No part of this book may be reproduced, or stored in a retrieval system, or transmitted in any form or by any means, electronic, mechanical, photocopying, recording, or otherwise, without express written permission of the publisher.

Contents

Foreword Nirmala Sitharaman	ix
Introduction Aishwarya Pandit	xv
Rethinking Indian Democracy Tony Abbott	1
India and the Arab World under PM Modi Waiel Awwad	9
India, Britain and Lessons for Democracies Aman Bhogal	27
The Indian Economy, Capital Markets and Society under PM Modi Ashish Chauhan	32
Britain–India Defence Relations in the New Age of Shared Threats and Global Insecurity Robert Clark	53
India's Future: Global Leadership Scot Faulkner	59

A Decade of Transformation: The Moment of India's True Independence *Antonia Filmer*	78
Advancements in Technology and the Digital Revolution in India *Jonathan Fleming, Namit Choksi and Vinit Parikh*	88
Revolutionising Infrastructure: Bridging the Human Connect *Bharat Kaushal*	116
India that is Bharat: A Decade of Change *Avatans Kumar*	124
A New Chapter in Education in India *Rajiv Kumar*	136
The Health Revolution *Ann Liebert*	148
India–Japan Ties and the Security of the Indo-Pacific *Satoru Nagao*	159
Replacing the 'Idea of India' with the 'Idea of Bharat' *Madhav Das Nalapat*	176
India—Now More Than a Partner in Principle *Grant Newsham*	186
Dismantling a Legacy *Aishwarya Pandit*	203
Indian Re-emergence: The Foreign Policy Boom *Cleo Paskal*	223

The Redeemer's Rite: How Narendra Modi Has Redefined Power *S. Prasannarajan*	237
America and India: Brothers in Democracy, Only Cousins in Geopolitics *Don Ritter*	245
Vasudhaiva Kutumbakam: India and the World *Samir Saran*	259
The Disruptor vs the Inheritors *Priya Sahgal*	269
The Catalyst *Kartikeya Sharma*	279
India's Transformation from 2014 to 2024 *Penny Street*	292
The Decade of Progress for US–India Relations *Raymond E. Vickery, Jr*	303
Modi—Taking the BJP from Strength to Strength *Pankaj Vohra*	308
India Under Transformation *Taguchi Yoji*	320

Foreword

Congratulations to Dr Aishwarya Pandit for her commendable work on the book *Indian Renaissance: The Modi Decade*. This publication explores the transformative era ushered in by Hon'ble Prime Minister Shri Narendra Modi and covers various significant aspects of governance and policymaking.

This book, coinciding with ten years of the Modi government, is enriched by perspectives from a wide range of authors and narrates the story of a nation and its citizens surging forward, not in isolation, but as a vibrant part of the global family.

Since 2014, the approach to governance has undergone a decisive shift. Ensuring access to basic necessities—such as housing, water and sanitation—has been a driving imperative for PM Shri Narendra Modi-led government, the implementation of which is being seen on the ground.

In the last decade, every household has been electrified, and over 4 crore poor families now have the dignity of owning a pucca house under Pradhan Mantri Awas Yojana. Clean drinking water has reached over 11 crore families through the Jal Jeevan Mission. Over 11 crore household toilets have been constructed, achieving complete saturation in rural areas. More than 10 crore families have been provided cooking gas connections under Ujjwala Yojana, safeguarding women and children from the health hazards of smoke-filled kitchens. Through Ayushman Bharat, more than 34 crore people have been provided free health insurance coverage.

More than 52 crore people have been brought into the formal banking system through Jan Dhan Yojana, enabling them to access financial services, such as small savings schemes, insurance and affordable credit for the first time. Access to collateral-free credit has allowed micro-enterprises and young entrepreneurs to establish and grow their businesses—more than 47 crore entrepreneurs have been supported under PM MUDRA Yojana, and over 63 lakh street vendors have availed loans under PM SVANidhi.

As the foundational elements of a dignified life are secured and the vicious cycle of poverty and debt is broken, over 25 crore people have come out of poverty.

A strong and stable India benefits not only its citizens but also the broader international community. The Modi government's focus on stability and inclusive growth promotes regional peace and development, contributing positively to global affairs.

India's foreign policy under Prime Minister Modi has been both pragmatic and reflective of the nation's civilisational ethos. The principle 'Vasudhaiva Kutumbakam'—the world is one family—is deeply ingrained in Prime Minister Modi's diplomatic endeavours and resonates through the efforts to build a world that celebrates diversity, encourages cooperation, upholds mutual respect and seeks collective prosperity.

India's increasing confidence and recognition on the global stage are evident. Under Prime Minister Modi, the country has seen a rise in influence and stature, forging strong international relations and becoming a key player in global affairs.

India's successful hosting of the G20 Summit showcased its leadership and commitment to addressing global challenges, particularly those facing the Global South. The unanimous adoption of the G20 New Delhi Leaders' Declaration highlighted India's ability to build consensus among a diverse array of countries, showcasing PM Modi and India's diplomatic acumen and leadership on the global stage.

Prime Minister Modi's leadership has been pivotal as his government navigated through a host of significant challenges that it inherited upon taking office in 2014, along with new issues that have since emerged. Back in 2014, India was labelled as one of the 'Fragile Five' economies by a prominent financial services firm—a term that referred to emerging economies burdened with weak macroeconomic fundamentals such as sluggish growth, soaring inflation, high external deficits and faltering public finances. Additionally, a series of substantial corruption scandals seriously tarnished the credibility of India's governance, both at home and on the international stage. Through decisive leadership, corruption-free administration and agile policymaking, Prime Minister Modi ensured that India capably addressed the extraordinary challenges of the COVID-19 pandemic, highlighted by a robust vaccination drive and crucial support for those in dire need.

Prime Minister Modi has consistently made bold decisions and implemented reforms with the national interest at heart. These initiatives have strengthened governance, enhanced transparency and fuelled economic reforms, paving the way for a more robust Atmanirbhar Bharat.

Under Prime Minister Narendra Modi's leadership, India has experienced a leap in the creation and completion of infrastructure projects, even those that had been stalled for decades due to the lackadaisical attitude of the previous governments.

New roads, railways, airports, metro rails and digital connectivity have not only enhanced 'ease of living' for its citizens but also stimulated economic growth and accessibility across the nation.

Overcoming legal and governance hurdles, Prime Minister Modi has smoothly handled several cultural and civilisational issues that were left unattended for centuries. Recognising the role of regional languages, the use of technology has strengthened their use in education at all levels. Promotion of iconic tourist sites, enabling global recognition for traditional Indian knowledge systems, medicine, yoga and wellness are essentials in the story of the Indian renaissance.

With visionary policies and transformative reforms, India is progressing towards becoming a developed nation by 2047, as envisioned by Prime Minister Narendra Modi. This vision for a 'Viksit Bharat' is driven by technological advancements, sustainability and inclusive growth, marking a new era of development under Prime Minister Modi's leadership.

This book aptly provides a comprehensive overview of the Modi government's transformative initiatives and achievements, which have been instrumental in shaping a new era for India. Best wishes to Dr Aishwarya Pandit and the contributors for their diligent efforts in capturing this significant phase of India's history and contributing to the discourse on India's path to progress.

PM Modi had famously said in 2014: we have not come here to enjoy the fruits of being in power. We are here to undertake fundamental and transformational changes for India to realise its full potential.

Indian Renaissance has truly begun.

Nirmala Sitharaman

Introduction

In a recent interview with *Newsweek*, Prime Minister Narendra Modi fighting for a third term conveyed a strong sense of confidence on trouncing his opponents in the election. He certainly will be India's fifteenth prime minister when he is administered an oath in June. Critics would point out what is the use of such predictions when pollsters have often been proved wrong in the past as they were in 2004. But 2024 is not 2004 and Narendra Modi is not like his predecessor Atal Bihari Vajpayee. His confidence stems from his decade of governance, which I can conveniently define as the 'Modi Decade'. When asked why I was writing another book on the PM when so many other exist on the rise of Narendra Modi and his term in office, I felt the need for a book that captures all aspects of his years in office. Asked why I called it *Indian Renaissance* and why now, the compelling answer is that no other theme or title would capture the enormity of the cultural, social, political and economic transformation of the nation. I needed a title that captured its scale, its substance and yet also its fault lines and the challenges that make our nation reinvent itself every time and emerge greater. For those who may ask how this book is different, the answer is that while it seeks to map out the transformation that has taken place under Narendra Modi, it does not gloss over the challenges that the country still faces. *Indian Renaissance* captures varied perspectives from across the globe about India and her path to becoming a developed nation, and it includes converging viewpoints on different aspects of the last ten years. For a diverse country like ours, ten years is too short a period to completely alter the landscape and free the nation of its problems, but long enough to set changes in motion. In his own words, PM Modi is not yet done and he has a plan for what he intends to achieve in the next two decades.

While you may find people who agree or disagree with the politics of Narendra Modi in equal measure, they are in agreement that politics in the country would never be the same. The party in power is not a product of the Congress system, the opposition is not the same even though comparisons with 1977 are inevitable. But this is not India of 1977 either politically, socially or culturally. The challenges are far greater than before, along with the worsening climate crisis, rise in prices and challenges of job creation for a constantly rising young population. There are other challenges, too, that the country faces with an aggressive China and a destabilised Pakistan on the international front, but Narendra Modi's government has made a departure from the foreign policy of his predecessors. While there have been some remarkable successes, especially in how India is perceived abroad and its reception among the Indian diaspora, the challenges of unstable and aggressive neighbours remain. Internally, Indian politics has always been fractious and challenging due to the caste, regional and religious divisions. There is no denying that Narendra Modi has inherited these problems from years of policy paralysis, caste-based politics, rising regionalism and mixing of religion and politics. He is seeking a re-election on his record of governance, his foreign policy successes and his ability to override caste and religion dynamics. While the country and Narendra Modi himself have been beneficiaries of the social media revolution and availability of cheap data, he is cognizant of its dangers too. He acknowledges the human costs of this revolution and has been conscious of using himself as a platform and influencer to warn us of its dangers. Another key challenge is that of transparency in the political space, something he has been conscious about and has addressed especially the questions about electoral bonds and political funding which many in the nation are concerned about. In fact, he is the first Indian PM to discuss the issue of political funding. But it is not just the national-level political parties that need to be open about political funding. Regional parties too have much to discuss, especially when it comes to governance, championing of narrow interests and caste politics as these divides are bound to deepen and become a challenge to democracy in the coming years.

Another deep imprint and transformation apart from the field of governance is the changing nature of the Bharatiya Janata Party (BJP) under Modi. Under Modi, the BJP has become the largest political organisation in the world and it is also under Modi that a kind of ideological balance with its parent organisation, the Rashtriya Swayamsevak Sangh (RSS) has been achieved. It is under Modi that the party has been centred on the personality of one person as the principle vote getter, yet under him we have seen the rise of strong regional leadership within the BJP. Contrast this with the other national and the grand old party, the Congress, where regional leadership is fast shrinking, sacrificed at the altar of a centralised coterie which has nothing to do with the character of the party and that of its founding fathers. The regional parties that are offshoots of the Congress are still based on strong regional aspirations, driven by caste calculus , such as the Bahujan Samaj Party (BSP) and the Samajwadi Party (SP). This has led to prolonging of caste-based politics, which was the reason for their rise in the first place. The parties have not progressed further than the agenda of their founding fathers and thus command a narrow vote base. The challenges of mixing religion and politics and the ever-shrinking faith of the voters in the electoral process remain. Narendra Modi in particular has tried to bridge these gaps that exist and appeal to a rising and highly aspirational young voting population and recruit them in nation building.

There is no denying the fact that historians of the future will analyse India before Modi and India after Modi as the impact of the personality in every aspect of the country's polity, society and economy has been transformational. I leave it to the readers and their judgement to analyse all aspects of the decade and draw their own conclusions.

Aishwarya Pandit

Rethinking Indian Democracy

TONY ABBOTT

Our global future will be brighter or darker, depending on whether or not India engages beyond the subcontinent, and whether or not it commits to the wider cause of freedom under the law. After decades of non-alignment, India is now leaning towards solidarity with its fellow democracies via the Quadrilateral Security Dialogue (Quad). Should this continue, there is little doubt that India will become one of the leaders—eventually perhaps *the* leader—of the free world. Should it be interrupted though, or reversed, the long-term future of liberal democracy will be in considerable doubt, given all its contemporary challenges.

It was always premature to declare the 'end of history', the absence of great power conflict in the future, and the permanent global ascendency of liberal democracy and market capitalism, in the wake of the fall of the Berlin Wall. Still, the 'unipolar moment' did usher in globalisation, with goods, people and ideas freer than ever before to move between countries. This brought about a period of remarkable prosperity, such that the world at the beginning of 2020 had never been more free, more fair, more safe, and more rich for more people, due to the long peace fostered under the Pax Americana. A few statistics are instructive: in 1990, more than 30 per cent of the world's population lived in absolute poverty; 30 years later this had dropped to under 10 per cent. In 1990, over 30 per cent of the world's population lacked access to safe drinking water, but by 2020, this was under 10 per cent. More wealth in dollar terms was created in the 25 years leading up to 2020 than in the previous 25 centuries. Few countries have made more of these good times than India. Unlike China, which has also done remarkably well over the past few decades, at least while it was economically liberalising, India has advanced as a full-fledged democracy.

Right now, though, early 2020 looks like the high-water mark of freedom and prosperity. The response to a relatively mild global pandemic severely curtailed daily life for the best part of two years. It slashed production, forced people into a form of house arrest, and generally sapped people's resilience and self-reliance. Then Russia's attack on Ukraine severely disrupted global energy and grain markets and threatened a new Cold War in Europe. This was followed by the Hamas atrocity against Israel, which has gravely destabilised the Middle East and poses a threat of a wider war with Iran and its proxies. Finally, there is China's growing belligerence to its neighbours, its obvious intention to seize democratic Taiwan and the oft-declared aim to be the world's dominant power by the middle of the century. There is an alliance of convenience between militarism, Islamism and communism, which an increasingly fragmented and polarised West will find hard to meet on its own.

This is where India becomes immensely significant. If India is to side with its fellow democracies against the 'might is right' dictatorships, the global balance decisively shifts. If, on the other hand, its traditional friendship with Russia, pragmatic engagement with Iran, and ability to hide behind the Himalayas from China causes India to be even-handed between democracy and dictatorship, geopolitical disrupters everywhere will be emboldened to take advantage of a relatively weaker and poorer United States that is starting to resent being the world's policeman, and increasingly thinking that others have been the main beneficiaries of its strength and goodwill.

Currently, India's wealth per person is roughly a third of China's, and India has nothing like China's current capacity to project military power. However, its population, scientific base and industrial strength—coupled with the inherent creativity associated with a democratic system under the rule of law—give it at least as much long-term potential for economic and military strength. Even now, after the US and China, and perhaps Russia, as a nuclear power with a large army, navy and airforce, India is probably the world's third or fourth strongest military. So far, at least since Independence, it has never deployed its troops much beyond the subcontinent. But this could change given Modi's self-confidence as a leader and the seeming lack of the Independence generation's instinctual resistance to cooperation with the West.

There is no doubt that Modi's India has put the 'licence raj' well behind it and is now roaring down the runway to economic take-off. The challenge will be to take a global position commensurate with its growing economic strength and moral standing and to be prepared to make common cause with like-minded countries on the right issues.

India is already the world's fifth largest economy and will be the third largest within a couple of decades. It is still a developing country, but at least 80 per cent of Indians—or something like 1.1 billion people—now have access to proper sanitation, over 90 per cent have access to good drinking water, and 97 per cent have access to reliable power. While these may be small things in a geopolitical context, they make a massive difference to people's lives.

Thanks to the digital revolution, nearly every Indian adult is now economically and socially connected. There has long been a legendary rail network, but India is now building airports at the rate of eight a year, urban metro systems at the rate of one and half a year, and national highways at the rate of 30 km a day. Last year, India became only the fourth country to land a space probe on the Moon. Indian companies such as the Ambani group, Tata and Infosys are among the world's largest, there are three Indians amongst the world's fifty richest people, and there are now any number of ethnic Indians at the helm of major global businesses.

And India isn't just the world's largest democracy; it's also one of the oldest, having been continuously democratic—with just one small wobble—for more than three-quarters of a century. India's democracy is older than Germany's and Spain's; it's older than France's Fifth Republic. India has had more changes of government than Japan. Its media is as free as America's, and its judiciary as robustly independent as Britain's.

India has long proven that a country need not be rich to be free. And it's now proving that freedom is no obstacle to rapid economic development. Yet, mysteriously, India often ranks well down the global democracy lists, produced by Freedom House and others. Perhaps that is because they think of Prime Minister Modi as a 'Hindu nationalist' when he's better called an Indian patriot who necessarily takes Hinduism seriously as by far the country's biggest creed. Sadly, faith in God and country is pretty rare in Western think tanks, which is why they often find India's democracy easier to caricature than to understand.

As the Australian prime minister, a decade back, I used to describe India as 'the world's emerging democratic superpower'. That was both a recognition of India's leadership potential and the fond hope that these possibilities might soon be realised. Under PM Modi, India is no longer a bystander but increasingly a force in the world as one of the two democratic superpowers. And if there is to be a leader of the free world fifty or a hundred years hence, it is as likely to be the Indian prime minister as the US president.

After all, India has always been the superpower of the subcontinent. It has never been the aggressor in regional wars and tensions, which it always tried to resolve quickly, fairly, and in ways that allowed others to be the best they can. And now global leadership is beckoning.

For a long time, India was a leader of the Non-Aligned Movement, trying to stay aloof from big global struggles. Now, it is a leader of the 'Global South' and, as such, speaks up for poorer countries to get the fair go they deserve. For all to have the respect and the national independence that India won for itself, against the superpower of the day, which was slow to acknowledge India's right to be free.

To that end, India has helped form a new partnership for freedom and development. Unlike the North Atlantic Treaty Organization (NATO), the Quad is not led by America. Indeed, it would not exist but for Shinzo Abe's foresight and determination, which was then matched by Narendra Modi's perception and magnanimity.

Unlike NATO, the Quad is not a military alliance. Unlike NATO, it lacks formal structures. It is a bit like the Five Eyes, a largely informal network based on shared values, common interests and high ideals that has nonetheless helped to keep global peace for seven decades.

As India's Foreign Minister S. Jaishankar said recently, the Quad is 'here to stay, here to grow, and here to contribute.'[1] If that works out, with annual leaders' summits and regularly scheduled officials' meetings, it could be the most important strategic initiative since NATO. Even though it is not against anyone. It is for the rights of all to be free, and aims to help all to be better off, in a world where there is peace, national freedom and international cooperation, to tackle global problems like underdevelopment, infrastructure poverty and environmental degradation.

But that means standing strong against those who would breach the peace: the militarist, Islamist and communist dictatorships that think they have a right to impose their systems on others; and that could, if mishandled, plunge the world into a new dark age.

The Russian dictator thinks he is on a mission from God to destroy Ukraine, even though its people have every right to look West rather than East. Apocalyptic Islam seeks a new holocaust, expunging Israel from the river to sea. Communist China bullies its neighbours, even India, as part of its oft-declared intention to be the global hegemon by 2050. Its next step is taking, by force, if necessary, Taiwan, a practically independent country of 25 million people, a country that's never been under Communist rule, that's hardly ever been governed from Beijing, and that is a living, breathing proof that there's no totalitarian gene in the Chinese DNA.

As a backpacker in India forty years ago, I spent three weeks in Bokaro Steel City, as a kind of teacher's aide at St. Xavier's School. I understand the practical help that the old Soviet Union gave to India, at a time when the US, unwisely, was tilting towards Pakistan. I can understand why India is reluctant to be publicly critical of Russia, for historical and practical reasons, although PM Modi did indeed upbraid the Russian dictator, at Samarkand, for using war as an act of national policy. Even so, I have yet to meet an Indian unconvinced that the wanton destruction of Ukrainian cities without the slightest attempt to minimise civilian casualties is simply evil.

With greater strength comes greater responsibility; that's my sense of where PM Modi is taking India, and it couldn't have come at a more critical time. When India helps to preserve freedom of navigation in the Arabian Sea, it is not taking America's side against Iran; it is protecting the global commons. Likewise, any country that helped Taiwan resist a Chinese invasion wouldn't be on the side of America against China, but on the side of democracy versus dictatorship. Were India to help Taiwan, a bit like it helped Bangladesh five decades back, far from playing the great power politics it has always deplored, it would be helping the weak against the strong, in the eternal struggle to heed the better angels of our natures.

The best hope of avoiding great power conflict in the coming years is for free peoples everywhere to make it clear that an attack on one small country is an attack on everyone. There is no doubt that this will be an Indo-Pacific century; but with its commitment to democracy and the rule of law, it would be better for all if it turns out to be more India's than China's.

History can be both an inspiration and an inhibition. Rome in the first and second centuries, Britain in the nineteenth century and the US in the twentieth century are instances of how the leading polities of their day can shape the wider world; overall, much more for good than ill. And there's China, which long considered itself the 'Middle Kingdom' with no call to look beyond its immediate neighbourhood, but which now has its designs on the world. Inevitably, there will be some who count the costs of leadership more than its benefits, and who feel constrained rather than empowered by the past. But destiny is calling India to be a global exemplar of the democratic freedom that it has so well assimilated and made its own.

Tony Abbott served as the twenty-eighth Prime Minister of Australia from 2013 to 2015. He has held office as the leader of the Labour Party of Australia. He is also the advisor to the UK Board of Trade.

NOTES

1. Yeshi Seli, '"Quad is Here to Stay, Grow and Contribute": Dr S Jaishankar', *The New Indian Express*, 24 February 2024, https://www.newindianexpress.com/nation/2024/Feb/24/quad-is-here-to-stay-grow-and-contribute-dr-s-jaishankar.

India and the Arab World under PM Modi

WAIEL AWWAD

The relationship between India and the Arab world is a testament to the enduring bonds forged between the two over decades. It is characterised by a multifaceted engagement encompassing diplomatic, economic, cultural and strategic dimensions. Rooted in shared historical ties and mutual respect, this relationship has evolved into one of the most robust and dynamic partnerships in the international arena.

The relations between India and the Arab world are characterised by civilisational and cultural communication throughout the ages. These relations began in the first millennium BC when India and the Arab world were centres of trade and civilisation. Archaeological ruins in cities such as Harappa, Mohenjo-daro and Hariya in the Indus Basin attest to the trade and cultural relations between India and Arab regions since ancient times.

The relics also indicate the existence of trade in incense, aromatic herbs, food and clothing between the two sides. These relations have developed throughout the various stages of history and have contributed to the exchange of knowledge, literature and science between the two cultures. The legacy of these relations is still present today, as cultural, commercial and scientific exchanges continue between India and Arab countries, strengthening ties between peoples and cultures in the region.

This cultural communication was not limited to kings and rulers; it also existed between peoples, as is evident from several books written by Arab travellers and researchers such as Abu Al-Rayhan Al-Biruni, Abu Zaid Al-Sirafi, Jahiz, Suleiman Al-Tajer, Ibn Battuta, Al-Masoudi, Ibn Al-Faqih, Al-Tabari and others who translated many Indian manuscripts and books since the time of Al-Mansur in AD 772.

Relations were strengthened in the twentieth century after India and the Arab countries gained their independence, making India one of the countries closest to the Arab world and supporting just Arab causes. This increased the appreciation of the Arab people and their governments for Indian positions in international forums towards the Arab–Israeli conflict in general and the Palestinian issue in particular. The Indian government was the first to recognise the Palestinian state and opened an embassy in the Indian capital, Delhi.

India and the Arab world share deep historical ties that date back to ancient times. In India, the Harappans, Dravidians and Aryans cultivated vibrant cultures and civilisations, leaving behind a legacy of innovation and intellectual exchange.

Sitting at the southern coastal shore of Kerala is a testament to the enduring bonds between Arabs and India. This relationship has significantly enriched the cultural landscape of the region. This coastal region, known for its vibrant communities and bustling trade, reflects the interconnectedness of both societies across vast geographical distances. It serves as a living reminder of the dynamic nature of historical interactions and the profound legacy of cross-cultural fertilisation.

The presence of Arab settlements along the coast of Kerala speaks of centuries of maritime trade and cultural exchange between the Arab world and the Indian subcontinent. These settlements facilitated trade and served as centres of cultural diffusion. Through interactions with local communities, Arab traders brought diverse customs, traditions and religious beliefs, which gradually integrated with the rich tapestry of Indian culture.

Kerala's cultural landscape bears witness to this cross-cultural exchange, which reflects in its cuisine, language, architecture and religious practices. The influence of Arab merchants can be seen in traditional Malabar cuisine, which features a blend of Indian spices with Arabic flavours, and in the architectural styles of mosques and other structures along the coast.

Furthermore, the enduring legacy of this historical interaction is reflected in the social fabric of Kerala, where Arab influences have seamlessly woven themselves into the region's cultural identity. This cultural fusion has enriched Kerala's diversity and fostered a spirit of tolerance and mutual respect among its inhabitants.

The southern coastal shore of Kerala serves as a living embodiment of the deep-rooted connections between the Arabs and India. It symbolises the resilience of human interaction, the fluidity of cultural boundaries and the capacity for societies to thrive through mutual exchange and collaboration.

The world has witnessed the three oldest civilisations preserving their legacies throughout the ages. These civilisations include the illustrious Indian civilisation, the pioneering

Sumerians and the enduring civilisation of Egypt. These ancient cultures have left behind remarkable tangible artifacts and contributed to the foundations of human progress through their principles and manifestations. It is only natural to recognise the interconnectedness among these civilisations, as they shared ideas, technologies and cultural practices, influencing each other in profound ways.

In contemplating the relationship between India, the cradle of one of the earliest civilisations, and the Arab world, which holds the heritage of the other two ancient civilisations, one finds a convergence of historical narratives. This connection is solidified by shared pillars of knowledge, innovation and cultural exchange, which have supported the development of both regions. This bond is not merely a product of geographical proximity but a testament to the enduring ties between the peoples of India and the Arab world since time immemorial.

Similarly, in the Arab lands, civilisations such as Babylon, Assyria, Syria, Palestine, Arabia, Egypt, Sumer and Elam flourished, laying the foundations of human civilisation. These ancient societies were hubs for trade, culture and learning, fostering connections and interactions across vast distances.

For instance, the people of the Indus Valley Civilisation had intimate relations with the civilisations of Sumer. They traded extensively with Egypt and Crete, demonstrating the early roots of India's engagement with the Arab world. These historical ties formed the basis for enduring cultural exchanges, economic partnerships and diplomatic relations between India and Arab countries, shaping their relationship over millennia.

The historic ties between India and the Arab world provide a broader perspective on the depth and continuity of their engagement, highlighting the resilience and adaptability of their relationship across different epochs of history.

Diplomatically, India and the Arab countries have cultivated strong ties based on sovereignty, non-interference and mutual cooperation. Regular high-level visits, bilateral dialogues and diplomatic exchanges have reinforced trust and understanding between the two sides, facilitating collaboration on regional and global issues of common interest.

Economically, the relationship between India and the Arab world has flourished, driven by a burgeoning trade and investment landscape. Both sides have capitalised on complementarities in key sectors such as energy, infrastructure, information technology and agriculture, resulting in mutually beneficial partnerships that have fuelled growth and development in both regions.

Culturally, the ties between India and the Arab countries run deep, enriched by centuries of cultural exchanges, shared traditions and mutual appreciation. Cultural diplomacy initiatives, including festivals, exhibitions and academic exchanges, have further strengthened these bonds, fostering a sense of kinship and camaraderie among the peoples of India and the Arab world.

Strategically, India and the Arab countries have recognised the importance of security cooperation and strategic alignment in safeguarding regional peace and stability. Collaboration in counterterrorism, maritime security, defence cooperation and intelligence-sharing has underscored their commitment to addressing common security challenges and advancing shared interests.

The relationship between India and the Arab world is a shining example of partnership and solidarity founded on mutual respect, equality and shared aspirations. As both sides continue to deepen their engagement and collaboration across various domains, the prospects for further strengthening and diversifying this relationship remain bright, promising a future of enhanced cooperation, prosperity and stability for India, the Arab countries and the wider region.

INDIA AND ARAB WORLD'S RELATIONS POST INDEPENDENCE

The relationship between India and the Arab countries during the Congress party's tenure in power, mainly from India gaining independence in 1947 to the early 1990s, was characterised by a mix of diplomatic engagements, economic cooperation and shared interests on international issues.

Following India's independence from British rule in 1947, many Arab countries were among the first to recognise and establish diplomatic relations with the newly formed Republic of India. This marked the beginning of formal diplomatic ties between India and the Arab world. In 1961, India's active participation in the Non-Aligned Movement (NAM) served as a platform for engagement with Arab countries, promoting principles of non-alignment, sovereignty and peaceful coexistence. India's alignment with Arab nations on various global issues further strengthened diplomatic relations.

India has consistently supported the Palestinian cause and the rights of the Palestinian people to self-determination and statehood. India's stance on the Palestine issue has been a cornerstone of its foreign policy in the Arab world, fostering solidarity and goodwill among Arab nations.

Over the years, India and Arab countries have forged strategic partnerships and signed numerous bilateral agreements covering various areas of cooperation, including trade, investment, defence, education, culture, and science and technology. These agreements have provided frameworks for enhancing bilateral ties and fostering collaboration in key sectors. In the 1980s, high-level visits and diplomatic exchanges between India and Arab countries played a crucial role in strengthening bilateral relations and deepening mutual understanding. Visits by heads of state, government officials and business leaders helped identify areas of mutual interest and explore opportunities for cooperation.

Trade ties between India and Arab countries have witnessed significant growth in recent decades. Both sides have capitalised on energy, infrastructure, IT, pharmaceuticals and agriculture complementarities, leading to increased flow of bilateral trade and investment. Cultural and people-to-people exchanges have played a vital role in enhancing mutual understanding and friendship between India and Arab countries. Cultural festivals, academic exchanges and tourism initiatives have promoted cross-cultural dialogue and fostered goodwill among the peoples of both regions. India and Arab countries have strengthened security cooperation and counterterrorism efforts to address common security challenges and threats. Collaboration in intelligence-sharing, capacity-building and joint exercises has contributed to regional peace and stability.

Contemporary history and geopolitical changes have also significantly influenced the diplomatic relations between India and Arab countries.

THE PARADIGM SHIFT

In the twenty-first century, India's emergence as a global economic powerhouse and geopolitical player has led to greater engagement with Arab countries. The country's growing influence in international affairs, including its membership in forums like the G20 and BRICS, has elevated its profile and enhanced its diplomatic relations with Arab nations.

India's main objective is to strengthen relations with the Arab world based on three factors: food, oil security and the safety of the Indian diaspora. India has pursued strategic partnerships with key Arab countries, particularly in the Gulf region, with members of the Gulf Cooperation Council (GCC), such as the UAE, Saudi Arabia, Oman, Bahrain, Qatar and Kuwait. Enhanced defence cooperation, joint military exercises and security dialogues have strengthened bilateral ties and contributed to mutual security interests in the face of everyday challenges such as terrorism and maritime security threats.

India's 'Look West' policy and the efforts of the Arab countries to diversify their economies have led to an expansion of economic cooperation between the two. This has increased trade volumes, investment flows and joint ventures, particularly in energy, infrastructure, technology and healthcare sectors.

The Indian diaspora residing in Arab countries, particularly in the Gulf region, is crucial to the strengthening of the ties between India and the Arab world. With over 8 million Indians living in the GCC and more than 14 million Indians visiting the region annually, this community contributes significantly to the economies of the host countries through their remittances. India's practical approach to regional dynamics, while maintaining its commitment to stability and non-interference, has enabled the country to navigate complex geopolitical challenges and maintain constructive relationships with all regional stakeholders.

India's growing energy needs continue to drive its engagement with Arab countries who have vast reserves of oil and gas. Diversification of energy sources, investment in renewable energy, and cooperation on energy security issues remain critical priorities for India and Arab nations.

These contemporary dynamics in diplomatic relations between India and the Arab countries reflect the evolving geopolitical landscape and the shared interests, aspirations and challenges facing both regions in the twenty-first century.

While India maintained a policy of non-alignment during the Cold War, it pursued strategic alignment with Arab countries on various international issues, including disarmament, human rights and global governance. Diplomatic coordination and collaboration between India and Arab nations on these issues strengthened bilateral relations.

Overall, the relationship between India and Arab countries during the Congress party's rule was characterised by diplomatic solidarity, economic cooperation, and shared values and interests. While there were occasional differences and challenges, particularly in regional conflicts and geopolitical dynamics, both sides worked towards promoting peace, stability and development in the Indo-Arabic region.

The Modi brand represents a significant shift in India's foreign policy approach, particularly in its relations with Arab countries. Under the leadership of Prime Minister Narendra Modi, India has adopted a proactive stance, prioritising economic diplomacy as a key pillar of its foreign policy agenda. This shift is evident in the renewed emphasis on enhancing trade and investment ties with Arab nations, focusing on key sectors such as energy, infrastructure, technology and defence.

One of the hallmark initiatives of the Modi government is the 'Make in India' campaign, which aims to promote domestic manufacturing and attract foreign investment. This campaign has been extended to Arab countries, where Indian start-ups and businesses are encouraged to seek investment opportunities. By leveraging India's strengths in sectors such as technology and defence, PM Modi has sought to deepen economic partnerships with Arab nations.

In addition to economic diplomacy, PM Modi has prioritised cultivating strategic partnerships with Arab countries, particularly in security, counterterrorism, maritime cooperation and defence collaboration. This strategic alignment is reflected in India's growing defence ties with countries like the UAE, Saudi Arabia and Oman, where India is increasingly viewed as a key security partner.

Cultural diplomacy also significantly influences India's engagement with Arab countries under PM Modi's leadership. Efforts to promote Indian culture, yoga, Ayurveda and Bollywood films serve to strengthen people-to-people ties and enhance India's soft power in the region. Prime Minister Modi has actively engaged with the Indian diaspora in Arab countries, recognising their contributions to India as well as their host nations. The diaspora bridges India and Arab countries, facilitating economic, cultural and diplomatic exchanges.

Overall, PM Modi's leadership has brought about a strategic realignment and elevation of India's relations with Arab countries, characterised by increased economic engagement, strategic partnerships, cultural exchanges and diplomatic cooperation. This paradigm shift reflects India's growing prominence on the world stage and its commitment to fostering mutually beneficial relations with Arab partners. Through these efforts, India aims to deepen cooperation, foster mutual prosperity and contribute to peace, stability and development in the Indo-Arabic region and beyond.

STRATEGIC OBJECTIVES

The strategic objectives of India's foreign policy, such as enhancing India's regional influence, ensuring energy security, countering terrorism and promoting stability in the Indo-Arabic region, are the main forces driving Modi's foreign policy towards Arab countries.

Unlike his predecessors, Modi's initiatives with his vision of India has led to extensive diplomatic engagements with Arab countries, including high-level visits, bilateral meetings, and participation in regional forums and summits, focusing on trade, investment, energy collaboration, infrastructure development and economic reforms. His policy is characterised by strategic pragmatism, diplomatic finesse and a commitment to advancing India's strategic interests. Some significant economic initiatives were witnessed in bilateral trade volumes, investment flows, job creation and economic growth in India and Arab nations. The Gulf Cooperation Council stepped up its efforts to strengthen ties with India by signing major gas and oil deals to meet India's demand. In addition, joint defence ventures and Indian projects led to billions of dollars flowing into the Indian market.

In recent years, PM Modi's foreign policy approach towards the Middle East has undergone a significant transformation. It is marked by a departure from traditional paradigms and a shift towards a more comprehensive and multifaceted engagement.

This evolution is characterised by the cultivation of stronger bilateral ties with individual nations from the Middle East and a concerted effort to engage with the region as a collective entity.

Historically, India's relations with the Middle Eastern countries were often centred on energy cooperation, given the region's significant oil and gas reserves. However, under PM Modi's leadership, there has been a notable diversification and expansion of the bilateral agenda, encompassing a wide range of strategic, economic, diplomatic and cultural dimensions.

One key aspect of this transformation is the strengthening of bilateral ties with individual Middle Eastern nations. Prime Minister Modi has pursued proactive diplomacy, characterised by high-level visits, strategic dialogues and enhanced cooperation across various sectors. This has led to deepening of economic partnerships, investment collaborations and defence engagements with countries such as Saudi Arabia, the United Arab Emirates, Israel and Qatar, among others.

Moreover, PM Modi has continuously emphasised engaging with the Middle East as a collective entity, recognising the region's growing geopolitical significance and potential to shape global affairs. India has actively participated in regional forums such as the Arab League, the GCC and the Organization of Islamic Cooperation (OIC), fostering dialogue, cooperation and mutual understanding.

Notably, the relationship between India and the Middle East is now more than solely defined by energy needs. While energy cooperation remains essential, both sides have expanded their collaboration to include trade, investment, technology transfer, counterterrorism, cyber security, healthcare, education and cultural exchanges. This diversified engagement reflects India's recognition of the Middle East as a vital partner in advancing shared interests and addressing common challenges on the global stage.

In conclusion, PM Modi's foreign policy towards the Middle East represents a remarkable transformation characterised by a broader and more nuanced approach to bilateral and regional relations. By leveraging India's historical ties, economic potential and diplomatic acumen, PM Modi has positioned India as a key player in shaping the future trajectory of the Middle East and advancing mutual prosperity, security and stability in the region and beyond.

HOW DO ARABS VIEW INDIA?

Many Arab countries view India as a strategic partner with shared interests in security, counterterrorism, energy cooperation and regional stability. India's stance of non-alignment and focus on multi-alignment resonate with Arab nations, which value India's independent foreign policy approach.

While there may be challenges and occasional differences in India–Arab relations, such as on regional conflicts or economic issues, there is a recognition of the broader strategic significance of, and the mutual benefits arising from, the relationship. Arab countries see India as a rising global power and a key player in shaping the future of the Indo-Arabic region. They view India under PM Modi's leadership as a valuable partner with shared interests, common values and immense potential for cooperation across multiple domains. The relationship between India and Arab nations is characterised by mutual respect, trust and a commitment to advancing shared goals of peace, prosperity and stability in the region and beyond.

CONCERNS

The possibility of India aligning with the US-led security architecture in the Middle East has raised concerns among some Arab nations. Such an alignment could result in perceived risks associated with India's involvement in regional conflicts and power struggles. One potential risk is the perception of entanglement, where Arab countries may view India as being embroiled in regional disputes, thereby potentially undermining its traditional policy of non-alignment and efforts to maintain strategic autonomy in regional affairs.

Strategic balancing is important in regional politics. Some Arab countries may perceive India's alignment with the US-led security architecture as a strategic balancing act to counter regional rivals or advance specific geopolitical interests. Such perceptions could lead to concerns about India's role in potentially exacerbating regional tensions or fuelling regional instability.

Moreover, it is essential to consider the potential impact on diplomatic relations. Depending on the situation, this could potentially strain a country's relationships with certain Arab nations that have stronger ties to rival powers or hold differing strategic priorities. This could lead to diplomatic tensions or frictions that could hinder bilateral cooperation and dialogue, ultimately impacting the ability of countries to work together towards common goals.

Apart from political and social implications, strained relations between India and Arab nations could also have potential economic consequences. Restrictions on trade, investment or energy cooperation could harm bilateral trade flows, thus impacting mutual prosperity and development. It is, therefore, important to address any issues and work towards maintaining solid and positive relationships.

Furthermore, Arab nations seeking to promote peace and stability in the region value India's perceived neutrality and impartiality in regional conflicts. If India was to align with any security architectures or military alliances, it could alter the regional dynamics and power structures in the Middle East. This would potentially reshape existing alliances, rivalries and security arrangements, leading to shifts in regional geopolitics and security calculations, consequently also having an impact on Indo-Arabic relations.

India's relationship with Israel can have implications for the Palestinian cause, although the extent of the impact depends on various factors, including India's diplomatic approach, regional dynamics and international relations. India has traditionally maintained a balanced approach on the Israel–Palestine conflict, supporting the establishment of a sovereign and independent Palestinian state alongside Israel through peaceful negotiations. While India has strengthened its ties with Israel in recent years, it has also reaffirmed its commitment to the Palestinian cause and expressed support for a two-state solution.

Overall, while there may be perceived risks associated with India's alignment with the US-led security architecture in the region, it is essential for India to carefully navigate these dynamics, maintain open and transparent communication with Arab countries, and uphold its principles of non-alignment, sovereignty and mutual respect in its foreign policy engagements. Striking a balance between strategic partnerships and regional interests will be crucial for India to advance its security objectives while preserving stability and cooperation in the Indo-Arabic region.

While India has emerged as a key player in regional security dynamics, particularly in South Asia and the Indian Ocean region, it would be challenging for India to directly replace the US as a global security manager, or to fill the vacuum left by the USA. India's engagement with Israel is conducted in a manner that does not undermine its support for Palestinian rights or its advocacy for a peaceful resolution of the conflict based on internationally recognised parameters. As such, India's ties with Israel are unlikely to significantly alter its stance on the Palestinian issue or its broader approach to peace and stability in the Middle East.

FUTURE PERSPECTIVE

The ongoing war between Israel and Palestine in the Gaza Strip and West Bank overshadows the prospect of a stable Middle East, threatening regional peace and stability, especially when all trends indicate the widening of this war into the Red Sea, Lebanon, Syria, Iraq and Iran. There is little hope of de-escalation or a diplomatic solution. Strengthening defence ties through military exchanges, joint training programmes and procurement of defence equipment can enhance regional security.

India has emerged as a key defence partner for several Gulf countries, providing defence technology, expertise and support. Cooperation in border security and management can help address challenges related to illegal immigration, cross-border smuggling and transnational crime. India and Gulf countries can collaborate on border surveillance, information-sharing and capacity-building to secure their borders more effectively. Given the volatile security environment in the Middle East, effective crisis management mechanisms are essential for responding to emergencies, conflicts and humanitarian crises. India and Gulf countries can work together to coordinate humanitarian assistance, facilitate evacuations and promote stability in times of crisis. Promoting peace, stability and conflict resolution efforts in the region is in the interest of both India and the Gulf countries. Diplomatic engagement, dialogue facilitation and support for multilateral initiatives can reduce tensions, resolve disputes and foster regional cooperation.

The future perspective of India–Arab ties holds significant promise and potential for further deepening and diversifying cooperation across various domains.

Indeed, the geographical link between India and the Arab world, facilitated by the sea, has been pivotal in fostering communication, trade and cultural diffusion between these regions. However, the connection between these two shores transcends mere physical proximity, rooted in the deep historical interactions that have occurred long before recorded history. The ancient maritime routes connecting the Indian subcontinent with the Arabian peninsula served as conduits for exchanging goods, ideas and cultural practices, shaping the collective heritage of both regions.

From the early maritime trade routes to the spread of religious and philosophical ideas, the historical relationship between India and the Arab world has been characterised by mutual curiosity, cooperation and cross-cultural fertilisation. This enduring bond continues to resonate in contemporary times, manifesting in various forms such as diplomatic engagements, economic partnerships and cultural exchanges. Thus, the historical connection between India and the Arab world is a testament to the enduring power of human interaction and collaboration across civilisations.

The outlook for India–Arab ties, the dynamic nature of historical interactions and the enduring legacy of cross-cultural fertilisation are characterised by this strong foundation of civilisational links, coupled with shared aspirations for peace, prosperity and development. By leveraging their respective strengths, addressing challenges and seizing opportunities for collaboration, India and Arab countries can build a resilient and dynamic partnership that benefits their peoples and contributes to regional stability and prosperity in the years ahead.

The need for proactive risk-taking and the challenges posed by alternative regional initiatives such as the Belt and Road Initiative suggest that India must navigate these dynamics carefully to maximise its influence and capitalise on the opportunities presented by its relations with West Asia.

Dr Waiel Awwad is a senior journalist and West Asia strategist. For more details, visit www.waielawwad.com.

India, Britain and Lessons for Democracies

AMAN BHOGAL

'We are dealing with an absolute political phenomenon.'

That is how Boris Johnson, then foreign secretary and later the prime minister of the UK, described the Indian Prime Minister Narendra Modi in 2019. And that is how PM Modi has led India both domestically and internationally.

Under Modi's leadership, India has levelled up on all fronts, from roads, railways and planes to the fintech revolution of unified payments interface (UPI) for digital payments, the streamlining of taxation with the goods and services tax (GST) reforms as well as the freeing of the market to deliver cheaper but better-quality goods. These positive domestic changes along with deft and dependable diplomacy—first directed by the exceptional Sushma Swaraj and then by S. Jaishankar—have resulted in India transforming into the 'New India' that is Bharat.

With the world's fastest-growing, make-in-India economy that is powering the reforms and resurgence led by PM Modi since 2014, India has finally begun to meaningfully leverage the dividends of freedom and independence to realise its long-standing potential.

Around the same time, we saw a surge in support for a referendum to answer the Brexit question, with the UK Independence Party winning the most seats in the 2014 European parliamentary elections in the UK and the Conservative Party promising a referendum in the 2015 general elections and then delivering it in 2016.

Truth is, here in Global Britain, we too had been encumbered with a puffed-up metropolitan liberal elite unable to look beyond its next deal, unwilling to govern the country as an independent nation and uninterested in taking responsibility for the ill governance it had inflicted upon the population through endless governments of no alternative.

People across the country had been clamouring for freedom and independence to take back control from the European Union and to be sovereign once again. That is the decision that the British people made in 2015 first with the first majority Conservative government since 1992 and then with the historic leave vote in the 2016 Brexit referendum, the biggest democratic exercise in British history.

However, the parallels between the resurgence in Indian freedom and democracy with the election of PM Modi in 2014, which finally ended the era of shaky horse-trading coalitions, and the wins for the 2015 Conservative majority and Brexit is where the shared story of taking back control and making those who govern and rule in our name accountable takes two different paths.

India is democracy-driven with a focus on minimising government and maximising good governance. It boasts of a steady slew of reforms of all that needs to be fixed and strong and stable leadership. In the UK, on the other hand, we had until

2019 been beseeched by instability and dithering directionless travel of seemingly trying to get Brexit done but without actually having the civil service and foreign service, let alone most of the out-of-alignment Parliament, wanting to get Brexit done.

Much like PM Modi, it took the leadership of Boris Johnson to finally emerge victorious with a stonking eighty-seat majority and go with the mood of the nation and get Brexit done, only then to be undermined by a political class where the Right was more interested in diluting conservatism as some pound shop version of Blairism and the Left more interested in re-running the battles of yesterday as some silver bullet to the problems of tomorrow. Not to mention the prevailing orthodoxy of the institutions and the great blob of the civil service quangocracy fighting solely to preserve its leaching hold on the levers of power.

Now this is where Global Britain has much to observe and learn from our friends in New India. The world's oldest democracy can learn from the world's greatest democracy on how to make democracy matter again. The world's oldest and most successful political party, the Conservative Party and Unionist Party, must see how PM Modi and the world's biggest political party, the Bhartiya Janata Party, has doubled down on the one idea that brings people together—the national interest. And as one civilisational nation, the UK needs to learn from another civilisational nation, India, on how to overcome the challenges to deliver a national resurgence where people feel proud to be nationals and not just residents. And as much as any of this, the UK needs to learn how to deliver much of what both the Boris-led victory of the Conservatives in 2019 promised electors— good governance. We need, as PM Theresa May promised in the 2017 general elections, a strong and stable government.

Ultimately, any government is a product of three things: the people who elect, the people who stand for election and the people that deliver the manifesto they campaigned for. That is the most important lesson to be learnt from the absolute political phenomenon that is PM Modi. A simple glance at the core team that has strengthened PM Modi's hand in shaping this New India tells us that he and the BJP have got their candidate selection largely spot-on, matching up ministerial portfolios to a lifetime of experience and enforcing accountability of ministers to ensure promises are delivered.

Be it the Indian finance minister or the foreign minister or the minister for IT or the railways and roads ministers, each and everyone is delivering three core ingredients of good governance—competency, stability and accountability. This, in turn, is delivering strong and stable governance, which is the mainstay of meaningful reforms, economic growth and the democratic dividend. This, by allowing free enterprise to get on with the job of delivering free trade powering the aspirations of the Indian people, is strengthening free democracy.

All this is further augmented by a deft and dependable diplomatic miracle that is India's international relations since 2014. Put aptly by S. Jaishankar at the Munich Security Conference 2024, 'If I am smart enough to have multiple options, you should be admiring me. Is that a problem for others? I don't think so.' This is possible solely because in this Modi era India is putting one ideal as its hallmark left, right and centre—the national interest first.

This is the number one priority that we in Global Britain ought to be learning and putting into practice in building a post-Brexit UK, which fully leverages our newly found Brexit freedoms to deliver in Britain's national interest—securing our borders, reforming the orthodoxy holding back good governance and conserving our national inheritance.

We campaigned for Brexit to look beyond the European Union, and our natural partner, our friend of old, a New India of free democracy is one to work together with to deliver for people in the national interest. And for our two nations, we are unique in the world as our national interests coincide with each other on nearly every graph and every path. This is made true by our shared values, shared languages and shared ideas of what prosperity and peace mean, as we head into what very much looks likely be the third historic win for PM Modi.

So, let's skill India with British innovation, let's bring in Digital India to level up British public services, and let's build a Global Britain which takes a leaf out of New India's book to secure our Brexit freedoms, national interest and sovereignty.

Together, Global Britain and New India matter to the world. What matters to us is freedom to be, independence to do and enterprise to achieve and it has been made possible because Modi matters to India.

Aman Bhogal is the Founding Chairman of Global Britain Centre, UK. He stood for parliament in the 2015 UK general elections.

The Indian Economy, Capital Markets and Society under PM Modi

ASHISH CHAUHAN

A LESSON IN HISTORY

In 2014, India was at a crossroads, emerging from a phase of economic sluggishness and policy stagnation. India was categorised as part of the 'Fragile Five', a term denoting emerging markets with poor economic indicators such as sluggish growth, rampant inflation, low foreign exchange reserves, huge corruption scandals and weak fiscal health. The country faced numerous challenges, including infrastructural deficits, sociopolitical complexities and a legacy of financial imbalances such as substantial bad loans and a significant current account deficit. The population of India grappled with issues like poverty, limited access to healthcare and inadequate education infrastructure. Narendra Modi's ascendancy to the Prime Minister's office brought with it a promise of change, a vision of India that was not only economically vibrant but also socially inclusive, corruption-free and globally influential.

Before him, for over sixty years Indian state had demonstrated very little implementation capabilities. Over the last forty to fifty years, previous governments had given up on creating even basic infrastructure due to rampant corruption and huge time and cost overruns. The state (central and state governments) demonstrated that they had very little capability on the ground. For this very reason, in 2004, the government led by Dr Manmohan Singh began talking about public–private partnerships for infrastructure and social sector projects, assuming that the private sector would create the infrastructure capabilities. It didn't help develop infrastructure or reduce corruption in social sector schemes from 2004 to 2014 and instead increased the leakages with very little to show in terms of achievements. Bank balance sheets had gone bad due to lending to public–private partnerships where a large part of the money was siphoned off and not used for the intended purpose. Corruption scandals were rampant, and the concept of accountability and shame had disappeared from Indian governance. Corruption scandals of more than Rs 1,00,000 crores were being reported with no one in charge almost daily.

Indian governance had started getting known as announcement-based governance where implementation of projects and schemes had very little relevance. Media and the public were made to believe that creating policies and announcing schemes was the end goal of governance. Large sums were earmarked and spent on social projects. Only a small percentage, if at all, of the announced social schemes and infrastructure projects were implemented correctly and on time. Media hype was created for announcing policies that appeared good and later, after a few years, the same policies were announced with minor modifications as even more fantastic policies.

In the absence of any way to govern effectively, the governments started announcing rights, such as the Right to Information and the Right to Food, without having the ability to ensure that the benefits of these rights reached the general population. Instead of improving governance, its capacity, capability and accountability—all hard work—governance by announcements only came to be the rule. The pacification of special interest groups by making announcements and earmarking carve-outs for such groups became the norm and this came to be considered governance. Democracy and government became all about managing special interest groups and their specific interests.

DAWN OF A NEW ERA

When Narendra Modi became the prime minister, he was one of the rare prime ministers of India who had earlier experience of acting as a chief minister of a state for a reasonable period. He knew about the administration of the states. However, he had not been a member of parliament before. He was also considered an outsider and is still considered an outsider, due to his complete disinterest in creating wealth for himself or his family. In any country, the 'establishment'—sometimes known as 'deep state' and 'old elites'—works across party lines and can persuade most people to ensure that policy remains intact. Even international companies, countries and the international community want policy continuity to protect their commercial and geopolitical interests. Anyone not beholden to 'deep state' is considered an outsider and a person who is not interested in personal wealth is considered uncontrollable by them. PM

Modi is one such rare leader who got elected without the help or involvement of 'deep state'.

The first five years of the Modi government were spent cleaning up the balance sheet of the banking system that was reeling under repercussions of overlending to companies—known as 'phone banking'—by previous governments after the financial crisis of 2007-08. The Modi government also tried to resolve issues related to fiscal indiscipline that had crept in during the second half of the previous government being in power, after the global financial crisis, which created high inflation on one side and very low economic growth towards the end of 2013, in addition to high oil prices and low exports leading to worries about the balance of payments.

PM Modi's second five-year term was marred by COVID-19, a once-in-a-century health issue affecting the entire world. Even the best and the richest international countries and thinkers advocated and implemented lax fiscal policies. The Indian government adopted a more controlled fiscal policy despite the need to provide adequate support to the population in one of the toughest periods for humankind in the last hundred years. Due to many other factors, including nationwide lockdowns, food management, vaccine preparation, etc., India came out of the pandemic much better than the rest of the world. During the period, India also managed the entire world's back office and provided vaccines free or at a nominal cost. The vaccines produced in India were very effective and easy to transport and administer. By sharing domestically produced vaccines with poor countries around the world, India enhanced its credibility among the world community.

The Modi government created a framework for monitoring the implementation of schemes and projects undertaken by them or announced by them in a manner that would control leakages. By implementing technology-based targeting and monitoring mechanisms, it managed to resolve the challenge of execution that had plagued the previous Indian governments. Jan Dhan Aadhaar (the number of Jan Dhan accounts) has grown to 51.74 crore in 2024 from zero at the end of 2013. A mobile framework was created using Aadhaar and unified payments interface (UPI) along with ubiquitous mobile connectivity available in the hands of each citizen. Direct benefit transfer (DBT), digital payments, the CoWin app, goods and services tax (GST), faceless direct tax assessment, PM Gati Shakti and many other interesting uses of technology for governance were implemented well and started showing results. The ability to execute schemes on time and within the estimated cost, and following all transparency measures to put a stop to corruption, has been of prime focus for the Modi government. Be it social schemes or infrastructure, project monitoring and implementation as per the measurement matrix is being done to enforce accountability.

When Narendra Modi became the Prime Minister of India, most observers thought that since he had never been exposed to issues of national importance like defence, banking and national finance (fiscal, banking, stock market), trade and foreign policy, he would have a tough time managing all four. These ten years have witnessed a paradigm shift in multiple facets of the nation, and PM Modi has excelled in all four areas, performing way beyond anyone would have imagined. India's gross domestic product (GDP) grew from Rs 112.3 lakh crore to an impressive Rs

296.6 lakh crore. This remarkable surge, representing a growth from 123.5 crore to 140.6 crore1 in population, was not merely numerical but indicative of the percolation of economic benefits to a broader demographic. The real GDP growth, averaging 7.2 per cent when excluding the tumultuous COVID-19–impacted fiscal year of 2020-21, is a testament to the effectiveness of the government's economic strategies. In nominal terms, per capita income more than doubled from Rs 89,796 to Rs 2,12,600, and in USD terms, it saw a significant increase from USD 1,494 to USD 2,566 as of FY2023–24. This leap in personal wealth indicates the growth of the middle-class with increased spending power, which is critical for the sustenance of a consumer-driven economy.

Government spending on infrastructure by the Modi government has increased from Rs 1.08 lakh crore during 2004–14 under Dr Manmohan Singh's governments to Rs 4.12 lakh crore from 2014–24 under the two successive Modi governments.[2] The effectiveness of infrastructure built at the government level went up by miles during the last decade. The pace of highway construction shot up, rising from 12 km per day to 28 km per day, showcasing the government's push to enhance connectivity and facilitate trade. The total road network expanded significantly, with national highways stretching over 1,44,634 km in 2024 from 91,827 in 2014. The railway electrification project also gained momentum, with 50,939 km of railway tracks electrified, aiming to increase efficiency and reduce the carbon footprint of one of the world's largest rail networks. The Modi government launched Vande Bharat Express, a premium medium-distance superfast express service, which has been designed and manufactured in India. As of January 2024, forty-one Vande Bharat trains are in service. At the end of 2023, metro rail was also present in twenty-seven cities with a length of 860 km. The Mumbai–Ahmedabad bullet train corridor is also being developed, which will cover a distance of 508 km and achieve a maximum speed of 320 km per hour, reducing travel time to just two hours. This infrastructural leap was complemented by advancements in the aviation sector, where the number of airports rose from seventy-four to 149, and there was a substantial increase in cargo handling by major ports and airports, which went up from 555.5 million tonnes to 783.5 million tonnes and from 16.0 million tonnes to 25.0 million tonnes respectively, underlining the robust growth and modernisation of India's critical transport hubs.

The decade spanning from 2014 to 2024 stands as a significant chapter in India's modern history, a period marked by transformative changes under the leadership of PM Modi. This era, characterised by substantial economic growth, technological advancements and pivotal policy reforms, has reshaped India's global identity and internal dynamics. Most importantly, the executive capacity to implement large, complex social and infrastructure projects has become real, as evidenced by many visible successes.

The foundations have been laid during this period, characterised by economic growth, digital transformation and social development to meet the needs of its people and the environment. They have set the stage for India's continued ascent in the global arena. Let us look at certain aspects of this revolution in detail.

SOCIAL AND HUMAN DEVELOPMENT

The Indian government's proactive approach, from 2014 to 2024 during PM Modi's two successive terms, to improving the welfare and quality of life of its citizens, with a special emphasis on the marginalised and underprivileged sections of society, has caused an impactful transformation of India's social fabric.

Poverty alleviation was a cornerstone of the government's agenda. The percentage of the population living in multidimensional poverty reduced from 24.9 per cent to 15 per cent, indicating that roughly 13.5 crore individuals were lifted out of poverty during this ten-year period. Efforts to decrease the intensity of deprivation among the poor were successful, with the average deprivation score decreasing, as reflected in the Multidimensional Poverty Index. Urban poverty saw a reduction from 8.7 per cent to 5.3 per cent, while rural poverty declined from 32.6 per cent to 19.3 per cent. These declines were not mere statistics but reflect an improvement in living standards through better access to healthcare, education and economic opportunities.

In healthcare, the government's initiatives were aimed at improving sanitation and access to healthcare. The percentage of the population practising open defecation decreased drastically from 32 per cent to 11 per cent, reflecting the success of the Swachh Bharat Mission. Improved sanitation facilities rose to cover 70 per cent of the population, ensuring better health and hygiene. Healthcare expenditure per capita in terms of purchasing power parity (PPP) increased from USD 19.4 to USD 44.4, which contributed to the reduction in maternal mortality from 135 to 103 per 1,00,000 live births, thus improving overall health outcomes.

Women's welfare received heightened focus, with institutional births climbing from 78.9 per cent to 93.8 per cent, significantly reducing the risks associated with childbirth. The percentage of ever-married women who have ever experienced spousal violence reduced from 31.2 per cent to 24.2 per cent, indicating progress towards gender equality and the empowerment of women. Furthermore, there was a decline in the number of girls married before the age of eighteen, from 26.8 per cent to 14.7 per cent, a change that points towards a shift in societal norms and increased educational opportunities for girls.

In education, the gross enrolment ratio in higher education improved from 24.3 per cent to 27.3 per cent, reflecting the government's emphasis on education and skill development as key drivers of economic growth. The establishment of Institutes of National Importance increased from 75 to 165, providing high-quality education and research facilities that are expected to produce the next generation of skilled professionals.

The government also worked towards increasing accessibility and affordability of basic utilities and services. Active LPG connections doubled, making clean cooking fuel available to 31.4 crore households. The drive to electrify villages saw success, with 100 per cent of villages having electricity by 2024, compared to 96.3 per cent in 2014.

The MUDRA (Micro Units Development and Refinance Agency) loan scheme, launched by the Government of India in 2015, aimed at providing financial support to the non-corporate, small business sector. These loans facilitated credit up to Rs 10 lakh to foster entrepreneurship among grassroots business owners, including women entrepreneurs, SC/ST communities and rural businesses. By offering financial assistance without collateral, the scheme empowered these small units to expand and upgrade their infrastructure.

The data underscores significant strides made in poverty reduction, healthcare, women's welfare, education and access to basic services, which are likely to have long-lasting impacts on India's socioeconomic landscape.

Through these various initiatives, the government shifted the focus of welfare from entitlement-based support to the empowerment of individuals by integrating them into the formal sector. In providing for targeted credit, women's welfare, poverty alleviation and healthcare, the government has managed to provide a welfare umbrella, a basic safety net for all individuals under which they can strive to maximise their productivity and capabilities. It is noteworthy that in most of the developed nations of the world today, citizens expect, and are provided with, such a safety net. It is collectively known as social security. Building blocks for the Western-style social security framework have been built in India from 2014 to 2024 without the notice of media and intelligentsia. A nation which wants to become a developed nation must have an effective and all-encompassing social security framework for all its citizens. PM Modi has been building such a system during his first two terms, from 2014 to 2024. While it is still a work in progress, the basic framework of social security is now functional in India.

In the past decade, the Government of India, under PM Modi, has been instrumental in strengthening the social security fabric of the nation through a series of impactful schemes. The Ayushman Bharat Yojana, a flagship programme launched in 2018, stands as a testament to India's commitment to universal healthcare. It offers health insurance coverage of up to Rs 5 lakh per family per year, benefiting over 50 crore citizens and ensuring that the poorest and most vulnerable groups can access healthcare without the burden of financial hardship. The Pradhan Mantri Jeevan Jyoti Bima Yojana (PMJJBY) offers affordable life insurance, while the Pradhan Mantri Suraksha Bima Yojana (PMSBY) provides accident insurance, both of which have ensured protection for families against unforeseen events. Direct benefit transfer has been another game-changer, aimed at ensuring the efficient transfer of benefits directly into the bank accounts of beneficiaries, cutting down layers of bureaucracy and reducing leakage. Covering a wide array of welfare programmes, DBTs have reformed the subsidy system in the country, from LPG subsidies under the Pradhan Mantri Ujjwala Yojana to subsidies for farmers under the Pradhan Mantri Kisan Samman Nidhi Yojana. Additionally, the Atal Pension Yojana (APY) targeted the unorganised sector, offering a steady pension in the sunset years, thereby securing the future of the elderly. Furthermore, addressing the basic need for shelter, the Pradhan Mantri Awas Yojana (PMAY) has been ambitious in its aim to provide 'Housing for All', especially for the poor. Between April 2016 and February 2024, over 2.5 crore houses have been built in the rural areas under the Pradhan Mantri Awaas Yojana–Gramin (PMAY-G).3

These schemes collectively form a multifaceted framework of social security, significantly reducing vulnerability and creating a more inclusive society. They not only offer financial relief but also impart a sense of dignity and self-reliance among beneficiaries, contributing to the broader objective of eradicating poverty and fostering a more equitable development model in India.

Initiatives such as Stand-up India, widespread credit availability, skill enhancement of self-help groups (SHGs) and financial support to street vendors represent the concerted effort of the government to include individuals from all sectors of society in the economic fabric. Tailoring welfare schemes to the unique demographic and occupational landscapes including but not limited to women, youth, the differently abled and particularly vulnerable tribal groups, and artisans. This strategy doesn't just build necessary social infrastructure; it also equips individuals to advance up the socioeconomic ladder, seizing the opportunities that come with becoming a developed economy.

TECHNOLOGICAL AND DIGITAL REVOLUTION

Under the leadership of PM Modi, the nation embarked on an ambitious journey to harness technology for governance, financial inclusion and societal advancement. At the heart of this digital transformation was the Aadhaar initiative, which saw coverage expand to 138 crore individuals, effectively the entire population. This biometric identification system became the backbone of a new governance model, enabling the delivery of government services, subsidies and benefits in a targeted and leakage-proof manner. The system's efficiency and reach were crucial to creating a more inclusive socioeconomic environment where the benefits of India's growth could percolate to the last mile.

The mobile revolution played a pivotal role in this digital narrative. Mobile penetration surged to 71 per cent, reflecting not just the accessibility of technology but also its integration into the daily lives of citizens. This leap in connectivity empowered individuals with information, access to services, and a platform for economic opportunity. Internet penetration also witnessed a significant jump to 50 per cent, catalysing the rise of digital entrepreneurship, e-commerce and digital literacy, creating a connected and digitally savvy populace. The impact of this digital proliferation was most evident in the financial sector, where mobile money transactions per 1,000 adults witnessed an exponential rise to over 5,000 in 2022 from thirty-six in 2013.4 This remarkable increase indicates a massive shift towards digital payments, fostering a cashless economy and financial inclusion. This digitisation of transactions not only simplified commerce but also brought transparency and efficiency to financial operations, reducing corruption and stimulating economic activity. As per estimates, almost one out of every two mobile payments in the world now take place in India.

The capital markets too were revolutionised by this digital wave. With the introduction of digital and mobile platforms for trading, a new generation of retail investors emerged. The stock markets saw increased democratisation, as individuals from various socioeconomic backgrounds began participating in equity investment, drawn by the convenience and accessibility of digital tools.

The government's push towards digital banking was accelerated with initiatives like the UPI, which revolutionised digital transactions. By 2024, the widespread adoption of digital banking significantly enhanced customer convenience, reduced transaction costs and increased transparency. This digital leap was instrumental in combating corruption, increasing tax compliance and boosting the efficiency of financial transactions.

The Startup India initiative played a crucial role in India's transformation into a global innovation hub by fostering entrepreneurship and facilitating start-up growth. Aimed at creating a conducive ecosystem for start-ups, the initiative simplified business regulations, provided tax exemptions and introduced a 'Fund of Funds' to financially support burgeoning start-ups. By 2024, these efforts had propelled India to become the third-largest start-up ecosystem worldwide, with numerous unicorns emerging in sectors such as fintech, e-commerce and edtech.

In the realm of education, technology played a transformative role, with digital classrooms and online learning platforms becoming the norm. The pandemic-induced shift to online education underscored the criticality of digital infrastructure, which enabled continuity in learning and expanded the reach of quality education.

The digital revolution, spearheaded by significant initiatives and widespread adoption of mobile technology, has redefined the Indian landscape. With a robust digital foundation in place, India is well-positioned to leverage technology for greater prosperity and innovation in the future.

REGULATORY REFORMS IN THE FINANCIAL SECTOR

The decade from 2014 to 2024 in India was marked by significant regulatory reforms in the markets. These reforms were pivotal were critical in shaping a robust, resilient and inclusive financial system, essential for supporting the country's burgeoning economic growth and development.

In 2014, India's banking sector was contending with several challenges, including high non-performing assets (NPAs), insufficient capitalisation and limited reach in rural areas. The government tackled the issue of NPAs head-on, with measures to improve the health of public sector banks (PSBs). Indian banking system's NPAs went up from Rs 58,700 crore in 2004 to Rs 3.2 lakh crore in 2014. Bank lending to the infrastructure sector went up from close to zero in early January 2004 to Rs 8.95 lakh crore in December 2014, growing by a CAGR of 28 per cent during the United Progressive Alliance (UPA) regime. Most of the infrastructure lending in Indian banks slowly turned into NPAs and continued till very late in PM Modi's tenure given the long gestation period for loans becoming NPAs, especially in infrastructure. Public–private partnerships acquired a bad reputation. The Insolvency and Bankruptcy Code (IBC) introduced in 2016 was a game-changer, providing a robust framework for resolving insolvencies and improving the recovery of bad loans. This legislation, along with the recapitalisation of banks and stricter regulatory oversight by the Reserve Bank of India (RBI), helped in stabilising the sector and restoring confidence among investors and the public. The period also saw the consolidation of PSBs, aimed at creating stronger and more competitive entities capable of meeting the growing needs of the economy. The mergers were intended to enhance capital efficiency, diversify risk and leverage synergies in operations.

In capital markets, the government, along with regulatory bodies like the Securities and Exchange Board of India (SEBI), embarked on a series of reforms to address these issues and make the Indian markets more attractive to both domestic and international investors. One of the key areas of reform was improving corporate governance. The introduction of stricter norms for board composition, enhanced disclosure requirements, push for sustainable development goals (SDGs) and stronger regulations for related party transactions aimed to increase corporate transparency and accountability. These measures boosted investor confidence, especially among foreign institutional investors, who were seeking safe and well-regulated market environments.

The government and SEBI also focused on simplifying and streamlining regulatory processes to encourage participation in the capital markets. Efforts were made to ease the initial public offering (IPO) process with an accelerated T+3 listing cycle, making it more efficient and less time-consuming. This was crucial in enabling more companies, including start-ups and small to medium enterprises (SMEs), to access capital markets for funding. SEBI also took measures to strengthen the mutual fund industry, a vital component of the capital markets. India became the first country to implement T+1 settlement across the board in January 2023, setting new standards in capital markets around the world. To aid the SME ecosystem in India, both the major exchanges introduced a separate listing platforms, NSE Emerge and BSE SME. Since their inception, both Exchanges have helped list close to 870 companies on their SME platforms, raising approximately Rs 14,000 crore with market capitalisation surpassing Rs 2 lakh crore. Of these listed companies, more than 300 have migrated to the main board of the Exchanges as of December 2023. Since its inception, the year 2023 has marked the highest-ever SME listing on NSE Emerge, with 118 companies raising approximately Rs 3,469 crore.

Regulations were enhanced to improve transparency and risk management, ensuring better investor protection. The increased emphasis on financial literacy programmes also played a critical role in educating investors about the benefits and risks associated with capital market investments.

These reforms not only addressed the immediate challenges but also laid a strong foundation for the future, positioning India as a vibrant and well-regulated market in the global financial landscape. The focus on transparency, efficiency, investor protection and global integration was pivotal to attracting a broader investor base and facilitating the growth of the capital markets in tandem with the country's economic aspirations.

CAPITAL MARKET EVOLUTION

Over the past decade, capital markets in India have not just grown, but have evolved, matured and integrated with the global financial ecosystem. The regulatory reforms, technological advancements and proactive government policies have collectively contributed to capital ratio soaring from 60 per cent in FY2013–14 to an impressive 116 per cent in FY2023–24, and its share in global market capitalisation tripling from 1.8 per cent to 3.9 per cent.

As India looks to the future, its capital markets stand as a beacon of its economic success, reflecting the potential and promise of the nation's financial landscape. It is important to note that beyond performance, it is the notion of a safe, 'trust' market that is central to its conception. Regulatory efforts in the past decade, and especially so in more recent years, have always been always geared towards this objective.

GLOBAL STANDING AND FOREIGN POLICY

This era saw India, with PM Modi at the helm, asserting itself more confidently on the international stage, leveraging its growing economic might, soft power and diplomatic acumen to forge stronger ties and partnerships across the globe.

India's foreign policy during this decade was notable for its economic diplomacy. The country entered into several bilateral and multilateral trade agreements, with a focus on expanding its export markets and attracting foreign investment. Initiatives like 'Make in India' were aimed at positioning the country as a manufacturing and investment hub, aligning with global investors' interests.

India's Global Capability Centres (GCCs) doubled their presence, from 760 to 1,600, accounting for 45 per cent of all the GCCs in the world by 2024. This remarkable expansion reflected the nation's burgeoning role as a global hub for knowledge-based services, IT and IT-enabled services. Our service sector, buoyed by these centres, became a powerhouse, contributing significantly to the global services supply chain and showcasing the country's intellectual capital to the world. Foreign exchange earnings from tourism in India also saw a notable increase and the annual average number of foreign tourists ramped up to 93 lakhs before the pandemic (2015–20). This is a testament to the country's growing service industry and its capacity to attract international attention.

India's foreign policy during this period was characterised by a proactive and multidimensional approach. The government's 'Neighbourhood First' policy aimed to strengthen ties with the neighbouring countries, while the 'Act East' policy focused on enhancing relationships with the ASEAN region and beyond. India's engagement with major powers, including the United States, Russia, Gulf Cooperation Council and European countries, was recalibrated, aiming to strike a balance between strategic autonomy and pragmatic partnerships. Our relations with countries in the Middle East have never been better.

The government has also put a renewed emphasis on multilateralism, actively engaging with international organisations and at forums such as the United Nations and the World Trade Organization. India's G20 presidency, under the leadership of PM Modi, marked significant achievements that underscored the country's global leadership. PM Modi's decisive role was pivotal in bringing the voice of the Global South to the forefront, culminating in the historic inclusion of the African Union in the G20. This move, along with the unified approach to addressing global challenges, demonstrated India's commitment to a future of shared prosperity and collective responsibility. The presidency, commended for its hospitality, also made notable strides in digital initiatives, aiming to leverage technology for global progress. The summit was not only a diplomatic triumph but also a reflection of PM Modi's vision of unity, as global leaders converged to deliberate on a future that is interconnected and mutually supportive.

The G20 presidency saw India advancing significant initiatives, including developing a Middle East corridor. This strategic move is aimed at enhancing connectivity and fostering economic integration, reflecting India's broader foreign policy goals and its commitment to creating a multipolar world where regional partnerships are strengthened. The Middle East corridor initiative is expected to boost trade, open new markets and deepen ties with a region that is pivotal to India's energy security and geopolitical strategy, marking another milestone in PM Modi's tenure.

The future outlook for India is one of optimism and potential. Building on the achievements of the past decade, the country is well-positioned to address its challenges, capitalise on its opportunities, and continue its journey towards becoming a global economic powerhouse. The focus on sustainable and inclusive growth, digital innovation and strong governance will be pivotal in shaping India's trajectory in the coming years, and the route to our path towards 'Viksit Bharat' by 2047.

The building blocks of welfare via social security for all citizens, social inclusion, e-governance, public sensitivity, responsibility and accountability, fiscal restraint and infrastructure building will accelerate our next 10–15 years and act as an impetus for further growth and welfare.

My hypothesis is that if we continue on the path of progress using technology and continue to improve accountability and governance capabilities in public affairs, India should be able to reach GDP of USD 30 trillion from current levels of close to USD 4 trillion by 2047 and market capitalisation of USD 50 trillion in Indian listed companies from the current USD 4.75 trillion to become 'Viksit Bharat'.

Ashish Chauhan is the Managing Director and current CEO of the National Stock Exchange.

NOTES

1. World Bank.

2. 10 Year Average.
3. https://rhreporting.nic.in/netiay/homereports/HomeCumulativeDataReport.
4. https://data.imf.org/regular.aspx.

Britain–India Defence Relations in the New Age of Shared Threats and Global Insecurity

ROBERT CLARK

It is difficult to understand just how drastically different the world is now, in early 2024, compared to what it was just four years ago, in early 2020. An emerging global pandemic originating from an embarrassed and secretive China exposed just how reliant many of the West's critical supply chains—for everything from medicines to offshore manufacturing—were on Beijing. Russia had yet to fully reinvade its neighbour Ukraine, despite many alarming calls from Eastern European partners, fearful of Putin's murderous ambitions to carve Europe up once more. While Iran was reeling from the targeted strike in January 2020 of the all-powerful commander of the Islamic Revolutionary Guard Corps (IRGC), Qassam Soleimani, for his decades-long role in targeting US military personnel and interests across the Middle East, the Trump administration in Washington was enjoying some success in curtailing Iran's destabilising nuclear proliferation and wider terrorist-supporting activities, where other administrations had failed.

Now, having largely crushed the murderous and evil Islamic State in Iraq and Syria, Islamist terrorism is once more threatening peace in the Middle East, as a rejuvenated Iran, enjoying billions of dollars of assets which were once frozen, now seeks to militarise the region in pursuit of its strategic aims of destroying Israel and ejecting America from the Middle East. Industrialised total warfare is raging in Europe once more. On the other hand, China is seeking to leverage the Global South to remake the global order in its image, in the process threatening its neighbours from New Delhi to Tokyo. And then there is Iran, which is once more seeking to destabilise the Middle East and sow chaos in the region. In the midst of this, Britain must turn to existing strong alliances and partnerships to weather these stormy times.

There are not many as strong as the relations that Britain has enjoyed with India, which itself has undergone a decade of transformation under Prime Minister Narendra Modi. India is arguably London's closest ally in the Indian Ocean and the western Indo-Pacific regions, one of the most strategically vital maritime routes in the world. While it is of course important to acknowledge that the relationship with India has not always been as harmonious as it is today, Delhi nonetheless remains one of our closest natural allies and trusted partners, sharing many cultural and historical ties which have led to a forged relationship between the powers not found in many other partnerships, making ours a unique one steeped in history, common values, shared interests and respect. Given the many varied yet often interlinked threats facing both of our nations (supply chain reliance, energy insecurity, authoritarian threats to our democratic institutions, to name but a few), as we begin to charter a route through the challenges stated earlier and opportunities (including a strengthened domestic economic forecast combined with many post-Brexit trading opportunities) that 2024 is already presenting, both London and Delhi have a powerful opportunity to increase cooperation in several notable areas, particularly in trade, and defence and security.

While the details of a potential free trade agreement are being worked out by representatives of both governments, it is hopeful that a final agreement is not long away, with many previous obstacles overcome through hard diplomacy and compromise. Given the many seismic events threatening the prosperity and security of both nations, and broader global insecurity, attention must now turn to mutual cooperation in defence and security, where there is already a rich history of collaboration. This was recently demonstrated by India's Minister of Defence Rajnath Singh's visit to the UK in January 2024, the first defence ministerial visit in twenty-two years, poignantly signifying a 'reset' in bilateral defence ties. From New Delhi's perspective, the last few years of the relationship have been marked by Britian's disastrous so-called 'Golden Age' relations with China under the Cameron–Osborne years of the last decade, as well as the activities of pro-Kashmiri independence movements and pro-Khalistani extremism in the UK. Given this, India chose to instead deepen defence and security ties with France, the US and, notably, Russia—a concern for London as the British government has taken a lead in supporting the European ally Ukraine in its war against Russian aggression.

Despite these concerns, British and Indian strategic priorities have convened in the last four years, with a shared unease of China's belligerent actions in the Indian Ocean and South

China Sea, and disruptions to global energy supplies and more recently to global shipping lanes. Accordingly, in May 2021, Prime Minister Narendra Modi and the then Prime Minister of the UK Boris Johnson launched the 2030 Roadmap for India–UK Future Relations, a ten-year strategic plan for bilateral cooperation along five pillars, including defence and security, while elevating the relationship to a Comprehensive Strategic Partnership. Subsequent meetings between the two National Security Advisors, in 2022 and then again in 2023, helped solidify trust and advance progress in this emerging bilateral security relationship. All of these agreements and meetings culminated in Defence Minister Rajnath Singh's London visit at the start of 2024, which resulted in, amongst other announcements, the signing of a Letter of Arrangement between India's Defence Research and Development Organisation and the UK's Defence Science and Technology Laboratory. This letter of agreement focuses on next-generation defence capabilities, including several new joint initiatives on logistics exchange between the armed forces of the two nations. Britian also announced plans to send the Littoral Response Group to the Indian Ocean later this year, and plans to deploy the Carrier Strike Group to train alongside Indian forces in 2025.

Given the converging strategic interests of the two nations, the revived partnership between them should concentrate on solidifying military cooperation using existing channels of communication and by sharing best practices. This would mean the UK joining Indian maritime deployments and anti-piracy operations across the Indian Ocean, including a strengthening of the ongoing MILAN multilateral Naval exercise hosted by India. Similarly, India could contribute to the US- and UK-led operations in the Red Sea, where its Navy is already heavily deployed to the east, by providing intelligence and helping combat piracy. Increasing practical bilateral military exercises and deployments should also help the UK make a sound military aspirational case for joining the armed forces of India, the US, Japan and Australia—the so-called Quadrilateral, or Quad—in the separate annual military Exercise Malabar. Concurrently to strengthening existing military collaboration, an earnest review is now required to explore how best to rejuvenate defence industrial relations. This vital and as-yet missing component of the bilateral defence partnership will help to further deepen ties between London and New Delhi. In this age of increasing geopolitical risk and tension, likely interstate conflict and costly supply chain disruptions, prudent nations like the UK and India are likely to seek to rely on trusted alliances and partnerships in an ever-increasing capacity.

Seeing Modi's 'India-first' trade policies aimed at reshoring India's manufacturing base, including the flagship 2014 'Make in India' programme, there remains plenty of scope for collaboration between Britain and India on defence industrial issues. For instance, even 2020's 'Atmanirbhar Bharat' ('self-reliant India') policy, aimed at supporting India's defence-industrial base, seeks foreign technology collaborations with friendly nations like Britain. So far there have been no joint programmes under this framework. This becomes an increasingly missed opportunity for Britain, which would like to see India reduce its reliance on Russian military imports in the light of Russia's war against Britain's ally Ukraine. Exasperating the British reluctance to engage harder with India's defence industrial base are Treasury concerns over India's financial regulatory standards, amongst other fiscal worries. However, neither the US nor France, with the current governments of either not particularly well-known for financial risk-taking, sees comparable quibbles over Indian financial practices or standards when it comes to their far more developed and matured defence industrial ties. The UK government should order an independent review looking into Treasury concerns on these matters, with an eye for increased financial engagement going forward should such concerns be potentially unfounded or less severe than currently thought.

British defence manufacturers should be seen to have a greater footprint and engagement in India. Britain should be seen to be willing to increase investment in India's defence industry, where appropriate. India, in turn, should appreciate that it is no longer in their strategic interest to rely so heavily on outdated, and now evidently outperformed, Russian military imports and industrial partnerships. In its place, New Delhi will find a welcome and willing partner in the UK, ready and able to further foster an already burgeoning and history-rich cultural and diplomatic relationship. The strengthening of their ties would help both nations further develop their respective defence base—for the common good of each party and the security of their people. A new decade of opportunity between the two allies is within grasp and must now be seized.

Robert Clark is a Fellow at the Yorktown Institute in Washington, DC and a Senior Fellow at Civitas in London. Prior to this, he served in the British military.

India's Future
Global Leadership

SCOT FAULKNER

The current geopolitical environment provides a historic opportunity for India to solidify its leadership on a global scale.

The challenges facing democratic free-loving nations are immense and complex. Since 1917, the United States has taken the lead to inspire and implement actions to thwart tyrants and protect its allies. Unfortunately, the US can no longer be relied upon to fulfil this responsibility.

President Joe Biden's foreign policy, national security and intelligence teams are the weakest and least prepared to meet global challenges of any administration in American history.[1,2] Possible foreign influence and business ties between Biden's family members and China undermine the usual resolve to stand firm for democratic principles and honour treaty obligations.[3]

Equally disturbing, the rise of former President Donald Trump sends mixed signals. Trump enjoyed a close relationship with Indian Prime Minister Narendra Modi. Trump's India tour on 24–25 February 2020 was a triumphant high point in India–US relations. The rally in Ahmedabad, Gujarat amazed commentators across the American political spectrum.

However, Trump's sometimes chaotic foreign policy and the current campaign pronouncements have shattered the long-established Reagan era conservative consensus.[4]

Bush-era 'neo-conservatives' (neo-cons), often voiced by Senator Lindsay Graham (Republican Senator, South Carolina), refuse to admit their mistakes in Afghanistan and Iraq.[5] They retain their approach of ignoring national cultures and history to impose American-style 'nation-building'. This means trying to create representative democracy in a few years while overlooking that it took Western Europe over 1,300 years to achieve a similar result (end of the Roman era to nineteenth-century democracy).[6]

Reagan alumni maintain their more balanced approach of boldly standing up to tyranny while inspiring others. They continue to project America as the 'shining city on the hill' to embolden those seeking freedom to fight and win in their own way.[7]

The core of Trump supporters, in Congress, think tanks and the conservative media, are articulating a very different world view. While honouring the 'Abraham Accords' breakthrough in the Middle East, they universally espouse 'America First' isolationism. Many pro-Trump Members of Congress are openly hostile to continued funding for Ukraine. Most stand by Israel, but they are placing some limits on that as well. They want the priority to be sealing off America's southern border with Mexico to end illegal immigration.[8]

The weakness of the Biden team and the disarray among Trump's supporters are being closely watched by China and America's allies in the Indo-Pacific region.[9]

This growing concern is grounded in America's general approach to confronting international threats. Except during

Reagan's crusade to destroy the Soviet Empire and the Soviet Union, America has traditionally been reactive to foreign challenges. America's quick and overwhelming reaction to Pearl Harbor remains the basis of this view. As long as America can ramp-up and successfully fight back, it can wait and see.

To put it another way, America prides itself as being exceptionally good at 'Whac-A-Mole'.

Whac-A-Mole is an arcade game where toy moles (North American rodents that burrow into field and lawns) pop up at random through various holes on a board. The object is to hit the toy moles with a mallet and score points for each successful hit.[10]

Just like in the arcade game, America's foreign policy and national security establishments spend less time determining if there is a predictable pattern to the moles popping up than to perfecting the constant effort to react.

Alternatively, China is perfecting the game it invented—Go.[11]

Around 2306 BCE, Chinese rulers developed a game to teach strategic thinking. The object of the game is to place pieces to control ever larger sections of the board.

China's President Xi Jinping and his military, economic, intelligence and technology teams are playing a master's level Go game.[12]

This is the challenge of the twenty-first century. How can freedom-loving people prevail when China is playing championship Go and the US is failing at Whac-A-Mole?

CHINA'S ECONOMIC OFFENSIVE

The ultimate Go board was initiated with Xi's Belt and Road Initiative (BRI).[13]

China launched the BRI in 2013 as a massive infrastructure project establishing the ancient Silk Road as the epicentre of twenty-first century transport and trade. China has recruited 125 nations to participate and pledged USD 150 billion a year to make it a reality.[14]

The Belt and Road Initiative is part of an aggressive and comprehensive strategy to become the world's dominant economic power by 2050. In 2018, the nineteenth Chinese Communist Party (CCP) Congress openly espoused this goal.

During the 2023 BRI Summit, Chinese foreign minister Wang Yi reaffirmed China's commitment to project itself through development partnerships to create an alternative vision to America.

'Why don't we take a look at the international track record, in terms of who can build more roads, railways and bridges for developing countries, and who can build more schools, hospitals and stadiums for the people of developing countries,' he said. 'We have the confidence and the capability.'[15]

China's boasts are taken very seriously by leading scholars in the field. 'There are the systematic efforts [by China] to refine methods of converting economic influence into economic coercion throughout the Asia-Pacific and beyond.'[16]

China's 'New Era' strategy echoes the mercantile policies of the eighteenth- and nineteenth-century imperialism. Its world view builds on lessons learnt during the Cold War.

During the Cold War, the US and the USSR globally competed for strategic resources and control of sea routes. The Soviets were driven by a Communist world view to forcibly take over the world and crush Western democracy and freedom. Soviet military and intelligence assets toppled governments, supported insurgencies and undermined Western resolve.

The US responded with a tepid 'containment' strategy that ceded large swaths of the world to communist tyranny. Soviet 'agents of influence' obfuscated true intentions by labelling Communist guerilla bands as 'agrarian reformers'. 'Agents of influence' were recruited by the USSR drawn from likeminded liberals and leftists in American and European governments, academia and the media to confuse issues, overcomplicate solutions and bungle countermeasures. Both East and West framed much of their efforts as economic reform or development. The communists destroyed whole populations with murder and starvation. The West killed with kindness. Liberal academicians, instead of businesspersons, ran development agencies that spent trillions on poorly conceived and implemented projects. The Developing World is littered with empty buildings, rusting tractors and environmentally damaged landscapes.

China capitalised on the West's Developing World failures by promising a new, modern approach.

Starting in 2000, China began pouring money into highly targeted projects in Africa. They either directly built and ran the project or offered enticing loans.

The direct approach for China is to take over a natural resource, such as a mine, take over the port for shipping the resource, and build rail and road links between them. Chinese workers run everything. There is no effort to employ or engage 'host county nationals' (HNCs). One by one, China has solidified control over strategic mineral resources and ports throughout Africa.

When direct control was not immediately available, China initiated 'Debt Trap Diplomacy' (DTD).[17]

The most infamous DTD project was China gaining control of the Kenyan port of Mombasa.

Mombasa is the third-largest port in Africa. China's long-term power play started with loaning funds to the Kenya government, to develop the Standard Gauge Railway (SGR). The SGR links to the new Inland Container Depot in Nairobi, which receives and dispatches freight hauled on the new cargo trains from Mombasa. Eventually, China called in its loan, which it knew Kenya could not afford. In one act, China owns a key port on the Indian Ocean and its supportive infrastructure.[18]

The Mombasa seizure follows other China DTD activities. In December 2017, the Sri Lankan government lost the port of Hambantota to China, for a lease period of ninety-nine years. This happened after failing to repay billions of dollars in loans.

China's economic strategy remains unchallenged on making its vision of world domination a reality.

CHINA'S MILITARY OFFENSIVE

As master 'Go' players, Chinese leaders are not placing all their Go pieces in the BRI basket.[19] China's military has been busy developing another way forward.[20, 21, 22, 23] The main arena is the South China Sea. China has fully exploited the complex history of this region to assert territorial claims. They have moved diplomatically, legally and militarily to establish their dominance. Confronting Philippines' maritime sovereignty is a key test.[24]

China–Philippines confrontations intensified with claims relating to Scarborough Shoal (10 April 2012) and Fiery Cross

Reef in the Spratly Island chain (late 2013). Ultimately, China began expanding and fortifying these and other small atolls.[25]

Instead of direct confrontation and sanctions, President Barack Obama chose to mount Freedom of Navigation Operations (FONOPs), where U.S. Navy ships transited China's new maritime zones to challenge its claims.

This weak response did little to slow China's expansion.[26, 27, 28]

President Donald Trump mounted strong rhetorical and economic initiatives against China, but to little avail.[29]

America leaders, from both political parties, failed in grappling with China's aggression. At the same time, China bolstered its naval capacity. China's 'naval shipbuilding program ... put more vessels to sea between 2014 and 2018 than the total number of ships in the German, Indian, Spanish, and British navies combined.' The size of the Chinese navy now surpasses the U.S. Navy.[30]

Instead of rising up to meet China's expansion, US naval capabilities, and those of its allies in the region, are declining.[31, 32, 33]

China's aggression in the South China Sea positions it to accomplish its long-stated goal of 'reunification' with Taiwan.[34] It further positions China to dominate and intimidate all countries that border this body of water and control a vital international trade waterway.[35]

China's maritime expansion is mirrored by its territorial aggression. India is confronting China along its border [36] and so is Nepal.[37]

China sees Asia, and the Pacific and Indian Oceans, as its 'Go' game board. It is winning.

America's ineffective response to China has been slow and fragmented. This is partly because US leaders have no idea what America should be doing in the world.

Starting with the Spanish-American War, America had a clear idea of its role in the world. John Philip Sousa composed his famous *Stars and Stripes Forever* to honour Admiral Dewey's victory against the Spanish fleet in Manila Bay. It embodied the patriotic fervour that would propel America for the next ninety-four years.

Theodore Roosevelt earned a Nobel Peace Prize for settling the Russo-Japanese War. *The Yanks Are Coming* heralded America's entry into World War I. On 29 December 1940, President Franklin Roosevelt declared the US the 'arsenal of democracy' to help stem the tide of tyranny and lead to winning World War II. In the 1980s, President Ronald Reagan went on the offence by describing the US as the 'shining city on the hill' to serve as a beacon of hope, inspiring millions to topple the Soviet Empire.

Unfortunately, America has had no actionable global strategy since the Berlin Wall fell. China has filled the void.[38]

INDIA'S OPPORTUNITY

Prime Minister Modi can lead India and the Indo-Pacific in effectively countering China's aggression. He could deploy a holistic approach that addresses economic, cultural, political and military aspects of China's challenge. He can become the new 'Go Master'.

India has a tradition of balancing global power blocs.

At its very inception, India was a driving force in countering Cold War divisiveness. In March 1947, Jawaharlal Nehru organised and led the Asian Relations Conference to assess Indo-Asian regional issues.

Other international conferences followed, leading up to the Asian–African Summit on 18–24 April 1955 in Bandung, Indonesia.[39] The result was the Non-Aligned Movement, which served as a third sphere of influence during the Cold War.[40]

Today, India continues to be a pivotal influence centre as a member of the G20 and the host of its 2023 summit.[41] India is part of the BRICS nations,[42] which is redefining global relations.[43]

It is India's role in the Quad nations that may guide its future leadership in the region.

In 2004, the Quad nations were formed to address the historic tsunami that devastated the countries surrounding the India Ocean. Australia, India, Japan and the US found common cause in the region's recovery. In the process, they expanded regional cooperation to strengthen their socioeconomic and cultural bonds.[44]

The Quad became a typical activity trap for career diplomats to plan meetings and issue general policy statements. Under President Biden it has further fallen from relevance.[45]

The Quad was briefly revitalised through the close friendships among Prime Minister Modi, Japanese Prime Minister Shinzo Abe, Australian Prime Minister Scott Morrison and US President Donald Trump.

Modi remains the only member of this team still serving in office. He can harness the fundamentals of the Quad and its shared values to prevail in winning the hearts and minds of people throughout the Indo-Pacific region.

India's unique network of relationships within the BRICS and G20 can strengthen the Quad as a more cohesive force for peace and deterrence in the Indo-Pacific.

An India-led Quad revitalisation could focus on two complementary projects:

1. Promoting investment and partnerships
2. Promoting 'shared values' and a 'free and open Indo-Pacific'

INVESTMENT AND PARTNERSHIPS

The West realises its mistake in becoming dependent on China for manufacturing and pharmaceuticals. 'Decoupling' from China is the West's new goal.[46, 47]

Decoupling is complex and will take time. India can expedite this process and reap substantial benefits. Western firms are seeking supply chain partners that can assure consistency, quality and sustainability, while being cost-effective.

Pacific Rim nations have started to meet this need. Decoupling has spurred economic growth in Indonesia, Japan, the Philippines, South Korea, Thailand and Vietnam.[48]

Taiwan remains a viable alternative, especially for chip manufacturers.[49] However, the ongoing invasion threat from China is a fundamental uncertainty.

The future could be India's. A recent medical conference in Manipal[50] showcased India's emerging leadership in the critical medical equipment industry. The Manipal conference could serve as a model for other forums. These conferences could be bolstered, by government policy and incentives, to attract investment and partnerships throughout India across multiple economic sectors.

India could create investment funds, in cooperation with public and private sectors, utilising innovation, ingenuity and tapping the expertise of key experts in private equity and venture capital among the Quad nations.[51]

India could promote training for entrepreneurs seeking to utilise these human, technical and financial resources to prepare Indian professionals in digital technologies, including cybersecurity and aerospace.

India could incentivise students returning home after studying at US universities. A record 2,68,923 Indian students attended US colleges and universities,[52, 53] but 80 per cent remain in the US instead of returning to help the Indian economy.[54]

AWARENESS AND SUPPORT

India remains on the periphery of US political concerns. Indian-Americans comprise only 1 per cent of those voting.[55] Over 1.3 million Americans visit India each year, but the country remains 'exotic'. Few Americans are aware of India's economic vitality.[56]

'Indian Prime Minister Narendra Modi has made outreach to the far-flung Indian diaspora a signature element of his government's foreign policy. Modi's courtship of the diaspora has been especially notable in the United States.'[57]

India could develop a cultural and political outreach drawing on lessons learnt from China's Confucius Institute. China's programme was revealed as a hub of propaganda and espionage activities.[58] India could avoid this by endowing scholarly centres and faculty positions for studying India and Indo-Pacific history, cultural, economics and geopolitics. 'Sister School' partnerships could be expanded between India and US institutions. Funding fellowships supporting US students studying at Indian universities would boost awareness and affiliations.

India could replicate these academic exchanges with Japan and Australia to further promote the shared values of the Quad nations.

Indian research centres, including geopolitical and economic, could establish partnerships. Private companies and organisations could fund scholars at US 'think tanks' to aggregate, curate and disseminate research on India and the Indo-Pacific region. They could organise and sponsor policy forums on these topics.

The goal is to raise positive awareness about India and its emerging global leadership role with decision-makers, influencers and the media. This could include developing a resource network of Indian subject matter experts who would be available to speak at conferences, engage at forums and provide media commentary on issues and news arising from the Indo-Pacific region.

These ideas can become part of a long-term, holistic strategy for institutionalising India's role in promoting the Quad countries' shared values, transcending domestic politics. This includes clear and consistent messaging of the Quad countries' aspirational vision of a free and open society, universal economic opportunity, and regional peace and stability.

India's vision and role could be reinforced, reaffirmed, aligned and embedded through organisational development within government and private entities, education/professional development, economic/professional incentives, and cultural exchange.

No one action will assure India's leadership in the Indo-Pacific region and globally. Understanding the interrelated challenges, and identifying the way forward, would position

India to dominate the geopolitical 'Go' board of the twenty-first century.

Scot Faulkner is former Chief Administrator Officer, U.S. Congress and advisor on economic development. He was also Director of Personnel for President Ronald Reagan.

NOTES

1. Author's content and context are drawn from off-the-record conversations with current and former members of Congress, senior government officials and policy experts.
2. Simon Hankinson, '"Woke" Public Diplomacy Undermines the State Department's Core Mission and Weakens U.S. Foreign Policy', The Heritage Foundation, 12 December 2022, https://www.heritage.org/global-politics/report/woke-public-diplomacy-undermines-the-state-departments-core-mission-and.
3. Peter Schweizer, 'Chinese Elite Have Paid Some $31M to Hunter and the Bidens', *New York Post*, 22 January 2022, https://nypost.com/2022/01/27/chinese-elite-have-paid-some-31m-to-hunter-and-the-bidens/.
4. Bill Schneider, 'Trump and the Return of American Isolationism', The Messenger – MSN, https://www.msn.com/en-us/news/politics/trump-and-the-return-of-american-isolationism/ar-AA1gglnF.
5. Jeet Heer, 'The Abject Failure of Biden's Quiet Diplomacy Is Spreading Middle Eastern Chaos', *The Nation*, 29 January 2024, https://www.thenation.com/article/world/biden-quiet-diplomacy-failure-middle-east/.
6. Scott Faulkner, 'Fifty Shades of Republican', *Citizen Oversight*, 20 October 2013, https://citizenoversight.blogspot.com/2013/10/fifty-shades-of-republican.html.

7. Scott Faulkner, 'Of BRICS & Dragons', *Citizen Oversight,* 30 June 2013, https://citizenoversight.blogspot.com/2013/06/of-brics-dragons.html.
8. Jeet Heer, 'This Isn't Your Father's GOP. It's Your Grandfather's GOP', *The Nation – MSN*, https://www.msn.com/en-us/news/politics/this-isn-t-your-father-s-gop-it-s-your-grandfather-s-gop/ar-AA1jtEou.
9. Robbie Gramer and Christina Lu, 'ASEAN Snub: Biden Skips Key Summit, Angering Officials in Southeast Asia', *Foreign Policy*, 5 September 2023, https://foreignpolicy.com/2023/09/05/biden-asean-summit-us-china-southeast-asia-snub/.
10. Whack-A-Mole: Definition, Meaning, and Origin, https://usdictionary.com/idioms/whack-a-mole/.
11. 'The Ancient Chinese Game of Go', 7 June 2005, www.china.org.cn/english/features/Archaeology/131298.htm.
12. Rush Doshi, 'The Long Game: China's Grand Strategy to Displace American Order', Brookings, 2 August 2021, https://www.brookings.edu/articles/the-long-game-chinas-grand-strategy-to-displace-american-order/.
13. Scott Faulkner, 'China Rising', *Citizen Oversight*, 3 May 2019, https://citizenoversight.blogspot.com/2019/05/china-rising.html.
14. Felix K. Chang, 'China's Belt and Road Initiative: Politics Over Economics', Foreign Policy Research Institute, 19 September 2023, https://www.fpri.org/article/2023/09/chinas-belt-and-road-initiative-politics-over-economics/.
15. Simone McCarthy, 'Putin's Prominence and the Shadow of Conflict: Key Takeaways from China's Belt and Road Forum', CNN, 19 October 2023, https://edition.cnn.com/2023/10/19/china/china-bri-forum-key-takeaways-intl-hnk/index.html.
16. Rush Doshi, 'The Long Game'.
17. Scott Faulkner, 'China Rising'.
18. Fergus Kell, 'Kenya's Debt Struggles Go Far Deeper than Chinese Loans', Chatham House, 31 May 2023, https://www.chathamhouse.org/2023/05/kenyas-debt-struggles-go-far-deeper-chinese-loans.

19. Bloomberg, 'Xi Jinping's Vow of World Dominance by 2049 Sends Chill through Markets' The *Times of India*, 26 October 2022, https://timesofindia.indiatimes.com/business/international-business/xi-jinpings-vow-of-world-dominance-by-2049-sends-chill-through-markets/articleshow/95102018.cms.
20. John Feng, 'Xi Jinping Says China to Become Dominant World Power Within 30 Years', *Newsweek*, https://www.newsweek.com/xi-jinping-says-china-become-dominant-world-power-within-30-years-1605848.
21. David Axe, 'This Is China's 30-Year-Plan for Global Military Dominance', *The National Interest*, 6 September 2020, https://nationalinterest.org/blog/reboot/chinas-30-year-plan-global-military-dominance-168398/
22. Robert O. Work and Greg Grant, 'Beating the Americans at Their Own Game', Center for a New American Security (CNAS), https://www.cnas.org/publications/reports/beating-the-americans-at-their-own-game.
23. Robert Peters and Wilson Beavers, 'The Defense Department's China Military Power Report: The Threat Is Worse Than Advertised', The Heritage Foundation, 30 January 2024, https://www.heritage.org/defense/commentary/the-defense-departments-china-military-power-report-the-threat-worse-advertised.
24. Author's conversation with Chinese Foreign Ministry Officials, Beijing, PRC, 8 June 2013.
25. 'The Recent History of the South China Sea: A Timeline', Crisis Group, https://www.crisisgroup.org/asia/south-east-asia/south-china-sea/recent-history-south-china-sea-timeline/.
26. Associated Press, 'China Has Fully Militarized Three Islands in South China Sea, US Admiral Says', *The Guardian*, 21 March 2022, https://www.theguardian.com/world/2022/mar/21/china-has-fully-militarized-three-islands-in-south-china-sea-us-admiral-says.
27. 'Key Events that Led to the Latest US-China Confrontation in the South China Sea', *The Straits Times*, 27 August 2020, https://

www.straitstimes.com/asia/se-asia/key-events-that-led-to-the-latest-us-china-confrontation-in-the-south-china-sea/.
28. Center for Preventive Action, 'Territorial Disputes in the South China Sea', Global Conflict Tracker, 30 April 2024, https://www.cfr.org/global-conflict-tracker/conflict/territorial-disputes-south-china-sea/.
29. U.S. Naval Institute Staff, 'Report on U.S.-China Competition in East, South China Sea', USNI News, 6 February 2024. https://news.usni.org/2024/02/06/report-on-u-s-china-competition-in-east-south-china-sea-13/; 'U.S.-China Strategic Competition in South and East China Seas: Background and Issues for Congress' Congressional Research Service, https://crsreports.congress.gov/product/pdf/R/R42784.
30. China Shipbuilding Statistics, ChinaPower Project, https://chinapower.csis.org/data/china-shipbuilding-statistics/.
31. Steve Wills, 'End the Navy's 30-Year Slide in Capability and Capacity', Proceedings, April 2023 Vol. 149/4/1,442, https://www.usni.org/magazines/proceedings/2023/april/end-navys-30-year-slide-capability-and-capacity/.
32. Zamone Perez, 'US Military in Decline, Threats from China "Formidable," Report Says', *DefenseNews*, 18 October 2022, https://www.defensenews.com/global/the-americas/2022/10/18/us-military-in-decline-threats-from-china-formidable-report-says/.
33. Kim Beazley, 'Australia's Disappearing Surface Combatant Fleet', *The Maritime Executive*, 21 January 2024, https://maritime-executive.com/editorials/australia-s-disappearing-surface-combatant-fleet/.
34. Charlie Bradley, 'South China Sea Tensions Soar as China Warns "We Will Show Our Swords" against US', *Daily Express US – MSN*, https://www.msn.com/en-us/news/world/south-china-sea-tensions-soar-as-china-warns-we-will-show-our-swords-against-us/ar-BB1hW8y7.
35. Chad de Guzman, 'Why China Keeps Antagonizing Others in the South China Sea', *TIME*, 8 August 2023, https://time.com/6302515/china-philippines-south-china-sea-aggression/.

36. Aadil Brar, 'Deadly Border Clash Exposed China As "No. 1 Threat"—India Army General', *Newsweek – MSN*, https://www.msn.com/en-us/news/world/deadly-border-clash-exposed-china-as-no-1-threat-india-army-general/ar-BB1id68u.
37. Michael Bristow, 'China Encroaching along Nepal Border – Report', BBC, 8 February 2022, https://www.bbc.com/news/world-asia-6028800.
38. Jake Sullivan and Hal Brands, 'China Has Two Paths to Global Domination', Carnegie Endowment for International Peace, 22 May 2020, https://carnegieendowment.org/2020/05/22/china-has-two-paths-to-global-domination-pub-81908.
39. 'Final Communiqué of the Asian-African Conference of Bandung (24 April 1955)', CVCE Website, https://www.cvce.eu/en/obj/final_communique_of_the_asian_african_conference_of_bandung_24_april_1955-en-676237bd-72f7-471f-949a-88b6ae513585.html.
40. Britannica, Non-Aligned Movement (NAM), Definition, Mission, & Facts, https://www.britannica.com/topic/Non-Aligned-Movement.
41. Forbes India, 'G20 Summit 2023: Dates, Schedule & Agenda, Member Countries, Leaders, and More', *Forbes India*, 9 September 2023, https://www.forbesindia.com/article/explainers/g20-summit-countries-leaders-schedule-agenda/88051/1.
42. 'BRICS 2023 – BRICS and Africa: Partnership for Mutually Accelerated Growth, Sustainable Development and Inclusive Multilateralism', https://brics2023.gov.za/.
43. Faulkner, 'Of BRICS & Dragons'.
44. Shiela A. Smith, 'The Quad in the Indo-Pacific: What to Know', Council on Foreign Relations, 27 April 2021, https://www.cfr.org/in-brief/quad-indo-pacific-what-know.
45. Suhasini Haidar, 'Quad Summit More Likely after the U.S. Elections in November: American Envoy Garcetti', *The Hindu*, 6 February 2024, https://www.thehindu.com/news/national/quad-summit-more-likely-after-the-us-elections-in-november-american-envoy-garcetti/article67815260.ece/.

46. 'Understanding Decoupling: Macro Trends and Industry Impacts', China Center, U.S. Chamber of Commerce, https://www.uschamber.com/assets/archived/images/024001_us_china_decoupling_report_fin.pdf
47. J. Stewart Black and Allen J. Morrison, 'The Strategic Challenges of Decoupling from China', *Harvard Business Review*. May–June 2021, https://hbr.org/2021/05/the-strategic-challenges-of-decoupling.
48. Ronald U. Mendoza, 'Rebalancing vs Decoupling: China-US Economic Ties and the Global Economy', *The Diplomat*, 10 February 2023, https://thediplomat.com/2023/02/rebalancing-vs-decoupling-china-us-economic-ties-and-the-global-economy/.
49. Milton Ezrati, 'Like the United States, Taiwan Is De-Coupling from China', *Forbes*, 8 May 2023, https://www.forbes.com/sites/miltonezrati/2023/05/08/like-the-united-states-taiwan-is-decoupling-from-china/?sh=2b405d1a62c0.
50. 'MAHE and WALT Organized "World Association for PhotobiomoduLation Therapy (WALT) Congress 2023'. Daijiworld.com, https://www.daijiworld.com/news/newsDisplay?newsID=1120487.
51. These recommendations are drawn from a draft Quad Strategy Proposal developed for Quad leaders by Dr Sunil Chacko and the author, 6 February 2023.
52. 'The United States Remains the Top Choice for Indian Students Pursuing Higher Education Abroad - U.S. Embassy & Consulates in India', U.S. Embassy and Consulates in India, 13 November 2023, https://in.usembassy.gov/the-united-states-remains-the-top-choice-for-indian-students-pursuing-higher-education-abroad/.
53. 'Despite Layoffs, Indian Students Stay in the US', *The Economic Times – MSN*, https://www.msn.com/en-in/news/India/despite-layoffs-indian-students-stay-in-the-us/ar-AA1jPUzt/.
54. '80% Indian Students Studying in the USA Don't Return Back

India', Workassist.in, 27 April 2023, https://workassist.in/blog/indian-students-studying-in-the-usa-dont-return-back-india.
55. IANS, 'Ballot 2024: What Do Indian-American Voters Want', *The Statesman*, 4 February 2024, https://www.thestatesman.com/world/ballot-2024-what-do-indian-american-voters-want-1503266300.html.
56 'India: Foreign Tourist Arrivals by Country of Origin 2022', Statista, https://www.statista.com/statistics/207005/foreign-tourist-arrivals-in-india-by-source-country/.
57 Sumitra Badrinathan, Devesh Kapur, and Milan Vaishnav, 'How Do Indian Americans View India? Results From the 2020 Indian American Attitudes Survey', Carnegie Endowment for International Peace, 9 February 2021, https://carnegieendowment.org/research/2021/02/how-do-indian-americans-view-india-results-from-the-2020-indian-american-attitudes-survey?lang=en.
58. Pratik Jakhar, 'Confucius Institutes: The Growth of China's Controversial Cultural Branch', BBC, 7 September 2019, https://www.bbc.com/news/world-asia-china-49511231/.

A Decade of Transformation
The Moment of India's True Independence

ANTONIA FILMER

In 2012, India was in a mood of melancholy due to a catalogue of past injustices; a sense of victimhood framed the minds and outlook of many Indians. This was also the year of the shocking Nirbhaya case, which brutally epitomised the plight of women and directed the world's eyes on India.

Contrary to expectations, Prime Minister Manmohan Singh was labelled an 'underachiever'. Some 1,200 km away, the then chief minister of Gujarat was elected for a third term. This chief minister was Narendra Modi, reputedly the most efficient and organised pro-market individual on a mission to transform Gujarat into an industrial powerhouse. Under his growth strategies and policies, Gujarat blossomed and its success was recognised, as were Modi's leadership skills. With the aim of replicating the prosperity of Gujarat, Modi was a possible candidate for the Bharatiya Janata Party (BJP) in the 2014 Lok Sabha election; his work ethic and humble and devout background were a welcome contrast to the dynastic entitlement of some of his predecessors. The 2014 Modi campaign was a thoroughly researched and masterful enterprise that successfully reached all corners of India, breaking demographic and geographic barriers. His social coalition offered more equality than the United Progressive Alliance (UPA) government, which was essentially wiped out. In 2014, it was the BJP that mustered the momentum around Modi; in 2024, it is Modi who musters the momentum around the BJP.

For the past decade, Modi's image has been ubiquitous. His appearance and attire have calmed down and matured since 2014. While delivering speeches, he wears the traditional headgear of the region; from Nagaland to Punjab, from Gujarat to Andhra Pradesh, this individuality is very appealing to his audience. Modi is relentless about rallies and public appearances; he graces events and inaugurates a countless variety of projects, ports, hospitals, banks, sporting events, shopping and drone festivals, and museums and art galleries. Modi is visible and connected through *Mann ki Baat*, his outreach radio programme. He finds time to seek blessings or pray at temples across India, from Dakshineswar in Kolkata to Kedarnath in Uttarakhand, from Sant Tukaram Temple in Maharashtra to Guruvayur in Kerala, amongst a myriad of others. Modi also initiated the renovation of the Kashi Vishwanath Corridor project to rival Kyoto's presentation of Japanese culture. His faith is unquestionable and the ultimate manifestation of this is the realisation of the Ram Mandir in Ayodhya. In football speak this could be termed as 'Ram Lalla's coming home', an essential event for India that is Bharat, and a critical theme before the 2024 general elections.

Culture and Bharat's ancient civilisations are a significant part of Modi's nation-building process. India's education curricula is gradually being adapted to comprehensively include India's rich tradition of Hindu learning and knowledge. Right from primary education, students are introduced to astronomy, social sciences and the civilisational heritage of India, in addition to the basic subjects. At the secondary stage, students are being introduced to India's classical concepts of art, metallurgy and everything else, including the origins of geopolitics via the subcontinent's relations with other civilisations over time, such as those in Mesopotamia, Greece, Central Asia, China, Southeast Asia, Arabia and Eastern Africa. There is no division or separation of art and science subjects—they are seen as compatible. The *National Curriculum Framework for School Education* document[1] reveals the remarkable 360-degree penetration of the current education system, offering insights into the depth and rigour of Indian pedagogy.

Contrary to how it is interpreted, BJP stands for the Bharatiya Janata Party, not the Indian People's Party. The move to rename India as Bharat is part of the Government of India's strategy to reclaim the civilisational identity and pride of India, bringing it is a step closer to Akhand Bharat—meaning, undivided India—with all its connotations; it is also a rejection of colonial mores and serves to establish a new independence from past obligations. In fact, I would go as far as to say that now is the moment of India's true independence, the moment that Bharat's absolute sovereignty has become apparent to the world. This and other initiatives, which detractors in the West call 'nationalist', are what have made the population drawn towards Prime Minister Modi. The Left-leaning West, particularly the Leftist press, seems to have tagged a negative interpretation to 'nationalist'. The Merriam-Webster Dictionary defines 'nationalist' as 'a sense of national consciousness exalting one nation above all others and placing primary emphasis on promotion of its culture and interests as opposed to those of other nations or supranational groups'—what's not to like about this in the context of today's geopolitics?

Until the twenty-first century, foreign policy and defence did not figure much in general elections anywhere; barely anyone had heard of, or considered, geopolitics as a factor in elections. Now, geopolitics has led to geoeconomics, and it seems PM Modi was one of the first to navigate these choppy waters. His tactic of 'friendships', including with those who might be termed as difficult customers, and engaging with adversaries, means that in troubled times he could pick up the phone and conduct 'invisible diplomacy'. The most recent example of this was seen in the evacuation of Indian citizens in Yemen and Ukraine. In the ten years of his premiership, he has made seventy-three international visits—often to more than one foreign country at a time—and attended fifty multilateral meetings in person and fourteen virtually. Modi is engaged nationally, locally and globally; he has brought India onto the world stage; and he has made a difference for his country, which is surely every leader's dream. During his overseas visits he makes a point of uniting the growing Indian diaspora, praising their successes and reconnecting them to their heritage.

His style varies from demonstrably hugging allies to silent diplomacy, perhaps both simultaneously when one observes the developing strategic infrastructure plans in the Gulf Cooperation Council (GCC) and the Global South. The new India–Middle-East–Europe Corridor poses challenges for the Belt and Road (B&R), Suez Canal and the Grand Faw Port; the International North–South Transport Corridor between Moscow and Mumbai suggests that it not only improves connectivity but is of better value and is sanction-proof against Iran and Russia; the Chabahar Port rail project connects India to Afghanistan and will expand India's maritime footprint; the Chennai–Vladivostok maritime route opens up necessary maritime connectivity throughout the eastern Indo-Pacific region. India has discreetly countered China's seduction of the Pacific Islands; in 2015, Modi called the India–Pacific Islands relationship a 'partnership of equals' and since has been magnifying the voice of the Pacific's lower-income countries on global issues such as the blue economy and pushing for convergence. The Pacific Islands and ASEAN engagements are part of India's quest for peace, prosperity and stability in the Indo-Pacific Region. All these geostrategic projects have taken on a new lease of life under PM Modi's banner of 'Vasudhaiva Kutumbakam'.

Indeed through the presidency of the 2023 G20, India introduced the rest of the world to the perspective of the Global South—from countries that are likely more geographically southern than the Washington, DC list. India has expanded out of its neighbourhood and become a global influence.

Modi's embracing and emphasising of Vasudhaiva Kutumbakam, the Indian humanitarian theme meaning 'the world is one family', is both a local and a global entreaty for a more compassionate and harmonious global citizenry.

Modi's oratory performances are legendary and his motivational slogans are intended to be unifying and egalitarian. Starting with *'Acche din aane waale hain'*—meaning 'good times are coming'—which undoubtedly appeals to everyone, the principles of minimum government/maximum governance and 'India First' strike a chord with people who look to democracy to fulfil their expectations. Arguably, 'achhe din' have arrived, with a stable growth rate and predictions of India being the world's third largest economy by 2030, and, even with their criteria varying, analysts agree that India's middle class has grown. 'India First' is demonstrated by the emphasis on self-reliance and India's independent foreign policy, which, as seen in its stance over Ukraine and Gaza, confounds the West. The 'Make in India' and 'Ease of Doing Business' campaigns have stimulated both the services and the manufacturing sector, particularly telecom. Since June 2014, India has launched 395 satellites from thirty-five countries and the Indian hardware market is estimated at USD 1,977 billion in 2024. India is considered one of the most valuable nations for its pharmaceutical sector, producing 60 per cent of vaccinations worldwide and 20 per cent of global volume; the foreign direct investment (FDI) in pharma in 2023 was USD 2 billion. Today, expanding sectors include aerospace production and assembly (Boeing and Airbus) and vehicle manufacturing (Ford, Hyundai, Volkswagen, Renault, Citroen, Honda and Nissan—all made in India, with a growing trend for electric vehicles). India remains a preferred FDI destination; in 2023, Singapore was the top FDI investor in India with over USD 17 billion, followed by Mauritius and the US.

The year 2019 was the test to gauge if Modi's ideas still had legs, and the increased majority proved his personal popularity: over 11.3 million lavatories were installed by June 2023, and the this project to build a lavatory in every home obliterated open defecation and became a life-changer especially for women. The same can be said for the abrogation of 1,600 moribund laws, some of which prevented women from being eligible for jobs. Moreover, over a million urban migrants and the poor working in the industrial sector have been rewarded with affordable and dignified rental accommodation and smart cities have proliferated. During the COVID-19 pandemic, every poor home in rural communities was supported with 5 kg of rice/lentils per month, amounting to USD 47 billion—all at a cost to the Government of India—to avoid mass starvation. With the introduction of Aadhaar and the unified payments interface (UPI), Digital India has made personal lives, business transactions, e-governance and all financial matters swifter, more efficient and more transparent; it is also another societal equaliser.

Recent slogans are all related—'Make in India', 'Sabka Saath, Sabka Vikas, Sabka Vishwas, Sabka Prayaas' and 'Atmanirbhar Bharat'—and they have all borne fruit in terms of self-reliance. Today, international brands are manufacturing and assembling in India, and Indian start-ups have proliferated to approximately 70,000. Most importantly, Indians feel good about being Indian. Through the preservation of traditions and rituals, Modi appeals to a sense of belonging to something great that needs to be conserved. The 'sabka' slogan and the 'Atmanirbhar Bharat' campaign are an appeal for a joint effort from citizens. The prime minister cannot achieve his ideals without cooperation from the people; his vision of social responsibility is for their betterment and societal unity. Sometimes, 'betterment' is a bitter pill to swallow because implementation is complex, as was seen in the case of the goods and services tax (GST). However, when this was realised later, the approach was revised to allow for a smoother adoption.

No administration is perfect, and the BJP have had their fair share of political upstarts who have embarrassed the party; self-promotion and a criminal record seem unremarkable among the members of parliament. The prime minister's strategic silence on issues like the border incursions with China, support to Taiwan, communal chaos in Manipur or Bengal, the free pass to separatists to return to India during BJP's term and other important security issues are perplexing. As is the BJP communications department, which appears to dive into communicating policies without following the due process, how demonetisation was rolled out, taking everyone by surprise, being a case in point. Other examples include the Citizenship (Amendment) Act, which has such a terrifying name that it instantly received international kickback because the context of the Act was not apparent from its name; the repealing of the farm and agricultural laws, which were in part designed to eliminate corruption but the government was unable to enact them. Compared to other developed democratic countries and countries in Quadrilateral Security Dialogue (Quad), India has a relatively small number of taxpayers, which is typically the primary source of the government's revenue.

During Modi's incumbency, the Indian Space Research Organisation (ISRO) must get an accolade of outstanding achievement and ingenuity. In August 2023, Chandrayaan-3 landed on the moon. In the future, India plans to launch space missions powered through nuclear propulsion. On 6 January 2024, Aditya-L1, India's indigenous space-based solar study mission, was successfully launched into a halo orbit. The spacecraft is a fully Indian project. Also due to be launched soon is NISAR, a joint venture between NASA and ISRO. This low earth observatory will map the entire globe in only twelve days and provide data for, and a better understanding of, climate change, water levels, natural disasters and agriculture.

A welcome side benefit is that ISRO's successes have sparked a renaissance in STEM studies amongst India's youth.

Recently, my husband and I spent nearly three weeks driving around Rajasthan. Having been a frequent visitor to India, the new infrastructure was a revelation—wonderful new highways connecting the main cities and rural villages now have tarmac roads; India's national railway network of rolling stock and tracks have been upgraded; hotels and restaurants cater to Indian and international tastes; and a new airport in Jaisalmer has improved tourism exponentially.

We met and spoke to many people and the unanimous verdict after the recent state election was 'We need Modi', the implication being that all the progress made so far would be wasted if Modi or the BJP do not win the 2024 Lok Sabha elections. Having achieved so much in the ten years of his leadership, perhaps the next term will be about consolidation?

India is now home to 1.4 billion people. Imagine trying to coordinate governance for this number of people without being a dictator, providing free and fair elections, free speech and free press, plus opportunities and jobs; a disorganised but vociferous opposition without a figurehead and the misappropriated name of I.N.D.I.A. does not seem much of a threat. In 2024, it seems there is no leader to rival Narendra Modi.

Antonia Filmer lives in the UK and spends time in Kenya and India. Since 2012 Antonia has been the London Correspondent for *The Sunday Guardian*.

NOTES

1. Ministry of Education, Government of India, National Curriculum Framework for School Education, https://www.education.gov.in/national-curriculum-framework-school-education-2023.

Advancements in Technology and the Digital Revolution in India

JONATHAN FLEMING
NAMIT CHOKSI
VINIT PARIKH

Rapid technological developments over the last three decades have made technology an ever-constant feature of our daily lives, dominating all our interactions. This is evident from the fact that 90 per cent of the world's data that has ever been in existence has been generated since 2019.[1] The fusion of technology with global commerce has birthed an intricate economic ecosystem, fostering interdependence among nations. A recent study forecasts a mammoth USD 3.37 trillion valuation for cross-border e-commerce transactions by 2028, up from USD 1.92 trillion in 2023, attesting to the expansive influence of technology on commerce.[2]

The pervasive use of technology has not only accelerated the digitisation of information but also catalysed a transformative phenomenon known as digitalisation. India has demonstrated an extraordinary ability to adopt low-cost innovation for high-impact scaled commercialisation of emerging technologies, particularly in the realm of payments and other critical sectors. The nation's unique approach to innovation has enabled the rapid deployment of cutting-edge solutions that cater to the needs of its vast and diverse population, while also driving momentous commercial successes. The impact of digitalisation is not limited to online transactions. India has embraced innovative solutions across various sectors, leveraging the country's entrepreneurial spirit and digital infrastructure to address pressing challenges. From agritech to healthcare, start-ups and enterprises alike are harnessing emerging technologies such as artificial intelligence, Internet of Things (IoT) and blockchain to develop scalable and affordable solutions with significant societal impact.

This emphasis on low-cost innovations not only drives economic growth and helps in job creation but also democratises access to essential services, empowering millions of individuals. By prioritising affordability and scalability, India has positioned itself as a global leader in harnessing the transformative potential of emerging technologies for the benefit of its citizens and beyond.

Traditional occupations such as healthcare services have leveraged the advancements in technology to optimise the process of collection of data from patients, and made doctor–patient interaction more accessible through online consultations. As per a report by McKinsey & Company, 55 per cent of patients reported higher satisfaction with telehealth/virtual care visits than with in-person appointments.[3] In terms of implementation of technology to improve on the existing range of medical devices used in a plethora of ways across all aspects of the healthcare sector (such as diagnostics, collection of medical data, surgery, etc.), the global medical devices market is expected to grow to around USD 996.93 billion by 2032.[4] By definition, this transformation of technology creates enormous opportunity for India to benefit its population by increasing access, and by using technology to diagnose and treat diseases in a more cost-effective way. The same technology wave also offers countless opportunities for entrepreneurs to build large and profitable businesses to augment healthcare. In fact, the digital transformation market has been evaluated to be worth USD 880.28 billion in 2023, with its revenue likely to be USD 4617.78 billion by 2030.[5]

Given the growing importance of 'the digital' all around, it is imperative for countries to be proactive in harnessing the digital transformation wave that is currently underway, and devise policies to use digital technology for improving and uplifting the quality of life of all its citizens.

A BRIEF BACKGROUND OF INDIA'S CURRENT DIGITALISATION PUSH

India started its journey of digitalisation with the establishment of the National Informatics Centre (NIC) under the Ministry of Electronics and Information Technology in 1976. The government's aim with establishing the NIC was to provide technology-driven solutions to the union and state governments for the various governance issues they faced. The NIC's robust ICT network, NICNET, has been pivotal in facilitating governmental initiatives and e-governance programmes, enabling the government to extend its outreach in the field of social and public administrations across the nation, even before the age of the internet.[6]

The post-liberalisation era witnessed the most rapid transformation in terms of digitalisation and adoption of new, cutting-edge technologies. Recognising the need for regulating the increasing use of IT services to ensure continued benefits of advancement in technology and addressing the challenges it brought, the government enacted the Information Technology Act, 2000 to 'regulate transactions carried out by means of electronic data interchange and other means of electronic communication'.[7] The Act was modelled on the United Nations Model Law on Electronic Commerce (adopted by the United Nations Commission on International Trade Law), which recognised commercial transactions conducted electronically and aimed at providing countries with a model that could be implemented within their respective jurisdictions. The Act was a significant development as it addressed the issue of cybercrime and made various forms of cybercrime punishable under the extant law. However, since the Act was a product of its time, it lacked the vocabulary to have provisions addressing the breadth of issues that emerged with the advent of internet. This is not to say that India had remained completely oblivious to the increased presence of the internet and its advantages.

In recent years, India has witnessed a massive push towards digitalisation, with the Narendra Modi government actively advocating the increased adoption of technology in governance and enacting laws aimed at strengthening data-related activities in India. This surge in digitalisation is epitomised by the proliferation of smartphones, with the percentage of smartphone-equipped households soaring from 36 per cent in 2018 to a staggering 74.8 per cent in 2022. This remarkable increase in smartphone penetration underscores the government's efforts to bridge the digital divide and make technology more accessible to the masses.[8]

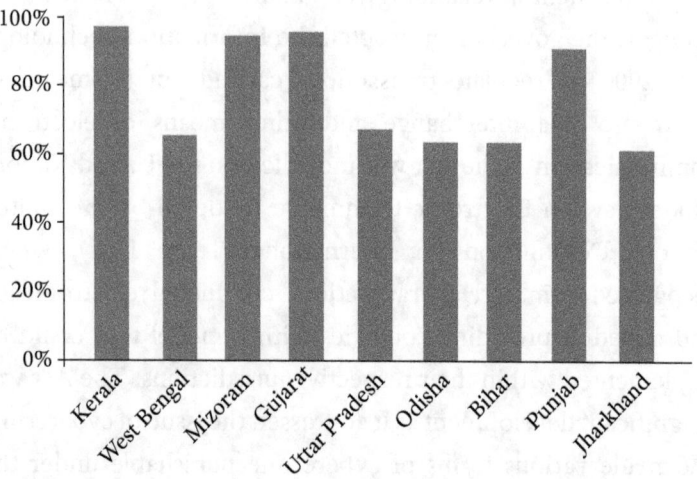

FIGURE 1: State-wise Penetration of Smartphones in India

Source: ASER

The following sections of this chapter shall look at some of the notable measures taken by the government since 2014 towards India's digitalisation, the scope of these initiatives and the impact they have had on the lives of Indians.

Digital India

Digital India is a flagship initiative launched by the Government of India in 2015. It consists of three major components: to develop stable and secure digital infrastructure; to deliver government services digitally; and to provide digital literacy. The aim of this initiative is to establish better connection between citizens and the government via e-services and deliver government services in a cost-effective and transparent manner. With its nine pillars, Digital India encapsulates the government's vision to transform India into a digitally empowered society and knowledge economy. These nine pillars are: 1. Broadband highways; 2. Universal access to mobile connectivity; 3. Public Internet Access Programme; 4. E-Governance: To reform the government via technology; 5. e-KRANTI; 6. Electronics manufacturing; 7. IT for jobs; 8. Early harvest programmes; 9. Information for all.[9]

Each pillar further has several components focusing on specific areas. For instance, Pillar 2 on universal access aims to increase the spread of mobile networks across the country. In keeping with this objective, the government has implemented the BharatNet Project under which gram panchayats would be provided with Wi-Fi or Fibernet. The target is to provide last-mile connectivity throughout the country. Accordingly, government's data shows that over 1.94 lakh gram panchayats are now service-ready and have a functioning broadband service.[10] The impact of this initiative is profound; it is helping students in rural India to access online education and other learning platforms. India has transformed its society by enabling communication, payment and transfer of data via internet.

This initiative has also gained the attention of the private sector, with players such as Reliance, Airtel, Larsen & Toubro, Cisco, etc. wanting to become stakeholders in the project.[11] Within the one-year period between 2020 and 2021, the project has led to an increase of 400 per cent in data consumption. With the entry of private players, the project has improved customer service and cost efficiencies as well.[12]

The *Internet in India Report 2022* pegs the number of 'active' internet users (AIU), that is, users accessing the internet at least once a month, at 759 million. Of these, 399 million are from rural India, while 360 million are from urban India. By 2025, the number of AIUs is likely to go up to 900 million.[13]

This is a remarkable shift from the early 2010s. In 2014, AIUs were reported to be at 232 million.[14] India has seen a rapid rise in its internet user base since the advent of Digital India, as can be seen from the graph in Figure 2.

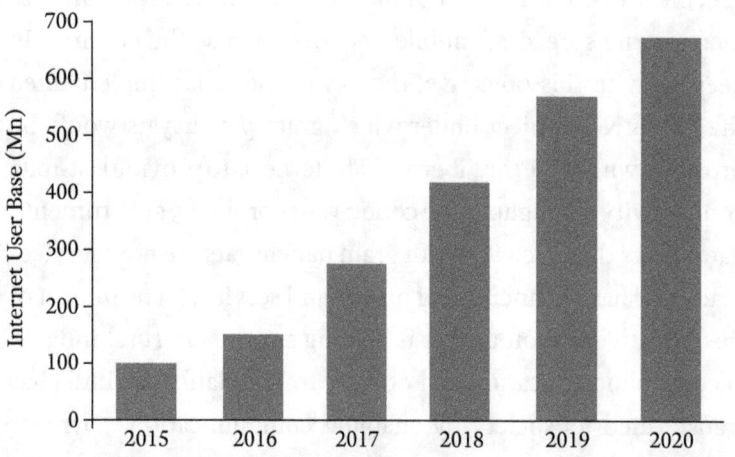

Figure 2: Rise in Internet User Base

Source: Yatti Soni, Inc42[15]

Another marker of increased digitalisation in India, especially in recent years, is the increase in the number of digital payments users to 338 million, which is a 13 per cent increase from 2021. A report published by IAMAI and Kantar in 2020 stated that in recent years, 46 per cent of Indians were using the internet to make digital payments.[16] The uptake of internet and smartphones is high in the rural regions as well. In 2022, it was estimated that by 2025, 56 per cent of new AIUs would belong to rural India. At present, AIUs from rural India make up 36 per cent of the users who make digital payments.[17]

Hence, it can be said that digital penetration has undeniably improved both in spread and depth. 'In terms of usage, digital entertainment, digital communications, and social media continue to be the most popular services in India. In fact, Indians are fast adopting social media platforms as the next e-commerce destination, with a staggering 51 per cent year-over-year (YoY) growth in social commerce.'[18] The report further said that 56 per cent of all e-payment are through unified payments interface (UPI)[19] and 99 per cent of all digital payment users are UPI users.[20] Smartphone penetration in India has seen a significant growth as well, with reports estimating that there will be 1 billion smartphone users in India by 2027.[21]

The government is taking well-thought-out measures to leverage the increase in the use of smartphones and the internet, which is transcending the urban–rural divide. Such is the extent of the use of smartphones that India's e-commerce market, which is primarily accessed via smartphones, is expected to reach USD 111 billion by 2024 and USD 200 billion by 2026. Additionally, India has gained 125 million online shoppers in the past three years, with another 80 million expected by 2025.[22]

While Digital India has made significant strides in transforming India into a digital powerhouse, concerted efforts are also being made to address the remaining challenges and ensure that the benefits of digitalisation reach every corner of the country. The following sections will elaborate on two very successful schemes of the Digital India initiative, one of which is related to digital financial service, UPI; while the other is related to the digital public platform, Aadhaar.

Unified Payments Interface

The unified payments interface has heralded a new era of digital transactions in India, revolutionising the way people send and receive money. Before the introduction of UPI, digital payments in India were made only by a certain class of people, with the option of making payments digitally limited to mid- to high-end stores, restaurants, etc. This was because, unlike in the developed countries, where everyday merchants, small retailers and even cab drivers had point-of-sale (POS) terminals, in India, the infrastructure to make digital payments was underdeveloped. Since its launch in 2016, it is the UPI that has played a key role in democratising digital payments.

As things stand today, UPI is the most popular digital payment method for end users. Its appeal stems from being free, safe, swift, seamless, flexible, and having features that are easy to grasp and convenient to use. With advancements in technology and as consumer preferences develop, the UPI payment ecosystem continues to evolve, offering greater accessibility, efficiency and security.

One of the reasons why UPI is so successful is because the government has emphasised on adding features to the existing system regularly, turning UPI into a service which constantly evolves, making payments easier and more accessible. For instance, the government took proactive steps to allow credit cards to be linked with UPI, eliminating the need to carry a physical card.[23] Additionally, users can make offline payments using UPI through the UPI123Pay[24] and enable recurring payments through UPI through UPI Autopay.[25] All these innovations have resulted in UPI emerging as the preferred mode of payment for users. That UPI is witnessing significant growth becomes all the more apparent from the fact that the YoY growth in the value of bank notes in circulation has decreased from 9.9 per cent in FY2021–22 to 7.8 per cent in FY2022–23.[26] In addition to revolutionising the field of digital payments, UPI has also bolstered India's soft power globally.

FIGURE 3: UPI Transactions Over the Calendar Years (2017–22)

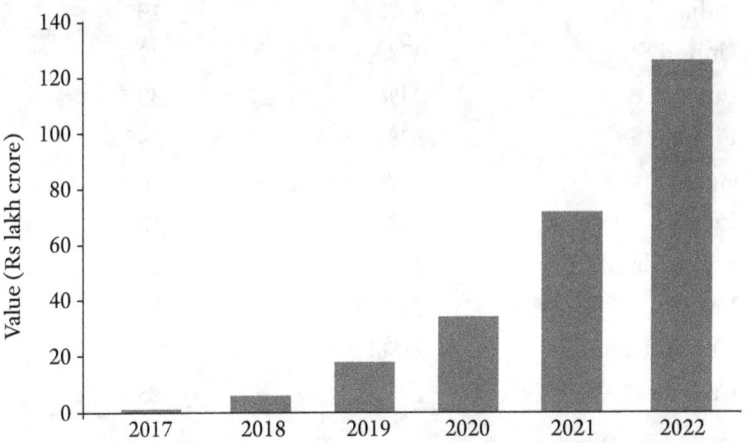

Source: NPCI[27]

Besides its domestic appeal, UPI has also been garnering acclaim internationally. During his two-day visit to India on the occasion of Republic Day 2024, French President Emmanuel Macron spoke positively about UPI, describing it as an innovation.[28] Soon after his visit, UPI was formally launched at the Eiffel Tower in Paris, allowing for payments at the Eiffel

Tower in Indian rupees.[29] India has signed MoUs with thirteen countries, including Malaysia, Thailand, the Philippines, South Korea and Japan to enable the adoption of UPI for digital payments.[30] As Table 1 shows, India tops the list of countries using Google Pay—which too can be used through UPI—by a wide margin.

TABLE 1: Country-wise Usage of Google Pay

Country	Usage of Google Pay at stores, restaurants and other PoS	Usage of Google Pay for Online Payments
India	83%	79%
United States	37%	32%
Poland	34%	39%
Finland	32%	29%
Germany	31%	16%
Italy	30%	18%
Switzerland	29%	27%
France	29%	15%
United Kingdom	28%	23%
Canada	27%	25%

Source: Statista[31]

Aadhaar

In India's digital ecosystem, the central pillar is the Aadhaar initiative. A biometric identification system, Aadhaar seeks to provide every citizen with a unique identification that comprises a twelve-digit unique identity number for individuals, which is linked to their biometric and demographic data.[32] The

Aadhaar ID enables people to become direct beneficiaries of government programmes by streamlining the process of availing the benefits and by eliminating the middleman. This initiative has resulted in streamlining the process by which people can access credit and financial facilities, simply by adopting the KYC process of linking their bank account with their Aadhaar numbers, eliminating the complex paperwork involved traditionally.

During the COVID-19 pandemic, the Aadhaar infrastructure allowed the government to enable migrant workers to get food grains from fair price shops by simply using their Aadhaar cards at the time of collecting their ration under the 'One Nation One Ration Care' plan of the Ministry of Consumer Affairs, Food and Public Distribution. As per the ministry, 94 per cent of the food grains were distributed in states and union territories under the Pradhan Mantri Garib Kalyan Anna Yojana between April and June 2020. The Aadhaar infrastructure enabled the government to ensure last-mile delivery of its services to a staggering 65 crore people, covering approximately 80 per cent of population that comes under the National Food Security Act, 2013. This ensured that the adverse impact of COVID-19 on the people was minimal.[33]

As per the Unique Identification Authority of India (UIDAI), the statutory body responsible for issuing Aadhaar numbers and safeguarding Aadhaar data under the Aadhaar Act, 2016, the government has launched 318 central government schemes and 720 state direct benefit transfers schemes under Aadhaar. Till November 2022, 135.2 crore Aadhaar cards had been issued by the UIDAI. As per the Economic Survey of 2023, '27.9 crore residents linked Aadhaar with cooking gas connection for LPG

FIGURE 4: Major Schemes Availed through Aadhar

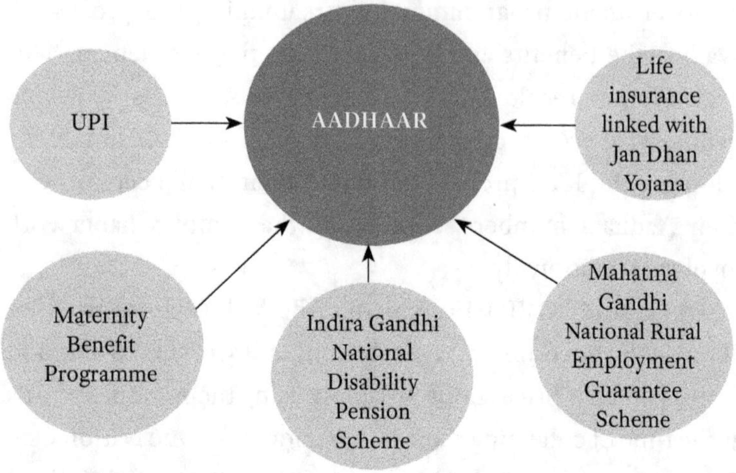

- UPI
- AADHAAR
- Life insurance linked with Jan Dhan Yojana
- Maternity Benefit Programme
- Indira Gandhi National Disability Pension Scheme
- Mahatma Gandhi National Rural Employment Guarantee Scheme

Source: *The Hindu*[34]

subsidy and 75.4 crore bank accounts are linked with Aadhaar, and more than 1500 crore transactions have taken place via Aadhaar Enabled Payment Systems (AePS).'[35] As per a report prepared by the Bank for International Settlements, the adoption of digital public infrastructures (DPIs) like Aadhaar, Jan Dhan bank accounts and mobile phones significantly contributed to the transition of transaction account ownership from approximately 25 per cent of adults in 2008 to over 80 per cent presently. This transformation, estimated to have spanned up to forty-seven years without the presence of DPIs, underscores the pivotal role played by these digital systems in enhancing financial inclusion. The surge in account ownership reflects substantial progress in promoting financial inclusion, highlighting the transformative impact of DPIs on socio-economic development in India.

National e-Governance Plan

Another milestone in India's transformative journey of rapid digitalisation is the introduction of the National e-Governance Plan (NeGP). Formulated by the Department of Information Technology (DIT) and Department of Administrative Reforms & Public Grievances (DAR&PG), the NeGP comprises twenty-seven mission mode projects (MMPs) and has ten components. Its aim is to improve access and delivery of services to citizens and businesses, as reflected in its vision: 'Make all Government services accessible to the common man in his locality, through common service delivery outlets and ensure efficiency, transparency & reliability of such services at affordable costs to realise the basic needs of the common man.'[36]

Building upon the framework laid down in the early 2010s, the central government has launched Phase II of the NeGP, including important projects such as the E-courts Mission Mode Project, which is aimed at making access to the justice delivery system more democratic and efficient. The government has also invested Rs 111.29 crore for the installation of a video conferencing infrastructure in over 18,735 district and subordinate courts across the country. Under phase III of NeGP, the government intends to move towards a paperless, online justice delivery system. The Union Budget has allocated Rs 7,000 crore to achieve this goal.[37]

Digitalisation of India's Healthcare Sector: An Analysis

A sector in which India's digitalisation is making great strides is healthcare. In a country as vast as India, where healthcare delivery to the grassroots has been a challenge, the push for digitalisation has come as a boon. The technological evolution has created a fertile ground for entrepreneurs to establish lucrative businesses focused on leveraging technology to innovate and augment healthcare services. Here are some examples:

1. Integration of medical devices with smartphones: In remote villages where access to healthcare facilities is limited, the integration of medical devices with smartphones has proved to be a game-changer. Devices such as portable ECG monitors, glucometers and digital thermometers can now be connected to smartphones, allowing individuals to monitor their health parameters from the comfort of their homes.

    This integration not only facilitates remote monitoring but also enables individuals to share real-time health data with healthcare providers for timely interventions. For example, a diabetic patient can monitor their blood sugar levels using a smartphone-connected glucometer and share the readings with their doctor for personalised treatment adjustments.

2. Telemedicine platforms for remote consultations: Telemedicine platforms have emerged as a lifeline for villagers who previously had limited access to healthcare professionals. Through these platforms, individuals can schedule virtual consultations with doctors, specialists and healthcare practitioners without the need to travel long distances.

    Follow-up appointments, routine check-ups and even specialist consultations can now be conducted remotely, saving time and resources for both patients and healthcare

providers. Additionally, telemedicine platforms enable patients to seek medical advice promptly, reducing the risk of delays in diagnosis and treatment.
3. Promotion of positive behavioural health practices: Digital platforms play a crucial role in promoting positive behavioural health practices among villagers. Educational content, interactive tools and mobile applications are utilised to raise awareness about preventive healthcare measures, healthy lifestyle choices and disease management strategies.

   For instance, villagers can access mobile apps or web-based platforms that provide information on nutrition, exercise, mental health and management of chronic diseases. These platforms offer personalised health tips, reminders for medication adherence, and motivational resources to encourage individuals to adopt healthier habits.
4. Efficient management of drug prescriptions and delivery services: Digitalisation has streamlined the process of managing drug prescriptions and ensuring timely delivery of medicines in rural areas. Healthcare providers can now electronically prescribe medications, reducing errors and delays associated with traditional paper-based prescriptions.

   Additionally, innovative delivery services such as drones and mobile dispensaries are being used to overcome logistical challenges and reach remote villages with essential medications. Patients can order medicines through mobile apps or call centres, and the medicines are delivered directly to their doorsteps.

5. Streamlining interactions with healthcare providers: Digital platforms facilitate seamless interactions between villagers and healthcare providers, enhancing the overall healthcare experience. Scheduling of appointments, management of medical records, and communication with healthcare teams can now be done online, eliminating the need for physical visits to healthcare facilities. Furthermore, digital platforms enable villagers to access health-related information, resources and support groups, fostering a sense of empowerment and engagement in their healthcare journey.

Global trends indicate that people are increasingly preferring to have their healthcare needs addressed telephonically or virtually. This is natural, considering how COVID-19 led to people being more vigilant about encountering other potentially unwell persons, and practising social distancing. India, too, has seen an increase in the uptake of telemedicine, with this industry valued at USD 5.4 billion by 2023.[38] This adoption of telemedicine is not an urban phenomenon. As per a 2023 report by Lybrate, the largest platform for online consultations in India, telemedicine witnessed a growth of 87 per cent in Tier 2 and 3 cities between 2021 and 2022.[39] This is significant considering that the last-mile delivery of healthcare services has been a concern. The government can bridge this gap through the effective addition of technological innovations in the healthcare system.

Apart from bringing villagers closer to doctors via virtual sessions, digitalisation also promotes positive behavioural health practices and allows access to medication using online platforms that help provide doorstep deliver of medicines based on prescriptions. It also enables people to track their own health via medical devices that can be attached to the body and that collect vitals without having to go to a medical facility.

The increase in the digitalisation of India's healthcare sector has been exponential in the last few years. The pandemic brought with it a set of unique, hitherto unseen challenges that governments across the globe had to tackle. In India, the Modi government took swift measures to develop two digital platforms, the Aarogya Setu and CoWin, both of which were crucial to India's strategy to curb the effects of COVID-19. Aargoya Setu is a contact tracing app, which, by using GPS and Bluetooth, gave users real-time data of COVID-19 cases in their neighbourhood, allowing them to ascertain and report any contact they had with persons who tested positive for the disease. The app also featured a colour-coded map that was based on the varying degrees of the spread of COVID-19 in different areas. The app was also used by the government for the dissemination of critical information pertaining to COVID-19. Aarogya Setu was immensely useful as it enabled the government to identify 84,36,524 suspected contacts in 322 days, in 2020-21. During this period, a total of 2,53,72,110 cases of COVID-19 had been reported on Aarogya Setu. It is estimated that over 33.35 per cent of India's COVID-19 cases were traced using the Aarogya Setu app.[40]

Aarogya Setu enabled the government to tailor its response and put in place measures to combat the rise of COVID-19 swiftly and with great efficiency while at the same time making citizens aware of the situation, which allowed them to make informed decisions. Given the large-scale data collection by this app, it is but natural that concerns about the potential misuse of the data and the violation of the right to privacy would be flagged. To counter such possibilities, the Aarogya Setu app was made open source in 2020 itself, enabling area experts to review the code of the app and identify possible vulnerabilities to which the application may be susceptible. The government incentivised people to identify loopholes in the application, announcing the Bug Bounty Programme for the application under which users who helped with the successful identification of issues with the app pertaining to data security, or who made suggestions that would improve the source code of the app, would be given awards starting from Rs 1 lakh to Rs 4 lakhs for every issue identified and reported.[41]

The other digital success story is the CoWIN platform. The platform was launched in 2020 to enable the government to roll out its vaccination drive in the most accessible and COVID-safe way possible. The CoWIN app helped users to pre-book slots for receiving doses of the COVID-19 vaccine at various government-run hospitals and institutions (schools, universities, etc.) and at private hospitals. The aim was to reduce potential COVID outbreaks due to mismanagement at vaccination centres. The CoWIN application streamlined the system, thus helping the government administer 1.5 billion doses of anti-COVID vaccines. This was more than the doses administered by the US, Japan, Brazil and Indonesia cumulatively.[42] The use of the CoWIN app goes beyond the role it played during the pandemic, with experts seeing it as a tool to be used in India's Universal Immunisation Programme. One of the key benefits of CoWIN that has been identified is its role in providing vaccinators with the patient details pertaining to previously administered doses, along with any reported adverse effects, etc., and even informing users about vaccinations they were scheduled to take. The CoWIN app can also enable the government to keep digital records that are easily accessible and micro plan immunisation drives with better efficiency.

The significant strides that India has made in digitalisation under the Modi government has ensured a robust push towards embracing digital technologies across various sectors. This would not have been possible but for the easy availability of smartphones and the internet. With the proliferation of affordable smartphones and the availability of high-speed internet connectivity, a growing number of Indians are gaining access to digital platforms and services. With the advent of Jio, last-mile connectivity of the internet has improved remarkably. From a mere 154 MB of internet data being used by the average mobile internet user in 2016, an astounding 15.8 GB of data per month is being consumed by users on an average at present, according to the Telecom Regulatory Authority of India (TRAI). This has democratised access to information, communication and online services, empowering individuals and communities to participate more actively in the digital economy.

Nevertheless, there are challenges that must be tackled by the government to fully utilise the potential of its vision of Digital India. As per a 2022 report, digital literacy in India continues to be low, with only 38 per cent of households being digitally literate.[43] This is concerning because it could result in a situation where several classes of people are not able to reap the benefits of government schemes due to access barriers in technology. To remedy this problem, the Modi government has formulated two programmes, the Pradhan Mantri Gramin Digital Saksharta Abhiyan (PMGDISHA) and the National Digital Literacy Mission (NDLM). The former aims to make one person from every rural household digitally literate. From its inception in 2017 to 2021, PGMDISHA has trained over 67 million persons, making them digitally literate. Similarly, NDLM sought to provide IT training to 53.5 lakh people, including Anganwadi and ASHA workers as well as ration dealers. Under these initiatives, over 4.2 crore people have been trained and certified by the government.[44]

Internationally, India's digitalisation has positive implications for its global image and can add to its soft power. For instance, India signed MoUs with eight countries, offering them the use of India Stack, which is 'a collection of open APIs (including Aadhaar and UPI) and digital public goods that aim to facilitate identity, data, and payment services on a large scale' to help with their move towards digitalisation, free of cost.

The way that the government has been leveraging this digital boom to use it to the nation's advantage is evident from the various policies and schemes that the Modi government has either introduced or improved upon since 2014. For a country whose IT boom started less than three decades ago, India has come a long way and is now seen as a pioneer for many aspects of digitalisation. In this journey, it is important to strike a balance between innovation, accessibility and inclusivity, so that no one is left behind. By creating an environment that optimally utilises technology, the government can ensure that citizens reap the benefits of India's digital infrastructure in a way that aligns with both individual and national interests.

Looking at the healthcare sector specifically, India stands as a global leader in digital innovation, and by leveraging its digitalised public infrastructure, India has been able to create an environment conducive to private sector innovation and entrepreneurship tailored to the needs of Indian consumers, particularly in rural areas where access to healthcare services has been limited. This collaborative approach between the government and the private sector has led to the emergence of groundbreaking solutions aimed at improving healthcare delivery in Indian villages. From telemedicine platforms to remote monitoring devices, private innovators are leveraging India's digital infrastructure to bridge the disparity gap in healthcare and enhance health outcomes for rural populations.

India's thought leadership in digital healthcare extends beyond its borders, inspiring other nations to embrace technology-driven solutions for addressing healthcare challenges. The success of initiatives such as Aadhaar-enabled services and UPI-based transactions has garnered international recognition, positioning India as a trailblazer in digital transformation.

In conclusion, the integration of digital technologies into healthcare delivery in Indian villages represents a paradigm shift in the way healthcare services are accessed and delivered. As these digital innovations continue to evolve, they hold immense promise in narrowing healthcare disparities and improving health outcomes for rural populations not only in India but also globally.

Jonathan Fleming is Senior Lecturer in the Martin Trust Center for MIT Entrepreneurship at the MIT Sloan School of Management. He is also a general partner of Oxford Bioscience Partners (OBP), an international venture capital firm specialising in life science technology–based investments, with offices in Boston and Connecticut.

Namit Choksi is currently leading the India and Asia-Pacific growth, strategy and expansion for a USD 1.7 billion California-based biotechnology company whilst pursuing his MBA at the MIT Sloan School of Management.

Vinit Parikh is an entrepreneur with more than twenty years of experience in the field of finance. He is chartered accountant by education and also an investor in a few start-ups.

NOTES

1. Petroc Taylar, 'Volume of Data/Information Created, Captured, Copied, and Consumed Worldwide from 2010 to 2020, with Forecasts from 2021 to 2025', Statista, 16 November 2023, https://www.statista.com/statistics/871513/worldwide-data-created/.
2. Matthew Purnell, 'Cross-border eCommerce: Key Trends, Regional Analysis & Market Forecast', Juniper Research, 17 July 2023, https://www.juniperresearch.com/research/fintech-payments/ecommerce/cross-border-ecommerce-research-report/.
3. Jenny Cordina, Jennifer Fowkes, Rupal Malani and Laura Medford-Davis, 'Patients Love Telehealth—Physicians Are Not So Sure', McKinsey & Company, 22 February 2022, https://www.mckinsey.com/industries/healthcare/our-insights/patients-love-telehealth-physicians-are-not-so-sure.
4. 'Medical Devices Market (By Type: Cardiovascular Devices, Orthopedic Devices, Diagnostic Imaging, MIS, IVD, Diabetes Care, Wound Management, Dental, Nephrology, Ophthalmic Devices, and Others; By End User: Clinics, Hospitals & Ambulatory Surgical Centers, and Others)—Global Market Size, Trends Analysis, Segment Forecasts, Regional Outlook 2023–2032', Prudence Research, November 2023, https://www.precedenceresearch.com/medical-devices-market.

5. 'Digital Transformation Market Size & Share Report, 2030, Market Anlaysis Report', Grand View Research, https://www.grandviewresearch.com/industry-analysis/digital-transformation-market.
6. Organisation Functions and Duties, National Informatics Centre (NIC), 2017, https://www.nic.in/wp-content/uploads/2017/03/organisation-functions-duties-0-2-1.pdf.
7. Information and Technology Act, Act No. 21 of 2000, Ministry of Law, Justice and Company Affairs (Legislative Department), Government of India, 9 June 2000.
8. *The New Indian Express*, 21 January 2023, https://www.newindianexpress.com/business/2023/Jan/21/number-of-smartphones-doubled-in-rural-india-frompre-covid-era-aser-2540034.html.
9. Press Release, Press Information Bureau, Cabinet, Government of India, 20 August 2014, https://pib.gov.in/newsite/printrelease.aspx?relid=108926.
10. '1.94 lakh Gram Panchayats Service Ready under BharatNet Project: Chauhan', *The Economic Times*, 26 July 2023, https://telecom.economictimes.indiatimes.com/news/policy/1-94-lakh-gram-panchayats-service-ready-under-bharatnet-project-chauhan/102141145.
11. Surabhi Agarwal and Kalyan Prabhat, 'Bharti Airtel, Reliance Infratel, STL, Cisco, L&T, Hughes eye BharatNet', ET Telecom.com, 17 August 2021, https://telecom.economictimes.indiatimes.com/news/bharti-airtel-reliance-jio-eyeing-bharatnet-second-phase/85389693.
12. 'Data Consumption Increased 400% in Rural India in the Past One Year', ET Government, 3 August 2021, https://government.economictimes.indiatimes.com/news/governance/data-consumption-increased-400-in-rural-india-in-the-past-one-year/84997210.
13. Internet in India 2022, Kantar and Internet and Mobile Association of India (IAMAI), April 2023, https://www.iamai.in/

sites/default/files/research/Internet%20in%20India%202022_Print%20version.pdf.
14. Internet in India 2014, Internet and Mobile Association of India, https://www.iamai.in/sites/default/files/research/Internet%20in%20India%202014.pdf.
15. Yatti Soni, Inc42, 14 August 2020, https://inc42.com/features/startupindia-how-digital-india-and-make-in-india-power-indias-tech-juggernaut/.
16. ICUBE 2020: Internet Adoption in India, Kantar, June 2021, https://images.assettype.com/afaqs/2021-06/b9a3220f-ae2f-43db-a0b4-36a372b243c4/KANTAR_ICUBE_2020_Report_C1.pdf.
17. 'Data Consumption Increased 400% in Rural India in the Past One Year', ET Government, 3 August 2021, https://government.economictimes.indiatimes.com/news/governance/data-consumption-increased-400-in-rural-india-in-the-past-one-year/84997210.
18. Ibid.
19. Shobhaa De, 'UPI Forms 52% of All E-Payments', *The Times of India*, 1 February 2023, https://timesofindia.indiatimes.com/business/india-business/upi-forms-52-of-all-e-payments/amp_articleshow/97503259.cms.
20. 'Over 50% Indians Are Active Internet Users Now; Base to Reach 900 Million by 2025: Report', *The Hindu*, 4 May 2023, https://www.thehindu.com/news/national/over-50-indians-are-active-internet-users-now-base-to-reach-900-million-by-2025-report/article66809522.ece.
21. TMT Predictions 2022, Deloitte, February 2022, https://www2.deloitte.com/content/dam/Deloitte/in/Documents/technology-media-telecommunications/in-TMT-predictions-2022-noexp.pdf.
22. Indian E-commerce Industry Analysis, February 2024, https://www.ibef.org/industry/ecommerce-presentation.
23. Press Release, Ministry of Finance, Government of India, 18 December 2023, https://pib.gov.in/PressReleseDetail.aspx?PRID=1987764.

24. Anshul Gupta, 'What is UPI 123Pay? How to Use It and How Is It Different from the Current UPI Interface?', *Wint*, 27 September 2023, https://www.wintwealth.com/blog/what-is-upi-123pay-how-to-use-it-and-how-is-it-different-from-the-current-upi-interface/#:~:text=In%20collaboration%20with%20the%20National,UPI123Pay%20on%20March%2008%2C%202022.
25. Pratik Bhakta, 'UPI AutoPay Top of Charts in Low-ticket Recurring Payments', *The Economic Times*, 22 December 2024, https://economictimes.indiatimes.com/tech/technology/upi-autopay-top-of-charts-in-low-ticket-recurring-payments/articleshow/106191068.cms?from=mdr.
26. 'Internet in India 2014, Internet and Mobile Association of India', https://www.iamai.in/sites/default/files/research/Internet%20in%20India%202014.pdf; Yatti Soni, Inc42, 14 August 2020, https://inc42.com/features/startupindia-how-digital-india-and-make-in-india-power-indias-tech-juggernaut/.
27. Moneycontrol News, 31 January 2023, https://www.moneycontrol.com/news/business/economic-survey-2023-upi-accounted-for-52-of-indias-total-digital-transactions-in-fy22-9970741.html.
28. Aman Sharma, 'Won't Forget the Chai With PM Modi, Because It Was Paid for by UPI, Says French President Macron', News18, 27 January 2024, https://www.news18.com/india/wont-forget-the-chai-with-pm-modi-because-it-was-paid-for-by-upi-says-french-president-macron-8755828.html.
29. 'UPI Services Launched In France At Eiffel Tower After Macron's India Visit', NDTV, 2 February 2024, https://www.ndtv.com/world-news/upi-services-launched-in-france-at-eiffel-tower-after-macrons-india-visit-4981830.
30. 'UPI to Enter North America, Other Middle-Eastern Countries Soon', *Livemint*, 17 July 2023, https://www.livemint.com/companies/news/upi-to-enter-north-america-other-middle-eastern-countries-soon-nipl-ceo-11689610413491.html.
31. Rohit Shewale, 'Detailed UPI Statistics 2024', DemandSage, 14 December 2023, https://www.demandsage.com/upi-statistics/.

32. https://time.com/5409604/india-aadhaar-supreme-court/.
33. Press Release, Ministry of Consumer Affairs, Food & Public Distribution, Government of India, 23 September 2023, https://pib.gov.in/PressReleaseIframePage.aspx?PRID=1658095.
34. K. Deepalakshmi, 'The Long List of Aadhaar-linked Schemes', *The Hindu*, 16 June 2017, https://www.thehindu.com/news/national/the-long-list-of-aadhaar-linked-schemes/article17641068.ece.
35. Press Release, Ministry of Finance, Food & Public Distribution, Government of India, 31 January 2023, https://pib.gov.in/PressReleasePage.aspx?PRID=1894916.
36. Press Release, Prime Minister's Office, Government of India, 1 July 2023, https://pib.gov.in/newsite/erelcontent.aspx?relid=96938.
37. BS Web Team, 'E-court Mission: Development of digital, paperless online courts in India', *Business Standard*, 14 September 2023, https://www.business-standard.com/india-news/e-court-mission-development-of-digital-paperless-online-courts-in-indi-123081100739_1.html.
38. Soumen Mandal, 'Why Telemedicine Is The Next Big Opportunity In Indian Healthtech, Datalabs', Inc42, 16 April 2020, https://inc42.com/datalab/telemedicine-market-opportunity-in-indian-healthtech/.
39. Sohini Das, 'Online Medical Consultations in Smaller Cities Grew 87% Last Calendar Year', *Business Standard*, 7 February 2023, https://www.business-standard.com/article/health/online-medical-consultations-in-smaller-cities-grew-87-last-calendar-year-123020701197_1.html.
40. Ashok Upadhyay, 'How Many Contacts Aarogya Setu App Has Traced in Fighting Covid-19? RTI Story', *India Today*, 23 September 2021, https://www.indiatoday.in/india/story/how-many-contacts-aarogya-setu-app-traced-fighting-covid-rti-story-1856217-2021-09-23.
41. 'Govt Offering up to 4 lakhs to Find Bugs in Aarogya Setu', *HT Tech*, 20 August 2022, https://tech.hindustantimes.com/tech/

news/govt-offering-up-to-4-lakhs-to-find-bugs-in-aarogya-setu-71590761280545.html.
42. Manish Pant, 'India's Fight against Pandemic Aided by Successful CoWIN App', United Nations Development Programme, 21 January 2022, https://www.undp.org/asia-pacific/blog/india%E2%80%99s-fight-against-pandemic-aided-successful-cowin-app/.
43. *India Inequality Report 2022*, Oxfam India, December 2022, https://d1ns4ht6ytuzzo.cloudfront.net/oxfamdata/oxfamdatapublic/2022-12/Digital%20Divide_India%20Inequality%20Report%202022_PRINT%20with%20cropmarks.pdf?3l.73PGQrpQfYrnwWeoXV3BFjhETfA_p.
44. Press Release, Ministry of IT and Electronics, Government of India, 23 December 2022, https://pib.gov.in/PressReleseDetail.aspx?PRID=1885958.

Revolutionising Infrastructure
Bridging the Human Connect

BHARAT KAUSHAL

A nation of colossal culture and historical significance, India has taken a stride towards distinguished transformation, which is setting exemplary yardsticks to build an inclusive yet empowered society. India, often depicted as the land of snake charmers and abundant heritage, is seen as consistently crossing significant milestones despite facing challenges and multiple impediments to growth. As the nation accelerated the pace at which it is moving to strengthen its unmatched universality, it not only leapfrogged ahead but set precedents to which the world is adapting.

We are fortuitous to have been a part of India's growth story—a proud story of reimagination, disruption, transformation and the building of a new narrative from being a follower to a leader. There have been several accomplishments, which have been instrumental in making India charter and revolutionise the varied aspects of distinctive dynamism not only for the world but for the nation that aspires to make progression an integral part of its success story.

Narendra Modi built on the foundations laid out for the New India that we all are experiencing today. It is remarkable to witness the transition of a nation with 1.4 billion people, and how the 'road to rekindle' has been oriented to amplify, acquire and augment a position that the world respects and follows.

The road to development is an unending one, but the milestones crossed by India so far are evident. Accessibility and empowerment have ignited the possibility of a better quality of life for its citizens. Whether it is about powering dreams by efficiently utilising natural resources under the 'Power for All' mission, the focus on green energy, or the ushering in of equal opportunities through a robust, large-scale digital solution, the futuristic aspirational journey has been scaling unparalleled heights.

This gradual acceleration is guided by a roadmap, and India's transformation in the last one decade is a testament to its burgeoning dominance across varied sectors and of its development journey being aspirational and ambitious.

India's ascendancy to a position of prominence at the world stage would be difficult without the push of its demographic dividend. Recognising this competitive advantage, the government has prioritised the health and well-being of its citizens. With the implementation of the government's National Health Mission, citizens' access to well-being is now quicker and wider, as nation- and state-wide initiatives in telehealth bridge the distances between health and healthier well-being with a click. Ayushman Bharat Digital Mission (ABDM) led by the National Health Authority has been able to digitalise healthcare for the first time. Envisioned along with user consent management frameworks, it places citizens at the core of the healthcare framework. The eSanjeevani initiative, conceptualised and implemented by the government during the challenging years of the global pandemic, has further strengthened the Digital Health ID (ABHA ID), serving as a testament to the revolutionisation of the healthcare infrastructure. Schemes including the Pradhan Mantri Jan Arogya Yojana (PM-JAY) have demonstrated the government's desire for achieving human inclusivity and good governance.

By putting citizen lifecycle needs at the centre of its operating layer, the government has ensured that its schemes and policies are effectually bridging the need gap.

The public transport system is the lifeline of billions. Over the past few years, India's public transport system, especially rail, has charted new horizons, offering safer and seamless commuting experience to its citizens and meeting the increasing demands of its burgeoning urban reality.

I recollect the time from my younger days where it was an accepted fact that trains would run delayed and freight movement through rail defied the transportation ecosystem. Fast-forward to the present and look at the transformation! From decongesting of high-density routes to building high-capacity dedicated freight corridors, the high-speed Vande Bharat trains and seamless travel in metros in twenty cities have ensured comfort and safety and made travel an extravagant experience.

Dedicated freight corridors are vastly improving the ease of doing business, by providing transportation that is fast, reliable and available at a competitive cost, ensuring necessities are met efficiently. In the words of PM Narendra Modi, 'These freight corridors will become a very big medium of Atmanirbhar Bharat. Whether it is industry, business, farmers or consumers, everybody is going to get the benefit.'[1]

The prime minister's vision is also propelling India towards becoming a leader in the blue economy. Inland waterways will play a crucial role in contributing to India's vision of achieving zero carbon emissions. The waterways transportation hadn't achieved prominence up until 2014 when the government made it a mission to reinvigorate the inland waterways system.

The government's Sagarmala Programme for the holistic development of coastal districts is pioneering a new era by serving as a growth driver for the national waterways, fuelling business realisations through the development of 106 notified waterways and the identification of 567 projects. This is true leveraging of India's natural resources.

India has the second-largest road network in the world, second only to the US. Since 2014, under the Modi government, the national highways in India have clocked an impressive growth rate of 59 per cent and there are more than 4,000 projects worth USD 347.16 billion underway.

With continued optimism, the government has prioritised the development of greenfield high-speed corridors, with twenty-one greenfield access-controlled corridors already in progress and approximately 3,336 km of work already completed.

Aspirations of a growing economy and people's aspirations are often at odds with urbanisation and infrastructure development. Rapid transition of rural to semi and urban cities is offering an opportune moment for fuelling infrastructural expansion. Previously, the focus on urban development was fragmented with limited technology integration. The rate of urbanisation in 2001–11 was 2.76 per cent. By 2011, 32 per cent of the population was urbanised, reflecting policies from Five Year Plans and central government initiatives. This was an especially tough area to bring order to. Some key policy enablers have been imperative.

The government's National Urban Policy Framework outlines an integrated and coherent approach towards the future of urban planning in India. UN-Habitat interventions are focused on inclusive planning and sustainable development through effective and participatory planning instruments at the city and regional scale.

As India embarks on its vision to achieve annual growth rate of 9–10 per cent and become a USD 5 trillion economy, providing electricity to all will be a key agenda. The last eight years have already seen tremendous development of the Indian power sector, and many of the measures taken by this government will ensure that reliable supply of power will keep pace with the requirements of rapid economic growth.

Over the past eight years, India has made significant strides towards achieving 'One Nation One Grid' by adding 1,66,080 km of transmission lines to connect and integrate the whole country under a single electric grid running on one frequency. As a result, the Indian grid has now emerged as the largest integrated grid in the world. Our transmission lines deploy some of the most cutting-edge technology in the world, such as the 800 KV HVDC, and are located in some of the most challenging altitudes in the world. Hitachi Energy, a world leader in HVDC technology, has been a key contributor to this.

Prior to 2014, more than 18,000 villages and hundreds of thousands of hamlets were yet to get electricity. Under the leadership of Prime Minister Modi, the target of electrifying every village was achieved in 987 days. The International Energy Agency called this the biggest news of the energy sector in the world in 2018. To achieve the target of providing electricity to every home in the country, the Modi government successfully provided electricity connections to 2.86 crore homes within eighteen months.

In a large country like India, logistics are crucial to the economy. Under the 'Make in India' initiative, the logistics sector has significant potential to grow, a realisation further enabled by the goods and services tax (GST). One of the challenges faced by our logistics system was the bottleneck at check posts where trucks spent approximately 16 per cent of their time just to pay state or entry taxes. However, since the implementation of GST, only an e-way bill must be generated and no other tax is to be levied. That is how GST eases the process of interstate trading. Today, more than 8 crore e-way bills are being generated every month.

India's financial inclusion landscape is witnessing an unprecedented transformation driven by the implementation of the country's digital public infrastructure (DPI), which includes Aadhaar (digital ID system), unified payments interface or UPI (fast payments system) and DigiLocker (digital document wallet). These initiatives have not only accelerated financial inclusion efforts in India but have also captured global interest and adoption.

At the much-celebrated G20 presidency of India in 2023, the *Financial Inclusion Plan* document acknowledged 'the significant role of Digital Public Infrastructure (DPI) in helping to advance financial inclusion' and applauded India for achieving 'over 80% bank account penetration, a journey that would otherwise have taken 47 years through traditional means'.[2]

Also leveraging the India stack to develop banking and payment offerings is India's fintech segment, which has witnessed a massive shift with more than 2,100 fintechs currently operating in the country, of which more than 65 per cent have been set up in the last five years.

The Modi government is continuously developing regulations, policies and initiatives such as account aggregator (AA) framework, open credit enablement network (OCEN), digital banking units, payment aggregator (PA) framework and cross-border UPI, which are all working together to drive both established companies and start-ups to reimagine what financial services mean to them.

As I cast my gaze towards the centennial celebration of India's Independence, I envision India ascending to become one of the top three global economies. This economic ascension is not only monumental but, more importantly, characterised by sustainability and equitability, where prosperity is not confined to select segments but resonates across the societal spectrum, especially with women and those confronted with economic and social disadvantages.

I see accessibility for industry and start-ups in the sectors of space and defence. Private participation in these sectors is bringing out the best from India's vast talent pool. Equipping our key national assets with the power of artificial intelligence (AI) and generative AI (GenAI) is now within reach, thanks to India's engineering talent base.

I see a digitally robust economy where technology is connecting humans with humans, actively participating in the growth of the digital economy. The synergy of technological prowess, societal engagement and environmental stewardship is propelling India towards a future where robustness and dynamism coalesce to redefine our place on the world stage. Indeed, this is India with a new cultural identity.

Bharat Kaushal is Managing Director, Hitachi India.

NOTES

1. Prime Minister's Office, 'English Rendering of PM's Address at Inauguration of New Bhaupur-New Khurja Section of Eastern Dedicated Freight Corridor', 29 December 2022, https://pib.gov.in/newsite/erelcontent.aspx?relid=217840.
2. *2023 Financial Inclusion Plan*, https://www.google.com/url?sa=t&source=web&rct=j&opi=89978449&url=https://g20.in/content/dam/gtwenty/gtwenty_new/document/G20_GPFI_FIAP_2023.pdf&ved=2ahUKEwjB9_HF3JeGAxXETGwGHSigC68QFnoECCoQAQ&usg=AOvVaw3E8L89OmYRktqwgHwc-9vq.

India that is Bharat

A Decade of Change

AVATANS KUMAR

The past decade of Bharat has been remarkably transformational. There isn't an aspect of Indian life that has remained untouched by these changes. While material shifts are easily discernible, those taking place at the sociocultural levels are subtle and subliminal yet definitive. It are these sociocultural transformations that are the focus of this chapter.

FROM THE NATION OF 'PIETISTIC GANDHIAN GLOOM' TO A USD 3 TRILLION ECONOMY

When the Nobel laureate V.S. Naipaul visited India in 1988, around the time he began his book *India: A Million Mutinies Now*, he found an India 'full of pietistic Gandhian gloom'.[1] It was an all-pervasive gloom, perhaps an outcome of nearly four decades of failed Nehruvian socialism. 'The talk among the talkers in the towns,' writes Naipaul, 'was of degeneracy, a falling away from the standards of earlier times.'[2] Hundreds of years of Islamic and British colonisation had turned an entrepreneurial society that, for most of its existence, had been one of the most prosperous societies in the world, materially and intellectually, into a wounded, defeated, despondent and fatalist one.

The economic liberalisation of the 1990s, pioneered by Prime Minister P.V. Narasimha Rao, opened up India's markets for foreign investments. However, after initial successes, the economic developments hit roadblocks.

Today, a sense of optimism is sweeping across India. In a post-COVID world plagued with inflation, rising food and energy prices, and the spectre of long-drawn-out wars in Europe and the Middle East, Indians are brimming with hope and confidence. There is also a hunger among Indians, old and young, to put India back to its precolonial eminence, both economically and civilisationally.

Standing atop the pedestal as the most populous nation, India is also the fastest-growing (7.6 per cent, Q2 FY24)[3] large economy. By providing access to electricity, cooking gas connections, toilets, bank accounts, housing, etc., the government of Prime Minister Narendra Modi has empowered the poor and the most marginalised of India in a way no government did in the past.

Digitisation and mobile connectivity have revolutionised the Indian landscape. QR code displays for digital payments at roadside stalls, kiosks and street vendors are standard across the length and breadth of the country. The unified payments interface (UPI) transactions in December 2023 rose to 117.6 billion in volume and Rs 183 trillion in value, an increase of 59 per cent and 42 per cent compared to the same month in 2022.[4] The combination of Aadhaar, the world's most extensive biometric ID system, and direct benefit transfer (DBT) delivers transparent government subsidies to the beneficiaries.

Another visible transformation has been in infrastructure development. Spending on roads and highways, bridges, tunnels, train tracks and train stations, metro rail projects, airports and seaports has exploded. Growing up, I never considered road trips from Patna to Delhi. Now my cousins do it all the time. There are more universities, Indian Institutes of Technology (IITs), Indian Institutes of Management (IIMs) and All India Institute of Medical Sciences (AIIMS).

THE NEW BHARAT IS FULL OF AATMVISHWAS

Beyond the economy, India has also made significant strides in other fields. From the artistic enterprise to scientific temper and from academia to sports and politics, 'changes are all over the place, and each one of us gets to see only slivers of those changes', said Ramesh Rao, Professor of Communication at the Columbus State University in the US.

According to Subhash Kak, the most significant and discernible change of the last decade or so 'is the abandonment of the old apologetic tone when speaking about [Indian] culture.' Kak is the Regents Professor of Computer Science at Oklahoma State University, in Stillwater, USA. He is a Padma Shri recipient and a member of Prime Minister Narendra Modi's Science, Technology, and Innovation Advisory Council.

While the 'abandonment' Kak mentions stems from the rediscovering and internalising of India's glorious heritage, the apologia is a direct byproduct of a deliberate Orientalist, Indologist and Marxist narrative.

THE ORIENTALIST, INDOLOGIST AND MARXIST NARRATIVE

As postcolonial India nursed its civilisational wounds, it became acutely aware of the prevalent blanket negative narrative about her people, past, culture, texts and traditions. That awareness manifested as a force to reckon with during the last decade.

When the Europeans—the British, French and Portuguese—colonised India, they began controlling India's intellectual discourse, and the directionality of information about India predominantly became 'outsider to insider'. As a consequence, the native 'insiders' of the tradition, according to Arvind Sharma, the Berks Professor of Comparative Religion at McGill University in Canada, 'began to be profoundly affected, even in their self-understanding of their own religious traditions, by Western [non-native outsider] accounts.'

The colonisers also created an Orientalist discourse about India. The discourse provided the basis for their political power, domination, racism and widespread colonisation. They primitivised Indians—Hindus by default—in their popular and academic presentations. Their need to portray Hindus as primitive, savage, uncivilised or vicious rose from their urgency to present themselves as civilised and 'enlightened'. They portrayed Hindu society as being riddled with malaise. They also claimed that the so-called 'social evils' such as 'sati' and 'caste' always have been part of Hindu society and Hinduism.

According to Vishwa Adluri, the Western Indologists, Germans in particular, believed that 'Indians lacked access to the "true" meaning of their [own] texts ... for Indians never developed scientific critical thinking.' Adluri, Professor of Religion and Philosophy at Hunter College, along with Joydeep Bagchee, has exposed the problems of German Indologists' so-called 'scientific method' in their much-acclaimed book *The Nay Science: A History of German Indology*.[5]

Post-Independence Marxists, on the other hand, consciously hid and denied any reference to India's past achievements and glory, claiming it might embolden Hindu extremism. They picked up from where the colonialists and missionaries left, in terms of demonising almost every facet of Indian society.

INDIAN KNOWLEDGE TRADITION

Overcoming the colonial narrative slowly but surely, there is a revival of interest in, and growing awareness about, the native Indian knowledge tradition (IKT). This awareness also includes looking at the tradition from a native 'insider' perspective. The Western world as well as the Indian elites who are burdened by their Western education and vested financial and other material incentives are finally willing to recognise India's rich cultural heritage, albeit grudgingly. Earlier, an expressed pride in Indian culture and its knowledge system most likely would have been 'painted in negative colors and the colonized Anglosphere [would have] continued to ridicule Hindu festivals and cultural practices [and more],' said Kak.

India, traditionally, has been a knowledge society. The Indian knowledge tradition is one of the longest-surviving traditions, with immense contributions in almost all fields of intellectual inquiry. For example, physician Sushruta described rhinoplasty surgery in 600 BCE in his book *Sushruta Samhita*. Similarly, according to the Fields Medalist mathematician Manjul Bhargava, the so-called Pythagorean theorem first appears in Bauddhayana's *Shulba Sutra*, around 800 BCE.

Indian mathematicians had mastered the basic mathematical algorithm of addition, subtraction and division at least a thousand years before the Europeans. The word 'algorithm' is associated with Al Khwarizmi, who borrowed and translated basic mathematical concepts and texts from India in his books. Calculus spread to the West through the Kerala School of Mathematics.

Ashtadhyayi, the treatise on grammar written by Panini in fourth century BCE, is the only complete, explicit and rule-bound grammar of any human language. Additionally, it has several formal features that directly parallel computer science. On the other hand, Yaska's *Nirukta*, written in seventh century BCE, is the first serious work on etymology. Yaska was also the first scholar to treat etymology as an independent science.

BHARAT, A CIVILISATIONAL NATION

More and more people, including those in media and academia, now recognise the fact that India is a civilisational nation, a rashtra with a history of several thousand years. It wasn't as if a group of 'founding fathers' got together one day and decided to form the republic. Bharatvarsha is sanatan, eternal. While liberty, equality and fraternity are the basis of Western democratic states, dharma is the basis of true democracy in Asia, according to Sri Aurobindo. 'Through Dharma,' wrote Sri Aurobindo in *Bande Mataram* (1908), 'the Asiatic evolution fulfils itself; this is her secret.'

The notion of the modern Westphalian state is relatively new. It is only a few centuries old and is based on the assumption that a common political entity best serves the aspirations of the nation's people. However, the notion of rashtra in the Indic civilisation is much older. It is also simultaneously different from the Eurocentric idea of a nation. The word 'rashtra' is used in the Vedic literature to describe the national identity of Bharatvarsha, a contiguous land mass between the snow-capped mountains of the Himalayas in the north and the deep sea in the south.

Bharatvarsha is also the land of the seven rivers, the Sapt Sindhu. It is replete with a sense of spirituality, divinity, sacredness and motherhood. In her *India: A Sacred Geography*, Diana Eck writes that India is a land of sacred geography that 'bears traces of gods and footprints of heroes. Every place has its own story, and conversely, every story in the vast storehouse of myths and legends has its place.'[6]

HINDUTVA

Many academics, scholars and activists have found a voice of resistance in Hindutva. For scholar-activist Sankrant Sanu, Hindutva is 'Hinduism that resists' the insider and outsider threats to Hinduism. The drumbeat of anti-India and anti-Hindu forces is now softened by the response of 'intelligent, smart, confident Hindutva voices who are pushing back with facts, data, reason, and challenges,' said Rao.

Hindutva is a Sanskrit word that translates to 'the essence'—the Hindu-ness—of Hindu dharma.

In his book *Who is Hindu?* (1923), V.D. Savarkar defines a Hindu as 'one who (1) regards the entire subcontinent as his (or her) mother/fatherland ...; (2) is descendant of Hindu parents ... and (3) considers this land holy.' Derived from this notion of a Hindu, her Hinduness—Hindutva—is then presented in terms of 'a common nation (*Rashtra*), a common race (*Jati*) and a common civilization (*Sanskriti*).'

Most Western and some Indian scholars, however, have misunderstood Hindutva. They consider it static and monolithic. According to Arvind Sharma, the reality is that 'its context, text, and subtext have changed over time, depending on the period involved ... and the person expounding it.'[7]

However, it is almost impossible to talk about Hinduism in favourable terms without being accused of being a Hindutva-vadi. In such a discourse, Hindutva is misused as a euphemism for Hindu supremacy, Fascism/Nazism, right-wing, Hindu nationalism, etc. According to philosopher-Indologists Vishwa Adluri and Joydeep Bagchi, the Hindutva smokescreen has often been used in academic circles 'to discipline non-conforming [Hindu] scholars.'[8] This characterisation had pushed many to the corner.

THE RAM MANDIR IN AYODHYA

The building of the Ram Mandir in Ayodhya was one of the most anticipated events in the history of postcolonial India and arguably the most important for Hindus in several generations. It indicates a new 'assertiveness' among Indians in general and Hindus in particular, according to Kak. Such assertiveness would have invited unfavourable consequences for individuals and institutions just a decade or two ago.

According to Pandit Vamdev Shastri (Dr David Frawley), the rebuilding of the Ram Mandir 'indicates a civilizational awakening in Bharat ... [and] Shri Ram and Ramrajya stand at the core of India's history, identity, and aspirations for the future.'[9]

Bhagwan Ram's Prana Pratishtha at the newly rebuilt Ram Mandir in Ayodhya was the culmination of a 500-year-long wait for the Hindus, and a long and fierce legal battle. The five-justice bench of the Supreme Court of India delivered its unanimous verdict to hand over the Sri Ram Janmabhoomi site to Hindus.

The temple's rebuilding signals the beginning of the healing process of a transgenerational trauma of the people of—to use Naipaul's expression—a 'wounded civilization'. More assertive Indians are now demanding to reclaim and rebuild their destroyed and occupied temples. They are also demanding that their temples be released from government control. 'Hindus wish to be treated as equal,' said Kak.

DHARMIC SCHOLARSHIP AND AUTHORSHIP

At a time when the Western education model is showing grave signs of strain due to woke left-wing ideology, corruption and irregularities, there is renewed interest in dharmic scholarship and authorship sweeping across India and in distant foreign lands. Recognising the conscious omission of crucial elements of the Indian texts, traditions and culture from the curricula led to a persistent demand for their inclusion. The establishment of the School of Sanskrit and Indic Studies at the prestigious Jawaharlal Nehru University heralded a new era of dharmic scholarship in India. The School was set up in 2017 after upgrading the Special Centre for Sanskrit Studies.

Indian scholarship, especially in academia, has been the monopoly of the Marxist left. The appointment of Saiyid Nurul Hasan, a left-wing historian and academic, as India's education minister by Prime Minister Indira Gandhi changed the course of India's education. Not only was the IKT kept out of curricula in India, but the leftist historians also significantly distorted the Indian subcontinent's history. Arun Shourie, in his seminal book *Eminent Historians: Their Technology, Their Line, Their*

Fraud (2014), exposed the academic corruption of Marxist historians. 'A Hindu resurgence,' according to Frawley, 'means the end of leftist intellectual domination not only in India but eventually in the entire world.'[10]

The last few years have seen an explosion of dharmic scholarship. Authors and public intellectuals such as Vikram Sampath, Sanjeev Sanyal and J. Sai Deepak have filled in the gaps in the narratives of the left historians. At the same time, academics, Indologists and researchers like Subhash Kak, Arvind Sharma, Makarand Paranjape, Pankaj Jain, Vishwa Adluri and Joydeep Bagchee have made considerable contributions to Indology, Yoga and consciousness studies, Vedanta and Indic environmentalism. Vishwa Adluri and Joydeedp Bagchee's masterful book *The Nay Science: A History of German Indology* exposed how India is studied in the Indology and South Asia departments of the universities in the West. Non-profits such as Indic Academy, of which the author is a trustee, offer courses on the various aspects of IKT and provides grants to researchers, scholars and authors.

The Sabarimala Mandir controversy brought a new breed of feminist scholars and activists who rejected antagonistic Western feminism. The Indic feminist scholarship and activism of people like Sumedha Verma Ojha, Shefali Vaidya, Angali George and Neha Srivastava are rooted in dharma. The 'Ready to Wait' campaign became a hugely successful social movement. Many Hindu women, including young women from all over India, supported the tradition regarding the entry to Swami Ayyappan temple. 'Smart, bright, learned women have begun to challenge the big-bindi communists think twice before they march out onto the streets,' said Rao.

The clash of civilisations is being played out at many levels and in different ways all across India. As the RSS Sarsanghchalak (chief) Dr Mohan Bhagwat once said, 'India's progress is not in making it like the U.S. or China. India should be India.' The 'transfer of power' from the colonisers to the colonised elites wasn't enough for true political, economic, social and cultural independence. In the past decade, India has seen a grassroots groundswell to place Hindu civilisation at the centre of everyday life. The needle is moving swiftly from India to Bharat.

A new dharmic awakening in India is a boon for humanity.

Avatans Kumar is a linguist and a recipient of the San Francisco Press Club's Journalism Awards.

NOTES

1. V.S. Naipaul, *India: An Area Of Darkness, a Wounded Civilization and a Million Mutinies Now*, Pan Macmillan, 2017.
2. Ibid.
3. Alekh Shah, 'India's GDP grew 7.6 per cent in Q2 FY24', *The Economic Times*, 30 November 2023, https://cfo.economictimes.indiatimes.com/news/economy/indias-gdp-grew-7-6-per-cent-in-q2-fy24/105628624.
4. Shine Jacob, 'UPI Scales New High in December; 2023 Value up 59% at Rs 183 trn', *Business Standard*, 2 January 2024, https://www.business-standard.com/economy/news/upi-scales-new-high-in-december-2023-value-up-59-at-rs-183-trn-124010100428_1.html.
5. Joydeep Bagchee and Vishwa Adluri, *The Nay Science: A History of German Indology*, Oxford University Press, 2014.
6. Diana Eck, *India: A Sacred Geography*, Harmony/Rodale, 2012.

7. Arvind Sharma, 'On Hindu, Hindustān, Hinduism and Hindutva', *Numen*, Vol. 49, No. 1 (2002), pp. 1–36.
8. Bagchee and Adluri, *The Nay Science*.
9. 'Dr David Frawley on Ram Mandir, says "Civilization awakening in India" | Converse India', https://www.timesnownews.com/videos/times-now/shows/dr-david-frawley-on-ram-mandir-says-civilization-awakening-in-india-converse-india/70279.
10. https://x.com/davidfrawleyved/status/1753429230988165168.

A New Chapter in Education in India

RAJIV KUMAR

India has an adult literacy rate of 69.3 per cent. By 2030, more than twenty Indian universities are anticipated to rank among the top 200 universities worldwide.

Rooted in the ancient learnings of the Vedas and the Puranas, the Indian education system has come a long way from the old-school gurukuls, where students resided with their teachers and received holistic instruction, to the new-age hi-tech academic institutions of today.

India's school system has a total of four levels, that is, lower primary, upper primary, high and higher secondary. In the recent past, the country has tried to bring significant changes through initiatives such as Sarva Shiksha Abhiyan and the Right to Education Act, which guarantees free and compulsory elementary education to children aged 6–14 years.

As India's education system continues to modernise, the introduction of international private schools is a noteworthy development. These schools aim to prepare students for global competition and equip them to pursue international opportunities. While the admission criteria tends to be more selective compared to public schools and the fee much higher, international schools have become an increasingly popular choice for parents seeking a global education for their children.

A recent news headline highlighted a concerning statistic: 25 per cent of rural children aged 14–18 years cannot read a standard second grade level text in their own mother tongue. The 2023 Annual Status of Education Report (ASER) further reveals that 43 per cent of this age group struggle with reading English sentences. Additionally, over half lack basic division skills, expected to be mastered by the third or fourth grade.

Paradoxically, the report finds that 90 per cent of these youngsters have smartphones at home, and 90.5 per cent have used social media (93.4 per cent boys and 87.8 per cent girls). However, only half are familiar with safety settings. The ASER survey focused on core competencies: basic reading, math and English; applying these skills to daily calculations, reading instructions and handling real-life finances.

It turns out that Humanities is the most popular stream among rural students aged 14–18 years, with 55.7 per cent in class 11 or higher opting for it, followed by STEM (science, technology, engineering and mathematics) at 31.7 per cent and Commerce at 9.4 per cent. Notably, the report identifies a gender gap in STEM, with girls (28.1 per cent) significantly underrepresented compared to boys (36.3 per cent).

This is a significant shift from the 2017 ASER report, where internet and computer usage were much lower (28 per cent and 26 per cent, respectively), and nearly two-thirds had never used a computer. Interestingly, the current report indicates that almost two-thirds of smartphone users use the phone for educational purposes, such as accessing educational content online, including educational videos, and for sharing notes or clarifying doubts.

This sets the tone not only for what needs to be rectified but something that really needs our serious attention, if we are to ensure equality and accessibility to education in every part of the country. The ASER report further clarifies that the aspirations of young boys and girls in the country's hinterland are deeply rooted in their roles in society. While more boys want to finish their studies by the 12th grade, girls are happy to remain in school as it gives them relief from the chores back home. One thing is clear—girls definitely prefer to complete their studies before getting married.

The message is clear: the younger generation recognises the importance of education for building a future for themselves and gaining upward mobility. This reality holds true across India, where even basic jobs require a school-leaving certificate. The intense competition for employment necessitates higher education, often reaching the undergraduate level. Making education compulsory for everyone under the age of eighteen and linking it to subsidies and financial schemes for families is crucial. Only through such a combined approach—compulsion for parents and incentives for students—can India achieve a well-educated population in the near future.

THE CHALLENGE OF ATTRACTING QUALIFIED TEACHERS IN INDIA

One of the most significant hurdles facing Indian schools, both government and private, is the lack of qualified teachers. Often, teaching becomes a career option pursued only after other avenues have been exhausted. This is further compounded by the fact that government school postings often lead to rural areas. Understandably, this discourages many teachers, who either request leave or seek immediate transfers. The situation in government primary schools is particularly concerning. Teachers are not only tasked with handling combined age groups in a single classroom, but they also face exhaustion due to long and demanding hours. This, unfortunately, contributes to the broader problems faced by government schools.

MULTIPLE FACTORS HINDERING EDUCATIONAL PROGRESS

There is a lack of well-trained teachers specifically for primary education. This poses a critical threat to the educational progress of young children. In some cases, there may be a lack of parental involvement, with children failing to receive adequate encouragement at home. There may be some instances where parents view their children as a source of additional labour and so they do not prioritise their education.

Furthermore, government schools often grapple with insufficient funding, neglect and a lack of accountability. Additionally, some teachers may not provide the necessary support for underprivileged children from disadvantaged backgrounds. Basic necessities like water and electricity can also be absent in these schools.

A GLIMMER OF HOPE: LEVERAGING TECHNOLOGY AND MULTILINGUAL LEARNING

Despite this seemingly bleak picture, there is a positive aspect to consider. India boasts of the highest rate of smartphone usage among children globally. This presents a valuable opportunity to utilise technology as a tool for improved, accessible and faster dissemination of education and information. Children's inherent adaptability to digitalisation can be a powerful asset. However, it is crucial to ensure that children remain proficient in their mother tongue. This fosters a sense of cultural identity and would help India retain the richness of its regional diversity and aspirations.

It is pertinent to point out here that in the final episode of *Mann ki Baat* telecasted in February 2024, Prime Minister Modi said that the Centre's endeavour is that language should not become a hindrance to education and the holistic progress of any child. 'In our country, many children would leave studies midway due to language handicaps. Our new National Education Policy is helping eliminate such obstacles to the process of learning and the holistic development of a child,' he said.

During his address, PM Modi also brought up the artificial intelligence (AI) tool Bhashini, which he used during the Kashi Tamil Sangamam earlier in the month for real-time translation for the benefit of his Tamil-speaking audience. It helped him establish an instant rapport with his audience. 'You can imagine the revolutionary change that could be brought about once this technology is used more widely in our schools, hospitals and courts,' he added.

The New Education Policy 2020 places a special focus on historically marginalised, disadvantaged and underrepresented groups. Let us recall the relevant principles for inclusion of all children in education:

- Recognising, identifying and fostering the unique capabilities of each student, by sensitising teachers as well as parents to promote each student's holistic development in both academic and non-academic spheres;

- Respect for diversity and respect for the local context in all curriculum, pedagogy and policy, always keeping in mind that education is a concurrent subject; and
- Full equity and inclusion as the cornerstone of all educational decisions to ensure that all students are able to thrive in the education system.

India's education system is in for a major overhaul. There is an attempt to bring in sweeping changes, including:

- revamped board exams;
- new curriculum with a focus on multiple disciplines;
- coding education for all students, including those with disabilities;
- stronger regulations for quality control;
- early childhood education with a fresh approach;
- greater emphasis on multilingualism; and
- improved assessment methods.

While some of these ideas may be familiar, NEP 2020 adopts a holistic approach. One key aspect is increased focus on online and digital learning, which is a significant departure from the existing policy, to ensure everyone has access to quality education. This policy aims to make India a global leader in education, leaving no social group behind.

Two years ago, the beginning of the war between Ukraine and Russia shattered the dreams of around 20,000 students, mostly medical students. It also exposed the shortcomings of our education system, which, due to limited accessibility and affordability, restricted opportunities available for talented students. Thankfully, most students were repatriated from

Ukraine in time, with few casualties. Imagine the struggles that parents of these children would have faced. They invested in their children's education, saving money for their studies abroad (admittedly not always in the best conditions), possibly even taking loans with long-term repayments. Then came the worry about job prospects and their children's integration into the workforce.

Recent headlines indicate that due to the ongoing conflict with Hamas, Israel is experiencing a labour shortage. This gap was previously filled in by Palestinian workers. To address this, Israel is inclined to recruit skilled workers from India at competitive salaries. This trend of high demand for Indian talent is likely to continue in Europe and other regions in the coming years. India's growing pool of IT professionals, engineers, doctors, business managers and bankers, along with its skilled and semi-skilled workforce, is becoming increasingly sought-after.

Indians are known for their adherence to rules and laws, which enhances their acceptance in foreign countries. However, this rise in demand isn't without challenges. Some anti-India pockets, fuelled by prejudice, resort to online abuse, or trolling, of Indian workers. A recent example involved Taiwan, where the Ministry of Foreign Affairs condemned racist remarks against Indian workers, attributing them to a deliberate attempt to damage India's image and its relations with Taiwan.

Statistics show that, in India, approximately 12 million young people enter the workforce each year. By the end of this decade, we could have a billion working-age individuals seeking employment. In stark contrast, many other countries will be facing ageing populations and labour shortages. India stands in a unique position, but there is still a gap to fill. Data reveals a significant shortfall of skilled and unskilled workers across various sectors in India, including for factories, engineering units and infrastructure projects.

A report by the Confederation of Indian Industries emphasises that, compared to 2021, the year 2022 saw a decline in migrant workers returning to cities. This creates a significant gap between the demand and supply of labour. The report also highlights a shortage of talent for white-collar jobs across all levels. This situation presents a clear challenge and opportunity for the private sector to bridge the skill gap by providing more practical, industry-oriented training. This will empower the workforce, drive innovation and propel India towards its goal of becoming a global manufacturing hub and economic powerhouse.

In the spirit of innovation, new diplomas and vocational courses have been introduced to give students a basic idea of what to expect from a degree course, and to provide them necessary grounding for skill-based education. These courses incorporate uniquely designed curriculums that support vocational training and polish the skills of students in a particular field. So, if you are looking for a course that will directly lead to professional occupancy in a well-paying job, you should definitely explore diploma courses after the twelfth grade. Thus, through these short-term courses, the chief goal of the current education system in India is to foster learning-focused pedagogy while promoting skill-based training programmes.

India has the third-largest education and development sector in the world, behind China and the US. It is abundantly clear that India's current education system focuses on theory rather than career. It lays great emphasis on exams—and, by extension, on rote learning.

The changes proposed by the NEP aim to make the Indian education system lively and skill-focused.

However, addressing the issue of shortage of skilled labour requires a multi-pronged approach involving collaboration between government bodies, educational institutions and industry stakeholders. Industry participation in curriculum design, training programmes and on-the-job training can enhance employability and align individual skills with industry requirements. For instance, a diverse set of specialised skills, encompassing expertise in robotics, automation, engineering, programming and various other technical domains, is essential in the manufacturing industry. Despite the growing reliance on machines and automation, there remains an unfulfilled demand for workers capable of operating and maintaining these technologies. Unfortunately, workers lack access to the training required to stay updated and adapt to evolving modern-day demands. There is, therefore, a need for refresher short courses and a tremendous opportunity in this.

Once again recalling the National Mission on Education, which is to focus on basic literacy and numeracy, the major reformations in pedagogical structure will not have any rigid separation between streams and between vocational, academic, curricular and extra-curricular studies. Moreover, Board exams will test the knowledge acquired instead of rote-learning skills. This is the one big change that one would see once the NEP 2020 is implemented in its right perspective.

Schools taught us how to read and write, pulled us through twelve years of education, but did not pay attention to developing a holistic personality through the different stages of our initial life. The New Education Policy proposes a new

5+3+3+4 structure of school education in India, which will replace the previous 10+2 system. This new system is mapped to the stages of mental development that a child goes through in these initial years of their life. Students will spend the first five years on strengthening their foundation, the next three years in the preparatory stage, then three years in the middle stage and the remaining four years in the secondary stage. The New Education Policy fosters holistic development of students, by integrating co-curricular activities, sports, arts and vocational education into the curriculum. It acknowledges that education goes beyond academics and aims to nurture well-rounded individuals.

Today, cricketers, Paralympians, those excelling in music, photography or even woodwork, and culinary experts are icons and well accepted in society. Our own opinion of what education a child must pursue for them to have a successful career has to change. Respect for all kinds of education, including excelling in craftsmanship, is required, which will give a child the confidence to choose from a very broad canvas of skills that could then be used to contribute to our economic activity and the expansion of business opportunities.

We need smart people in the food and hospitality industry, particularly for the 24x7 delivery of food, young legal experts in smaller towns to help deal with the legal formalities of setting up small businesses and to offer other legal advice—the list goes on. Girls are now driving cabs, even trucks, and schools need to give lessons on traffic rules and management and help every child get a driving licence before leaving school if they meet the age criterion for getting a licence. There was once a plethora of schools that would train flight staff for the aviation industry.

With the biggest aircraft orders emanating from India in the last few months, the sky is the limit, and private educationists must grab this opportunity.

Furthermore, technology has changed the way we read and absorb information. Once a school atlas was a significant book to understand where we were, and where was the rest of the world. But technology has outpaced the atlas and has also put on the backburner big encyclopaedias, with boundless information now accessible at the tap of a button on our mobile phones. Millions of videos are available on YouTube. They cover all sorts of topics—from scientific engineering to travel and tourism, personality development and acquiring new skills. Educators and teachers now have the option to teach with the aid of audio and visual devices. They can share subject-related videos rather than restricting themselves to textbooks and a theoretical approach. Should weather or external factors disturb the set patterns of school and college education curriculum, the same can be imparted through online classes. The disruption caused by the COVID-19 pandemic has helped us incorporate a new angle to learning and continuity from wherever we are.

The change for the better will be towards universalisation of access, from early childhood care and education (ECCE) to secondary education. It will mean that, instead of mere rote learning, students will acquire more practical knowledge, which is foundationally rewarding. They will have increased flexibility in the choice of subjects to study, which will allow individuals to focus on, and specialise in, their areas of interest. Coupled with this, the reduction of curriculum content will promote essential learning and critical thinking, thereby increasing reasoning skills and overall capabilities. This will help students nurture a scientific temper from a very young age and, by the time they complete their higher education, they will be at par with global standards. With foreign colleges setting up Indian campuses, there is already a shift for more global exposure, and with India revamping its education system, more foreign students are likely to choose India for education.

With greater importance given to practical assignments and skill development, including introduction to music, arts and literature, and students gaining greater exposure to vocational skills as well as coding—which may be taught as early as from the sixth grade—the Indian education system is all set to see a new wave of learning. Focused towards building a culture of critical thinking, along with scope of discovery, discussions and analysis, India will be adopting a specific action-oriented policy that is outcome-driven. There will be stress on research and funding to private institutions to usher in twenty-first-century skills in teaching, learning and assessment.

Change is always for the better. Both those teaching and the ones being taught have to make the best of these new, better opportunities that the NEP will usher in.

Rajiv Kumar is former Chief Producer, News and Current Affairs, Doordarshan. He is a Fulbright Scholar, Syracuse University, Upstate New York.

The Health Revolution

ANN LIEBERT

India, the world's largest democracy, with its fast-growing economy, has a major impact on world health, particularly with its formidable manufacturing base and its ability in recent times to offer treatment for the HIV epidemic in Africa when no other option was available. India is a world leader in many aspects of traditional medicine and is focused on combining it with modern advances in the field to offer all-inclusive healthcare.

In 2009, a bilateral strategic partnership was proposed between India and Australia. This was formalised ten years ago, in 2014, and was elevated in 2020 to a comprehensive strategic partnership. This partnership, based on 'mutual understanding, trust, common interests and the shared values of democracy and rule of law', led to the establishment of the Centre for Australia–India Relations to 'foster new ties and support expanding exchange and cooperation with India'.[1] The partnership defines many areas of cooperation, including terrorism, maritime safety and defence. In the area of enhancing science, technology and research collaboration, there is a commitment towards strengthening healthcare systems in the two countries and globally.

Both India and Australia recognise the importance of global cooperation for saving lives, managing the economic impacts of healthcare and alleviating future global challenges, including pandemics. Both nations are committed to sharing the benefits arising out of scientific and medical research and development, and the strengthening of healthcare systems. Both countries recognise the importance of collaborative efforts in research, innovation and healthcare delivery, to improve health outcomes not only within their borders but also on a global scale.

Under the partnership agreement, India and Australia have resolved to work through multilateral, regional and plurilateral mechanisms to strengthen and diversify supply chains for critical health and technology services. This is also consistent with the initiatives taken by India's G20 presidency and the G20 Health Ministers' meeting to identify the three major health priorities to strengthen the global health infrastructure and deliver universal health coverage. This will be done by consolidating the existing digital health initiatives and ensuring preparedness for future health crises of pandemics and antimicrobial resistance.

Within the healthcare system of both countries, there is an urgent need for better therapeutic interventions for many intractable diseases that have few or no pharmacological treatments, such as metabolic diseases, chronic kidney disease, diabetic wounds and ulcers, traumatic brain injury, concussion and stroke, neurodegenerative diseases and chronic pain. Included in this is long COVID or post–acute COVID conditions. While most people with COVID-19 recover completely, long COVID conditions can affect up to one in eight people, according to a large study published in *The Lancet*. However, a recent study suggests that numbers could be much higher in India, with up to 25 per cent of COVID patients having symptoms that persist for at least a year.[2] These symptoms could include brain fog, headache, sleep problems, dizziness, change in sense of smell, and depression or anxiety.

The incidence of chronic kidney disease in India ranges from less than 1 per cent up to 17 per cent, depending on the region. Further, incidence of the disease is increasing due to the nationwide rise in cases of diabetes.[3] This is a major health problem, with the only possible treatment options at the later stages of the disease being dialysis and transplantation, both of which are expensive and not universally available. Parkinson's disease is another cause of concern. While the incidence of this disease in India is low compared to Australia and the US, the absolute numbers are high due to India's large population. There are more than 7 million patients suffering from Parkinson's and only very few trained neurologists to take care of them.[4] Chronic pain is another problem in India, with up to 20 per cent of the population being affected. This places a significant burden on employment and the quality of life.[5] In the case of chronic pain, the effectiveness of the available modern medicine treatment of opioid and non-steroidal anti-inflammatory drugs is limited.

There is a need for alternative treatments for diseases and conditions that have few options in modern medicine. India, more so than Australia, embraces traditional, complementary and integrative (TCI) medicine, due to its multicultural society. There appears to be a growing trend to integrate TCI with standard medicine to offer holistic and more individualised treatment. This is consistent with the World Health Organization's (WHO) approach to TCI medicine with the traditional medicine strategy for 2013–24.[6]

Traditional, complementary and integrative medicines in India include Ayurveda, yoga, naturopathy, Unani, Siddha and homoeopathy, which are used by hundreds of millions of people, including in primary healthcare settings, either alone or alongside modern medicine. The history of Ayurveda massage treatments has strong parallels to manipulative physiotherapy as well as light therapy. The therapies that we research and use clinically are light-based therapies based on low-power lasers or LEDs, which is now called photobiomodulation (PBM). Photobiomodulation is well documented over the last thirty years to be an effective treatment for wounds that heal with difficultly, such as diabetic and venous ulcers, inflammatory conditions such as osteoarthritis, tissue repair such as tendinopathies, and for pain relief, including chronic pain. As such there is a huge opportunity for this therapy in India and PBM is currently being used and taught at several institutions across India.

It is worth emphasising the significance of international collaboration in driving advancements in medical research. I recently attended the World Association of PhotobiomoduLation Therapy (WALT) Congress at the Manipal Academy of Higher Education (MAHE), which was a fantastic example of international collaboration, underscoring the potential for transformative research and treatments, bringing together researchers and clinicians in the field of PBM from across the globe and opening up new opportunities to expand and promote PBM therapy. This was my first visit to India, and I was struck by the long and impressive history of both education and medicine as well as the strong interdisciplinary structure of the university with its dental, medical and allied health therapeutic fields.

MAHE was founded by Dr T.M.A. Pai as a private college in 1957, after the establishment of the Kasturba Medical College in 1953. It is an institution of eminence and a deemed university, with an international reputation for education, healthcare and pioneering research. The convenor of WALT was Dr Arun Maiya, who is an active researcher and contributor in the field of PBM and a strong advocate of collaborative research. The Manipal Hospitals attached to MAHE use PBM to treat patients with diabetic foot ulcers and wounds as well as patients of chronic kidney disease with neuropathy symptoms. Megha Nataraj, a PhD candidate, gave a very enlightening presentation on her clinical study of PBM and diabetes-induced kidney disease. Research conducted at MAHE also offers new understanding of the role of the microbiome in Parkinson's disease in the Indian population and the implications for treatment.[7]

Professor Rene-Jean Bensadoun, the president of WALT, recognised the contribution of MAHE to PBM by announcing the Centre for Podiatry and Diabetic Foot Care and Research at MAHE as a centre of excellence for PBM. It was also truly inspiring to attend the celebration for the inauguration of the first Chair of Photobiomodulation at MAHE, with our WALT colleague Professor Praveen Arany taking up the position. Professor Arany also teaches at the University at Buffalo in the USA and is a former president of WALT. I have been collaborating with him on research on PBM cellular mechanisms for over ten years. He has made significant contribution towards the acceptance of international guidelines for PBM in supportive cancer care.

I have had the opportunity to visit several hospitals in southern India and see first-hand the manner in which PBM therapies are being trialled and used clinically. I have also seen groundbreaking research being conducted on diseases such as Parkinson's disease and chronic kidney disease, including the connection between the gut microbiome and the brain in these diseases.

MAHE's commitment to the use of PBM and further research on its uses, the hospitals that I visited, the colleagues that I saw, and the emerging Indian med-tech industry representatives with whom I met presented a very promising story for an India-based collaboration to drive this exciting and necessary field going forward.

As an Australian clinician scientist and the head of a laboratory group in Sydney, I would like to outline a perspective on the importance of PBT for mitigation of intractable diseases and the opportunities that exist for global collaboration on innovation between Australia and India. I have a particular interest in many of the aspects of light therapy, which we now call PBM. We have been conducting clinical trials using PBM for various conditions as well as researching some of the basic mechanisms of how PBM works.

Light therapy has its roots in ancient times. The evolution of light as a therapeutic modality can be traced back to thousands of years to the Egyptians and to the practitioners of Ayurveda, or the science of light, which combines the healing powers of light and colour with plant extracts. The modern world embraced the use of light, including heliotherapy, in Europe in the nineteenth century and with the work of Florence Nightingale who advocated sunlight and fresh air. Indian scientists such as J.C. Ghosh, N.R. Dhar and Bawa Kartar Singh pushed forward the boundaries of photochemistry in the 1920s and 1930s and Manapurathu Verghese George established a photochemical research group in the early 1960s to study photo-organic transformations.[8]

The effectiveness of PBM as a medical treatment was first demonstrated in 1967 by Dr Endre Mester in Budapest. While investigating whether laser was harmful and could cause cancer, Dr Mester serendipitously found that when applied to a wound on a rat, laser caused the wound to heal more quickly and led to accelerated hair regrowth. Since that time, laser—and LED treatment, which is now known as PBM—has been quietly revolutionising healthcare practices. Despite its technical name, the concept behind PBM is elegantly straightforward. It harnesses the energy of light to influence cellular responses within the body, especially stimulating the mitochondria, which are the powerhouses of cells, to produce more energy. The process uses a low power of light and is non-thermal, but the wavelength or colour of the light is important, with certain red and near infrared wavelengths being the most effective to trigger a cascade of biochemical and cellular changes.

Central to the effect of PBM is the involvement of a vital enzyme known as cytochrome-C-oxidase, which plays a pivotal role in the electron transport chain within the mitochondria. When exposed to specific wavelengths of light, cytochrome c oxidase undergoes a series of conformational changes, leading to enhanced mitochondrial function. This process culminates in a plethora of physiological responses, including heightened energy production, improved oxygen binding, augmented cellular signalling pathways and reduced inflammation. The cellular effects that PBM produces makes it amenable to treating a multitude of conditions. Over the past five decades, PBM has evolved into a versatile tool for the management of various medical conditions, including tissue healing, particularly in the context of wounds, burns and chronic ulcers, in pain relief, deep tissue repair, such as for tendons and cartilage, and bone attenuation of inflammation in conditions such as osteoarthritis.

Photobiomodulation now has a small but important and increasing place in modern clinical practice. The increasing acceptance of PBM in mainstream medicine has been helped by it being established as an accepted treatment for the side effects of oral mucositis and radiation dermatitis, which are the side effects of radiation therapy and chemotherapy for cancer, under both the MACSS and NICE guidelines.

Recent years have witnessed the emergence of new areas of PBM therapy. Transcranial PBM or PBM directed to the skull and brain is an important area that has the potential to address a spectrum of brain-related ailments. Transcranial PBM has been shown in pre-clinical animal studies as well as in some clinical studies to be effective in treating traumatic brain injury (TBI) and stroke. It is also useful in managing neurodegenerative diseases and neuropsychiatric conditions, such as reversing cognitive impairment, post-traumatic stress disorder (PTSD), anxiety, depression, Alzheimer's disease and Parkinson's disease. Pre-clinical models have also underscored its neuroprotective and neuro-regenerative potential, offering new avenues for therapeutic intervention. Importantly, the safety profile of transcranial PBM remains exemplary, with reports of only minimal and transient side effects. The potential therapeutic benefits of PBM in diverse neurological disorders offer a ray of hope for patients confronting diseases with limited pharmacological options.

The importance of PBM therapy to the Indian population cannot be overstated. The proven effectiveness of PBM for healing of wounds, tissue repair and pain management shows that there is a place for PBM as a much-needed additional therapy for chronic pain, diabetic and venous ulcers, and other conditions that are prevalent in India. It is also projected that the number of people who will develop neurodegenerative diseases, including Parkinson's disease, will rise due to ageing population and increasing risk factors for the diseases, which makes PBM, a non-invasive, safe and potentially effective therapy, very attractive. By adopting PBM for mainstream diseases and conditions that Indian patients suffer from, India can build upon its leading role in the supply of generic medicines to poorer countries. At the same time, it can stake out a prominent position in the use of PBM.

There is no doubt that there is a very promising opportunity for local research and clinical collaborations to extend this exciting therapy in India. India is particularly well placed to make a substantial contribution to this burgeoning area of medicine and to deliver on many of the recent health aims and objectives articulated at the G20 summit and the Indian–Australian Comprehensive Strategic Partnership. International collaboration between India and Australia and the international research setting in PBM provides a framework for an exciting area of treatment of intractable diseases as well as providing further technological innovation that can address complex health challenges and be at the forefront of world health initiatives. As we navigate the complexities of modern healthcare, it is imperative to harness the power of collaboration and innovation to build a healthier and more resilient world.

Ann Liebert is a clinician/scientist and Coordinator of Photomolecular Research at the San Hospital, Sydney, Australia. She has research positions at Sydney University and the University of Western Sydney and teaches in the Diploma of Photobiomodulation at Universite de Montpellier, France. Ann researches the mechanisms of photobiomodulation and the treatment of Parkinson's disease and kidney disease and has published many papers on these and other topics. She continues to treat patients in her photobiomodulation clinic. Ann is Co-founder of the med-tech company SYMBYX Biome, which produces photobiomodulation devices to treat Parkinson's disease and other neurodegenerative diseases.

NOTES

1. https://www.foreignminister.gov.au/minister/marise-payne/media-release/centre-australia-india-relations.
2. Vignesh Kumar, Jency Maria Koshy, S. Divyashree, Suneetha Narreddy, Priscilla Rupali and Sowmya Sathyendra, '1370. Prevalence and Predictors of Post-COVID-19 (Long COVID) in India', *Open Forum Infectious Diseases*, Volume 10, Issue Supplement_2, December 2023, https://academic.oup.com/ofid/article/10/Supplement_2/ofad500.1207/7446786.
3. Santosh Varughese and Georgi Abraham, 'Chronic Kidney Disease in India: A Clarion Call for Change', *Clinical Journal of the American Society of Nephrology*, Volume 13, Issue 5 (7 May 2018), pp. 802–4, https://www.ncbi.nlm.nih.gov/pmc/articles/PMC5969474/.
4. Akhilesh Kumar Verma, Janak Raj, Vivek Sharma, Tej Bali Singh, Shalabh Srivastava and Ragini Srivastava, 'Epidemiology and the Associated Risk Factors of Parkinson's Disease among the North Indian Population', *Clinical Epidemiology and Global Health*, Volume 5, Issue 1 (March 2017), pp. 8–13, https://doi.org/10.1016/j.cegh.2016.07.003.
5. Ashok Kumar Saxena, Parmanand N. Jain and Sushma Bhatnagar,

'The Prevalence of Chronic Pain among Adults in India', *Indian Journal of Palliative Care*, Volume 24, Issue 4 (October–December 2018), pp. 472–77, https://www.ncbi.nlm.nih.gov/pmc/articles/PMC6199848/.
6. 'Traditional, Complementary and Integrative Medicine (TCI), World Health Organization, https://www.who.int/teams/integrated-health-services/traditional-complementary-and-integrative-medicine.
7. Sujith Pavan, Sankar Prasad Gorthi, Arvind N. Prabhu, Bhabatosh Das, Ankur Mutreja, Karthick Vasudevan, Vignesh Shetty, Thandavarayan Ramamurthy and Mamatha Ballal, 'Dysbiosis of the Beneficial Gut Bacteria in Patients with Parkinson's Disease from India', *Annals of Indian Academy of Neurology*, Volume 26, Issue 6 (November–December 2023), pp. 908–16, https://journals.lww.com/annalsofian/fulltext/2023/26060/dysbiosis_of_the_beneficial_gut_bacteria_in.13.aspx.
8. Srinivasan Chandrasekaran, Ayyappanpillai Ajayaghosh and Suresh Das, 'Photochemistry, Photophysics and Photobiology', *Journal of Chemical Sciences*, Volume 130, Issue 148 (2018), https://link.springer.com/article/10.1007/s12039-018-1557-6.

India–Japan Ties and the Security of the Indo-Pacific

SATORU NAGAO

India has been rising under the leadership of Prime Minister Narendra Modi since 2014. One of the pillars of the Modi government's foreign policy has been promoting India–Japan cooperation. The Indian prime minister's friendship with the former prime minister of Japan, Shinzo Abe, who was assassinated in July 2022, led the way in this regard. Recently, improved cooperation between India and Japan has become more evident. The two countries have been increasing their diplomatic exchanges, conducting joint exercises of their armed forces and seeking joint infrastructure projects. Therefore, it is logical to ask why the relations between India and Japan have strengthened recently. This chapter seeks to explore this by focusing on three questions: How have India–Japan relations developed? How the cooperation between the two countries will promote India's rise? How to deal with China, which has tried to prevent the rise of India?

THE DEVELOPMENT OF INDIA–JAPAN RELATIONS

The year 2007 was an important turning point for the relations between India and Japan. Japan was a pioneer in creating the concepts of the Quadrilateral Security Dialogue (Quad) and the Indo-Pacific identity. In a speech entitled 'Confluence of Two Seas' given in the Indian parliament in 2007, the former prime minister of Japan Abe Shinzo introduced these ideas. He said, 'By Japan and India coming together in this way, this "broader Asia" will evolve into an immense network spanning the entirety of the Pacific Ocean, incorporating the United States of America and Australia. Open and transparent, this network will allow people, goods, capital, and knowledge to flow freely.'[1] Initiated in 2007, the Quad is a security arrangement between Japan, the US, Australia and India.

An important feature of Abe's speech was that he introduced both the concepts of the Indo-Pacific and the Quad at the same time. The Indo-Pacific identity allowed Abe to include both the Pacific Ocean and the Indian Ocean in one concept, replacing the concept of 'Asia-Pacific', which did not include the Indian Ocean region. Because of rapid economic development, both the Pacific and Indian Ocean regions are increasingly emerging as influential regions in world politics. For example, the International Institute for Strategic Studies in the UK pointed out that nominal Asian defence spending (excluding Australia and New Zealand) overtook that of NATO Europe in 2012. Therefore, to explain current trends in world politics, Abe saw a need for new concepts that tied in all ascendant regions, including both the Pacific and the Indian Ocean regions.

However, this rising Indo-Pacific region has been under threat. Prime Minister Abe believed that it should not be a

China-dominated region. He explained this idea in his article 'Asia's Democratic Security Diamond', which was published in Europe just before he was sworn in as the prime minister for a second time in 2012.[2] The Indo-Pacific is a geographic concept that includes all the countries surrounding China. The Quad includes all the great powers except China.

In this case, Prime Minister Abe wanted to emphasise the importance of India and its integration into the Quad. Both Japan and Australia are long-time US allies with established modes of cooperation. India was the newcomer. To cooperate with India, Japan needed the security architecture of the Quad.

Since then, the relations between India and Japan have developed both bilaterally and multilaterally.

INDIA-JAPAN COOPERATION AND THE RISE OF INDIA

As stated earlier, Prime Minister Abe came up with the concepts of Quad and the Indo-Pacific because he wanted to promote cooperation with India. But, is the cooperation between India and Japan beneficial for India? Indeed, Quad and the Indo-Pacific are not only beneficial for Japan, they are vital for India. There are two reasons for this: first, India's rise relies on maritime security and second, India needs to deal with China, which could restrict its rise.

India's ascent relies on economic rise. However, the economy relies on maritime security, which is directly linked with the safeguarding of the sea lines of communication (SLOCs) of trade and energy import. Ships can carry huge products and energy without high cost. Compared with land routes, there are few terrorist-related problems on the SLOCs. Therefore, if India rises economically, it will rely more on maritime security.

Cooperation of maritime powers such as the US, Japan and Australia is beneficial to secure India's SLOCs.

In addition, India itself has the potential to become a maritime power. History is a testament to this. From the eighteenth century to the 1970s, Great Britain was the most influential country in the area. What gave the British their influence was their naval power, which enabled them to go anywhere and approach or attack various countries. Later, because the British could not maintain their naval power, they had to withdraw from the east of Suez in the 1970s.

Alfred Thayer Mahan, while analysing the case of British naval power, listed six important factors that make a country a strong sea power: geographical position, physical conformation (especially the length of coastline), the extent of territory (especially the balance of coastline and military power to defend), the number of population (for working at sea), the character of the people, and the character of the government.[3] In his opinion, the British dominated the sea because they did not need to concentrate to defend their land borders. They had a long coastline as well as sufficient military power to defend it, and there was enough population to work at the sea. This was why the British were able to adjust to new societies and develop these colonies: their government supported maritime expansion; and the British dominated the sea. Thus, if Mahan is right, these factors were crucial to Britain maintaining its influence in maritime affairs. By extension of this view, India has enough potential to become a sea power

India has a good geographical position, with high mountains separating the Indian subcontinent from Eurasia. History reveals how this can work to India's advantage. There are only three empires that dominated most of the subcontinent: Maurya Empire, Mughal Empire and the British Raj. The territories of these three empires were very similar, and were based on the line of mountains. The only exception was the Khyber Pass, which was used by Alexander the Great. Therefore, the Indian subcontinent is a kind of an island, and India can concentrate its naval forces if it has the required will to climb up the global order by becoming a sea power.

FIGURE 5: Influential Area of Empires in the Subcontinent

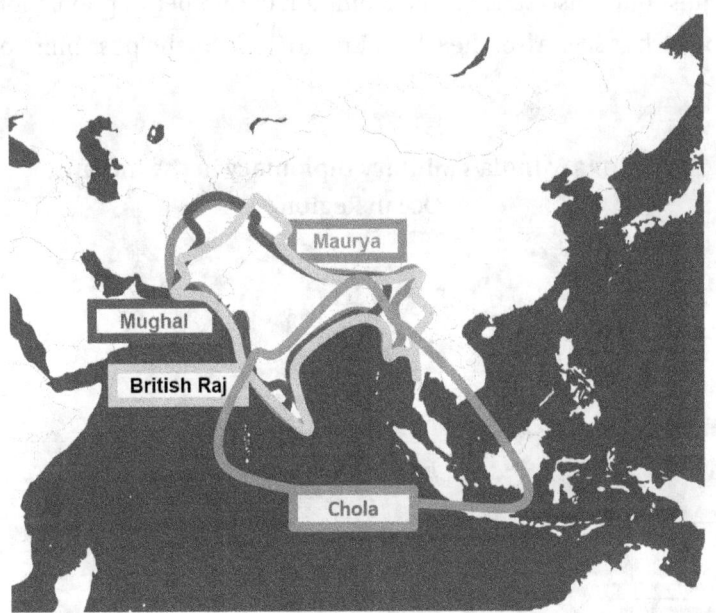

Source: Satoru Nagao, 'The Emerging India is Not a Threat, Why?: An Assessment from Japan', *Asia Pacific Journal of Social Science*, Vol. III, Jul–Dec 2012, pp. 99–109.

In addition, the history of Cholas indicates another geographical advantage of India. The Chola Empire, which was located in southern India, made an expedition to Southeast Asia in the eleventh century. Their area of influence expanded to the whole coastal area of the Bay of Bengal. This historical fact is another good example of India's geographical advantage. Since India is located at the northern centre of the Indian Ocean, the country can access not only Southeast Asia, but also all sides of the Indian Ocean, including the Middle East and East Africa.

India has physical conformation because of its 7,517 (only mainland 6,100) km of coastline. Moreover, India has been a reliable and important source of marine manpower in the world.[4] Thus, India also satisfies the condition of number of population to work at sea. Also, the Chola Empire reflects the possibility of

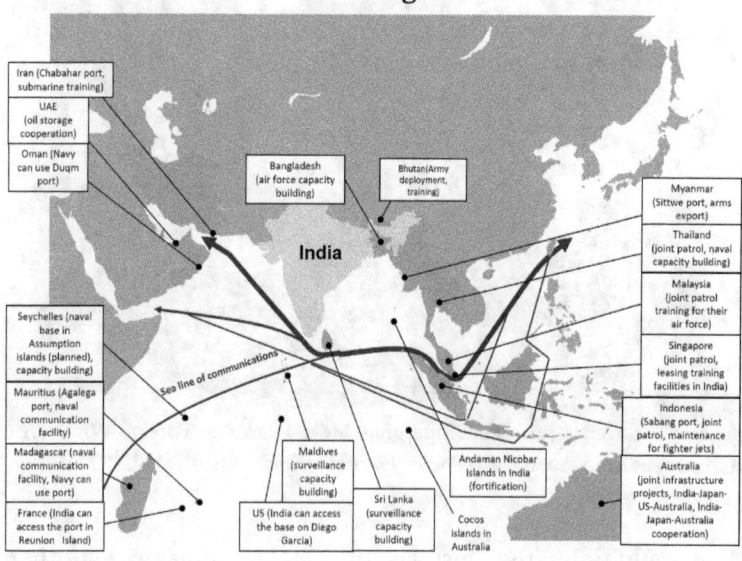

FIGURE 6: India's Military Diplomacy in the Indian Ocean Region

Source: Author

FIGURE 7: India's Military Diplomacy in the Southeast Asia

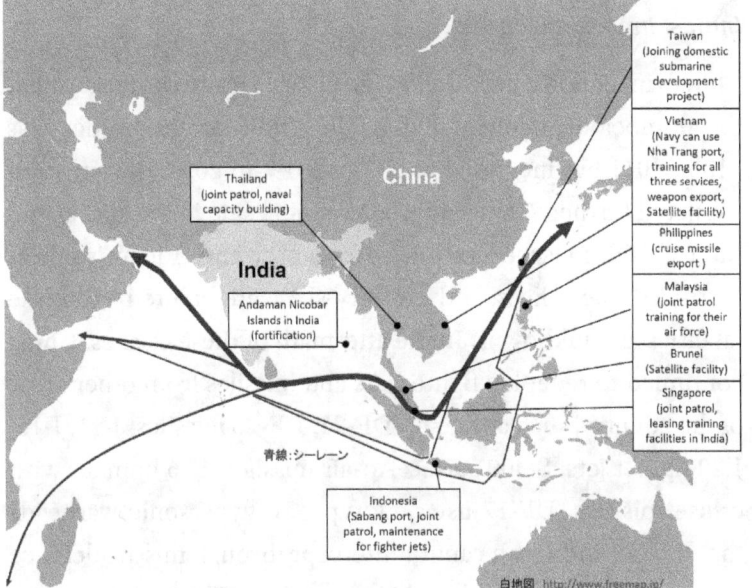

Source: Author

the people of India being oriented towards being a sea power. India's strategic objective should therefore be to emerge as a maritime power. India has been providing security in the Indian Ocean region (Figures 6 and 7). Thus, according to Mahan's theory, India has sufficient potential to become a sea power, which also indicates that India could become an influential country in the Indo-Pacific.

MANAGING CHINA

India's maritime potential, however, could face a threat from China, which has been increasing its activities around India.

China's Activities in the Indian Ocean Region

India–China Land Border

China's incursions increased in the 2010s. Figure 8 indicates that the number of incursions along the India–China border was 213 in 2011 but increased to 633 in 2019. In 2020, the situation escalated further. China entered the India side in the spring and the two sides clashed in June. At least twenty Indian soldiers sacrificed their lives and seventy-six were injured (Chinese fatalities are unknown). In the aftermath of these clashes, China continued to redeploy fighter jets and missiles from other areas of the country, such as DF-17, DF-21, DF-26 missiles, J-11, J-16, J-20 fighter jets, S-400 surface-to-air missiles, H-6 bomber with cruise missiles. DF-17 use new types of hypersonic warheads that the US and Japan cannot intercept through missile defence systems. J-20 is a stealth fighter jet. Thus, China is deploying the latest weapons to increase tensions on the border areas. Moreover, it is also building more than 600 villages, which could be military camps in the India–China border area.

Indian Ocean

China's activities in the Indian Ocean region are also a threat to India. China has invested in many infrastructure projects in the Indian Ocean region through the Belt and Road Initiative (BRI). Because China charges high-interest rates, it creates huge debt for recipients. (Generally, the World Bank and the Asia Development Bank charge 0.25–3 per cent as interest. In the case of China's BRI, the interest rate is 6–8 per cent.[5]) Thus China can wield strong influence over its loan recipients. For example, Djibouti, which has a huge debt to China, leased a big naval base from China. And Sri Lanka gave China the right to control their Hambantota port for ninety-nine years. In the case of Pakistan too, Chinese troops are deploying in the port developed by China.

China also provides weapons to this region. Their high-tech, sensitive machines are used under rough conditions and are prone to breakage. Thus, it requires constant maintenance and repair. If countries receive Chinese weapons, they rely on a supply line of repair parts from China. China exports submarines to Pakistan and Bangladesh, and provides frigates to Sri Lanka. Myanmar also got JF-17 fighter jets jointly developed by China and Pakistan. Through these arms exports, China has increased its influence on the recipient countries.

Figure 8: China's Activities in the Indian Ocean Region

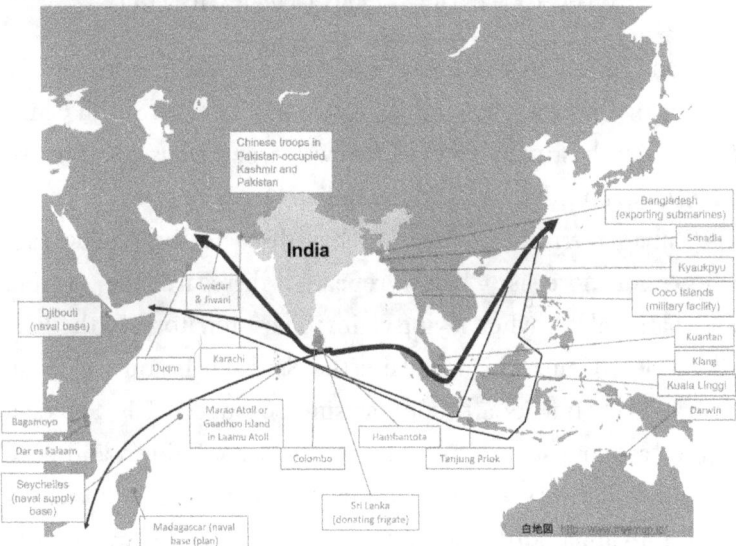

Source: Author

China is deploying its military in this region. Since 2008, it has deployed naval ships for counter-piracy measures off the coast of Somalia. It has started to deploy many submarines under the guise of 'anti-piracy', despite these submarines not being effective in dealing with piracy. Chinese naval fleets have already called at ports in all the coastal countries around India. And China has been continuously deploying six to eight naval ships in the northern part of the Indian Ocean.[6] When the pro-China government of the Maldives faced a serious situation in 2018, China sent fourteen warships to the Indian Ocean. Figure 8 shows China's activities in the Indian Ocean region. Along with its activities on its border with India, China's activities in the areas surrounding India is a ploy to restrict the rise of India's influence in the region.

WHAT CAN INDIA–JAPAN COOPERATION DO

The answer to this is likely influenced by China's territorial expansion in the sea around Japan, Taiwan and the South China Sea, which has many similarities with what it has done in the Indo-China border area and the Indian Ocean region.

China's territorial expansion has three features. The first feature of note is China's repeated disregard for current international law when laying claim to new territory. In the East China Sea, China did not claim the Senkaku Islands of Japan before 1971, but its attitude has since changed. The Senkaku Islands are in a strategic location to pressure Taiwan and have potential oil reserves. China continues to make incursions along the Indo-China border, although the Tibetan exile government has stated that these areas belong to India.[7] China has ignored current international law and expanded its territorial claim in all three areas.

The second feature of China's territorial expansion is timing. Whenever it has found a power vacuum, Beijing has exploited the situation. For example, China occupied half of the Paracel Islands just after France withdrew in the 1950s. In the 1970s, one year after the US withdrew from Vietnam, China occupied the other half of the islands. In the 1980s, China expanded its activities in the Spratly Islands and occupied six features there, just after the Soviet Union decreased its military presence in Vietnam. And in the 1990s, China occupied Mischief Reef three years after US troops withdrew from the Philippines.[8] These instances indicate that China tends to expand its territorial reach when military balances change and power vacuums are detected.

If that observation is true, China will continue to escalate its activities. Over the past decade, the military balance has been changing. According to the Stockholm International Peace Research Institute (SIPRI), China increased its military expenditure by 63 per cent from 2013 to 2022. During the same period, India increased its military expenditure by 47 per cent and Japan by 18 per cent.[9]

This data indicates that our observation about China is indeed true. A comparison between the number of Chinese vessels identified within the contiguous zone in the waters surrounding the Senkaku Islands in Japan and China's incursions in the Indo-China border area support this view. These incursions are similar to China's activities around the Senkaku Islands of Japan (see Figure 9).

A third feature of China's territorial expansion is non-military control. China's threat is bound up with the strength

Figure 9: Comparison of China's Incursions

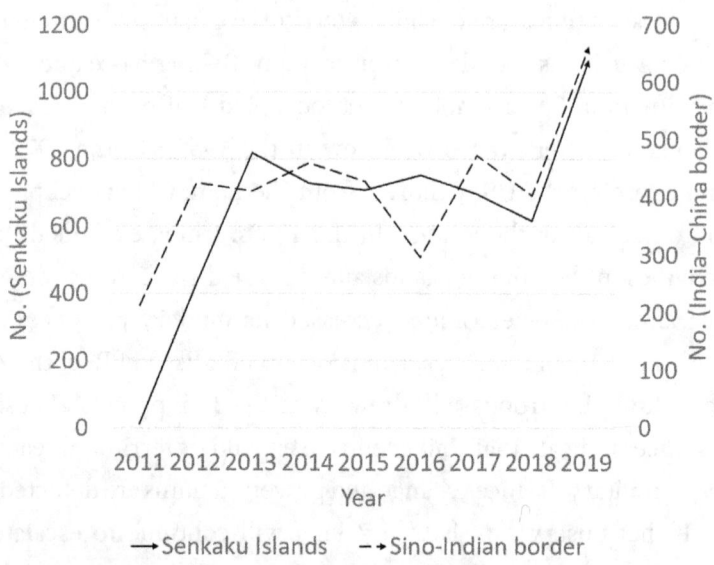

Source: Ministry of Foreign Affairs of Japan, 'Trends in Chinese Government and Other Vessels in the Waters Surrounding the Senkaku Islands, and Japan's Response', https://www.mofa.go.jp/region/page23e_000021.html and other media reports.

of its budget. China can change the status quo by force when its military power is stronger than others, and so maintaining a military balance is important. However, because of its strong economy and ample budget, China's military modernisation has outpaced other countries.

And if these countries depend too heavily on trade with China, their economies will be hostage to it. For example, when Australia insisted on an international investigation to identify the origin of COVID-19, China delayed processing Australian imports like wine and lobster. Dependence on the Chinese market is a powerful weapon for Beijing to expand its influence, and ultimately expand its territories.

In the case of foreign infrastructure projects, the situation is the same. China has used foreign infrastructure projects to expand its sphere of influence. Because of its favourable economic situation, China can invest heavily in these projects and create huge debts and obligations for recipient countries. Countries with significant Chinese investment and debt are hesitant to criticise China, even when it flouts international rules.

How Can the Quad Countries Gain Advantage

A lack of respect for international law, expansion of territorial claims where there are power vacuums, and attempts at economic dominance or other non-military methods to expand influence abroad are all common themes of China's exploits in the Indo-Pacific region. Thus, the question remains: how should the Quad countries, including India and Japan, respond? Knowing the pattern of China's behaviour points towards the answer: they should do the opposite of what China wants.

Respecting rules-based order

First, the Quad must continue to respect and insist upon a rules-based order grounded in current international law. The joint statements of both Quad summits mention that a free, open, rules-based order will 'meet the challenges to the rules-based maritime order, including in the East and South China Seas.'[10] These words carry great significance because China has tried to change the status quo by force and continually challenges international norms.

Maintaining military balance

Second, Quad countries need to fill perceived power vacuums by maintaining a military balance. To do this, they need to increase their defence budgets. But it is not an easy task.

What can the Quad do to discourage China's territorial expansion? If Quad countries coordinate well, they can force China to defend multiple fronts at once. In such a scenario, China would need to simultaneously make defence expenditures on its border with India as well as against Japan (and the US) on the Pacific side. This sort of cooperation would provide a way to maintain a military balance even if China's military expenditure were rising at a rapid pace.

In this case, offensive capability is key. If India and Japan (with the US and Australia) possess long-range strike capabilities, their combined capability forces China to defend multiple fronts. Even if China decides to expand its territories around the Indo-China border, it will still need to expend a certain amount of its budget and military force to defend itself against a potential attack from Japan (and the US). Currently, India, Japan and Australia are all planning to possess 1,000–2,000 km long-range strike capabilities such as cruise missiles and glide bombs. These moves could be critical.

Integrate military and non-military policy as one overall strategy

Third, the Quad needs to integrate non-military efforts into its overall strategy. China's military power relies on its ample budget. But China is a top-three level trading partner for India and Japan (with the US and Australia). Quad countries need to integrate their economic efforts and reduce their reliance on

China. Decoupling and risk-diversifying of supply chains and markets are necessary.

Japan has already begun to do so. With Japan relocating its factories from China to Southeast Asia and South Asia, the number of Japanese citizens living in China has decreased from 1,50,399 in 2012 to 1,01,786 in 2023. At the same time, the number of Japanese people living in the US has increased from 4,10,973 in 2012 to 4,14,615 in 2023.[11] Now, Japan and its allies and like-minded countries should relocate their factories and find new markets elsewhere. India is a new hope.

In the case of foreign infrastructure projects, the situation is the same. Even if purely for civil purposes, Japan's infrastructure projects are a useful way to neutralise China's influence in the Indo-Pacific region. For example, when China proposed the Sonadia port project to Bangladesh, Japan counter-offered with its own Matarbari port project, even though the two locations were very close together. Bangladesh ultimately chose Japan's Matarbari port project. Therefore, proposing alternative projects and financing sources can be an important step to neutralise China's influence. The Asia–Africa Growth Corridor led jointly by India and Japan, the Blue Dot Network led by Quad and the Japan-led Indo-Pacific Vision are very effective towards this end.

Former prime minister Abe Shinzo's speech to the Indian parliament in 2007 was the important turning point for India–Japan relations. Strong relations between these two countries can potentially lead to India's rise. However, combined with the India–China border, China's activities are surrounding India to contain its influences. India and Japan need to join hands to overcome the challenges from China. Considering the pattern of China's territorial expansion, cooperation among the Quad, particularly India and Japan, can be a solution. Insisting on respect for a rules-based order, maintaining a military balance, and integrating military and non-military policies into its overall strategy are essential for the Quad to achieve this goal. Now is the time to do so.

Dr Satoru Nagao is a Fellow (Non-Resident) at Hudson Institute, based in Tokyo, Japan. From December 2017 to November 2020, he was a Visiting Fellow at Hudson Institute, based in Washington, DC. Dr Nagao's primary research area is US–Japan–India security cooperation.

NOTES

1. Ministry of Foreign Affairs, Government of Japan, 'Confluence of the Two Seas: Speech by H.E. Mr Shinzo Abe, Prime Minister of Japan at the Parliament of the Republic of India', 22 August 2007, https://www.mofa.go.jp/region/asia-paci/pmv0708/speech-2.html.
2. Shinzo Abe, 'Asia's Democratic Security Diamond', Project Syndicate, 27 December 2012, https://www.project-syndicate.org/magazines/a-strategic-alliance-for-japan-and-india-by-shinzo-abe?utm_term=&utm_campaign=&utm_source=adwords&utm_medium=ppc&hsa_acc=1220154768&hsa_cam=12374283753&hsa_grp=117511853986&hsa_ad=499567080225&hsa_src=g&hsa_tgt=aud-963711451164:dsa-19959388920&hsa_kw=&hsa_mt=&hsa_net=adwords&hsa_ver=3&gad_source=1&gclid=CjwKCAiA7t6sBhAiEiwAsaieYjhlhaKYMtK500dBAlx3jH8jFsBp2QzYJ3MvVSnYp3tZ2eCrw2 CGghoCivEQAvD_BwE.
3. Alfred Thayer Mahan, *The Influence of Sea Power upon History, 1660–1783*, Little, Brown, and Company, Boston, 1898.
4. Directorate General of Shipping, Ministry of Port, Shipping of

Waterways, Government of India, 'Our Strength', https://www.dgshipping.gov.in/Content/OurStrength.aspx.

5. Dipanjan Roy Chaudhury, 'China May Put South Asia on Road to Debt Trap', *The Economic Times*, 2 May 2017, https://economictimes.indiatimes.com/news/politics-and-nation/china-may-put-south-asia-on-road-to-debt-trap/articleshow/58467309.cms?from=mdr.

6. Anirban Bhaumik, '6-8 Chinese Navy Ships Always in Indian Ocean', *Deccan Herald*, 10 January 2019, https://www.deccanherald.com/india/6-8-chinese-navy-ships-always-712273.html.

7. Central Tibetan Administration, '"Ladakh Belongs to India": Tibet Sides with India, Exposes China's Expansionist Tactics', 5 June 2020, https://tibet.net/ladakh-belongs-to-india-tibet-sides-with-india-exposes-chinas-expansionist-tactics/.

8. Ministry of Defense of Japan, China's Activities in the South China Sea (China's development activities on the features and trends in related countries), March 2023, https://www.mod.go.jp/en/d_act/sec_env/pdf/ch_d-act_b.pdf.

9. Nan Tian, Diego Lopes da Silva, Xiao Liang, Lorenzo Scarazzato, Lucie Béraud-Sudreau and Ana Assis, Trends in World Military Expenditure, 2022, Stockholm International Peace Research Institute, April 2023, https://www.sipri.org/publications/2023/sipri-fact-sheets/trends-world-military-expenditure-2022.

10. Ministry of Foreign Affairs of Japan, 'Quad Leaders' Joint Statement: "The Spirit of the Quad"', March 2021, https://www.mofa.go.jp/files/100159230.pdf; Ministry of Foreign Affairs of Japan, 'Joint Statement from Quad Leaders', 24 September 2021, https://www.mofa.go.jp/files/100238179.pdf.

11. Ministry of Foreign Affairs, Government of Japan, 'Annual Report of Statistics on Japanese Nationals Overseas (Japanese)', (Data is based on the numbers as on 1 October 2023), https://www.mofa.go.jp/mofaj/toko/tokei/hojin/index.html.

Replacing the 'Idea of India' with the 'Idea of Bharat'

MADHAV DAS NALAPAT

Horrendous losses were endured by Germany and Japan as a consequence of the misdeeds and horrors perpetrated on their own people and on other countries throughout the 1930s until 1945. Both countries were occupied by the US military principally, a reality that continues, somewhat anachronistically, to the present. Both countries were, as a consequence of their rulers at the time, battered to the ground, with their economies shattered. And yet, not for a single moment during those years (1945–52), when the debris of war was being replaced with new construction, their economies set on the path to revival, and their populace gaining in self-confidence as a consequence of the fact that the post-War settlement in 1945 was unlike that in 1919 after World War I, were they not regenerative but retributive.

As a consequence, Germany regained the democracy that had briefly flickered into life during the 1918–33 Weimar Republic period. Japan became a constitutional monarchy, thanks to the wisdom of both Emperor Hirohito as well as the victorious Allied forces led by General Douglas MacArthur.

Replacing the 'Idea of India' with the 'Idea of Bharat'   177

Not for a moment during the darkest moments of their lives did the people of Japan stop referring to their country within themselves as Nippon. Nor did the German people ever pause referring to their country as Deutschland among themselves. Only to the outside world were the two countries 'Germany' and 'Japan', never to their own people. While those in authority in Tokyo and Berlin may not find sufficient reason to change the external names of their respective countries to Nippon and Deutschland, there is a compelling case for changing India's name to Bharat, the original name of our ancient homeland. Perhaps the makers of the Constitution of India ought to have said Bharat, i.e., India rather than India, i.e., Bharat, that too as a temporary provision in the manner of the now extinct Article 370 rather than continue as a permanent part of the Constitution of, let us be clear, Bharat.

Shakespeare wrote 'What's in a name?' The answer is: a lot. It is telling that countries in Europe persist in referring to Myanmar as Burma. The latter was the name given to a colony; the former is the traditional name of a proud people. 'India' came into use much before the British, with some tracing it to 327 BC, when Alexander the warrior roamed with his soldiers across the Punjab before returning home, leaving behind several of his officers and soldiers to settle down in the territories that had been discovered and occupied by them. It is telling that the term 'India' is said to have originated during a period of conquest by a foreign army, and that it continued to be used by the British, who took over much of the subcontinent and administered it for the benefit of their own country and at an incalculable cost to the people of Bharat. While the appellation 'Bharat' brings to mind a land with a glorious and extraordinarily long history, 'India' awakens often subconscious memories of the period when Bharat was invaded and large parts of it occupied by foreign powers.

The concept of the idea of India has been presented by protagonists of the name in a romantic hue, which camouflages the reality that it was a term in common use not among the people of Bharat but among its conquerors. It is such a subconscious association with a glorious—as distinct from subjugated—past, which makes it not just desirable but imperative to replace the idea of India with the idea of Bharat. The process has been accelerated significantly during the Modi decade (2014–24) and is expected to become entrenched not only within the country but also internationally, should the Modi era continue for another fresh five-year term after the 2024 Lok Sabha polls.

The idea of India has been characterised as secular by its protagonists. Yet, in its operation, the idea is the reverse of secularism. After the bolting of the horse of Partition on the specious grounds of Hindus and Muslims being 'two nations' rather than a single people, a construct was created that sought not to erase differences but to emphasise them. Secularism is when religion does not play a role in policy.

During the Modi decade, multiple schemes have been rolled out that are of benefit to the needy, including the giving of free rations of grain to 800 million citizens of Bharat. There is no discrimination between those professing different faiths in these schemes; the criteria laid down is applicable to all citizens. Contrast such a secular approach with the UPA-era Right to Education (RTE) Act. Only institutions started by the 'majority community' are subjected to its provisions, while those created by 'minority communities' are exempt. Indeed, the concept of those belonging to a particular faith being from the majority community while those of other faiths are minorities merits examination in terms of the realities within the society of the country that is the most populous in the world. Income is a much more accurate measure of intra-population differences than faith. Individuals belonging to different faiths but having similar income levels have much in common that they do not at all share with those of their own faith. What is termed as the middle class is an example. Across the country, this group shares numerous interests, such that they mingle and deal with each other across the country in a truly secular way. Preservation, indeed the deepening of concepts of divergence that are based on the sole ground of the religion practised, is the converse of secularism rather than—as proponents of the idea of India claim—its affirmation.

At the heart of the secular ideal lies '*Sabka saath, sabka vikas, sabka prayaas*'—an entirely inclusive concept. Yet, the originator of this notion, Prime Minister Narendra Modi is traduced by many proponents of the 'idea of India' for supposedly falling short of that ideal. Ironically, these critics, who constantly divide people solely on religion grounds, consider themselves to be 'secular'. Equal treatment to people of all faiths by the governance mechanism is at the heart of the secular ideal. Which is why not just Egypt and Turkey but Western countries have a uniform civil code. Yet, when the same topic is barely touched upon in Bharat, it is condemned as a negation of secularism. There are many individuals in the country and outside who seem to prefer that the idea of Bharat remains synonymous with the idea of India, seen as a country where emphasis is placed not on the commonality of interests of all citizens but on assumed divergences between them on the ground of religion.

Every segment, each strand, of the variegated history of Bharat belongs to each and every citizen of the country, whatever be their faith. Accompanying the idea of India was an emphasis in textbooks of specific periods, such as the period since 1857, marked by a widespread revolt against British rule, or the period since 1915 when Mahatma Gandhi returned to Bharat and began to lead the non-violent stream of the popular movement against the British rule. Or the period since Robert Clive began expanding British influence through treaties and conquests in the mid-1770s. Or Babur's invasions beginning 1519 until 1523. Although more than nine-tenths of the history of Bharat took place before Babur stepped foot into the subcontinent, less than 10 per cent of history as it is taught in schools relates to that period. Believers in the idea of India apparently did not want any cognisance of that period, much of which was incorrectly described as myth during the British rule, and hence undeserving of mention in history books. Even as the idea of Bharat is gaining traction during the prime ministership of Narendra Modi, such self-imposed constraints and distortions in the teaching of the history of this land are melting away. Increasing emphasis is being placed on the entirety of the history of Bharat, a tapestry that belongs equally to every citizen of Bharat. The persistent emphasis on at most a tenth of the country's historical record has not, contrary to the claims made by those uneasy about the continuation of colonial-era pedagogy, been replaced solely by an emphasis on the initial nine-tenths, but rather a history of Bharat as a whole. No period has been neglected. Even once scarcely mentioned treasures from the past, such as the spread of the Chola Empire, have regained the prominence that should have been theirs from the start of the period since the Union

Jack was replaced atop the Viceregal Palace—which has been the Rashtrapati Bhavan since 1947—with the tricolour.

There is a difference between arrogance and pride. The first is exclusivist and destructive, while the other is inclusive and constructive. Ideas rooted not in reason but in prejudice, such as racial or religious supremacy, breed intolerance, while those based on understanding and acceptance promote the societal cohesion necessary for Bharat's leap into the middle-income tier of countries.

DNA mapping has shown that people across both sides of the India–Pakistan border are the same, although the trajectories of both countries are very different. Votaries of the idea of India remain silent about such phenomena as the disappearance of religious minorities in Pakistan, whether they be Sikh, Hindu, Christian or other. If quizzed, their reply is that 'India is not Pakistan'. Absolutely, which is why what is happening to essentially the same people but on the other side of the border need to be the concern of citizens of Bharat. What is happening there is a cautionary tale about what could happen if the fanaticism fuelled by religious exclusivism proliferates within a society and becomes normalised across the population. Both the UK and the US have large numbers of citizens who ethnically are Pakistani or Indian. Whether in tables relating to per capita income or in the per capita distribution in police records of crimes committed, the difference between the two is striking. Much of the first half of the twentieth century showed the pitfalls of exclusivist, supremacist approaches, habits of thought that engendered conflict and its attendant misery. Colonies were supposed to be the sources of whatever progress was made by countries in Europe that had built up vast empires. Yet, whether it be Spain, France, the Netherlands or the UK, the quality of life of the average citizen is far better in an era where colonies were lost, as compared to periods when conquered lands were there in plenty. Such a paradox illustrates the wisdom behind the emphasis on Vasudhaiva Kutumbakam, meaning the earth is one family, placed by the prime minister and made the central motif in 2023, the year of Bharat's presidency of the G20 comprising the largest economies of the world. As a consequence of the efforts of the 2023 presidency of the G20 by Narendra Modi, the African Union joined the European Union as a member of what is now the G21. In a way, such a change represents the shift away from the twentieth to the twenty-first century of Bharat during the past decade.

Emphasis has been placed not only in the entirety of history but in the entirety of the population. Whether it be smokeless kitchens, weatherproof homes or avoiding the need to use open spaces for ablutions, hundreds of millions of lives have been transformed over the past decade. This is a change that is visible everywhere, even to a casual visitor. All this has created a sense of pride in the country, a belief that each citizen has the potential to succeed in the way Narendra Modi, a lad from an underprivileged background in Vadnagar, Gujarat, has done. The odds were daunting, yet were met and overcome by a dauntless spirit based on knowledge of, and hence respect for, the idea of Bharat. If the idea of India can be compared to a lake, the idea of Bharat is an ocean, serving as a far greater motivator for individual excellence needed to achieve the double-digit growth rates necessary to uplift all its people from poverty to adequacy in living standards. A sense of empowerment is very different from a feeling of entitlement, such as that which is felt by those born

Replacing the 'Idea of India' with the 'Idea of Bharat'   183

with silver spoons in their mouths. An ambience is being created that engenders a sense of empowerment within each citizen, thereby giving them the courage and the determination to aim not for moon but the stars. Such an ambience has been created as a consequence of the life and work of Prime Minister Modi.

During the colonial period, only the state was considered deserving enough of an abundance of responsibility. Even after 1947, this mindset continued, such that it became a nightmare and very often impossible to set up and run within the country a private enterprise on the scale needed to compete globally. That period of discrimination is over, and in several sectors, the private sector is the leader rather than the follower. Segments of activity such as space research and defence production that were once barred to private enterprises have been thrown open, to the immense benefit of the country. Beginning from the 1970s, when Snamprogetti had overpowering influence over policy, and lasting until the 1990s, the domestic private sector was treated with contempt even as foreign suppliers were encouraged. As a consequence, by 2014 more than 80 per cent of critical defence needs were met by imports, thereby causing a chasm of vulnerability in the event of a conflict. That period began to melt away in 2014, and by 2029, Bharat will be on track to emerge as one of the top five, if not the top three, defence exporters of the world. From one nuclear power plant every decade to one every year, domestic production of critical items has been supercharged, again without any discrimination between the public and private sectors.

Secularism as practiced in India is contrary to the fundamental tenet of equality of treatment underpinning that term. Until 2014, there was no prospect of ensuring that Mathura, Ayodhya and Kashi, the three sacred locations of the Hindu community, were returned to what they were before Aurangzeb destroyed the temples standing on the birthplaces of Lord Krishna and Lord Ram, as well as the Kashi Viswanath temple that was standing on the spot consecrated by Lord Shiva. According to proponents of the idea of India, such a return was unnecessary and indeed unwelcome. Even the joy felt at the return of the Ram Mandir to its pre-Aurangzeb state was frowned upon as being almost anti-Indian. We are all children of the same Almighty power, and to treat a community of over a billion people whose country was vivisected by the British colonial masters in 1947 on the explicit grounds of faith was to treat them as 'children of a lesser god'. Such a mindset is not conducive to the self-confidence and determination required of citizens of Bharat to enable not just themselves but their country and indeed the world to prosper. Over the decade, individuals at the higher echelons of society who have such a discriminatory mindset have witnessed a diminution in their influence, a fact that has led them to make increasingly vehement denunciations of such a change. The expectation is that Kashi and Mathura will follow the path set by Ayodhya, and reclaim a past that was marred by the exclusivism and supremacist sentiment of the emperor who was responsible through his misdeeds for the collapse of the Mughal Empire. And that the British-era takeover of temples and their lands will be reversed, at least so far as Hindu temples are concerned. Far from promoting fanaticism and hatred in the way that votaries of the idea of India claim, such a move would lead to a steep decline in such sentiment within the populace, and in the harmony between faiths that was sought to be damaged by the British Empire.

Replacing the 'Idea of India' with the 'Idea of Bharat'

In the 1980s, when Prime Minister Rajiv Gandhi sought to make widespread the use of computers in India, there was an uproar similar to that which ensued when colour television was introduced in the country a few years earlier. Indians were seen as too backward to merit such innovations, or to operate them. Soon afterwards followed the period when India began to lead the world in the number of computer operators and software engineers. From the start, Narendra Modi has kept abreast of technology and understood the value of the country keeping pace with technological changes. This is why he made Digital Bharat a flagship initiative. Whether it be the creation of a home-grown COVID-19 vaccine or a soft landing on the south side of the lunar surface, Bharat has shown that a country that is at the centre point of the Global South can equal, and in several respects excel, the Global North in the twenty-first century. Foreign policy has been tailored to meet the challenge of ensuring progress in the milestones determined upon by Prime Minister Modi, whether it be inclusive growth domestically, catalysing growth internationally, or ensuring that the waterways of the Indo-Pacific remain free, open and inclusive. Bharat has stood up, and the people of Bharat have shown the world what a country that eschews the predatory ways of colonialism, both past and present, is capable of. It is a country that does not seek to expand its territories at the cost of others. Such has been the transformation of India into Bharat since 2014 when Narendra Modi was sworn in as the prime minister of the world's most populous country.

Madhav Das Nalapat is Editorial Director, itv network. He is also the UNESCO Peace Chair at Manipal University and Director of the Department of Geopolitics and International Relations.

India—Now More Than a Partner in Principle

GRANT NEWSHAM

The Indians and the Americans have a long-standing relationship. However, in recent years, the dynamic of the relationship has changed.

Usually, the nature and depth of defence cooperation between countries gives a good idea of the broader relationship between them. India's military engagement with the US forces took off from the 2000s, but it often seemed overly measured and sometimes had a pro forma aspect. India seemed at pains to avoid too deep ties or appear too close to the Americans. At least that is how it seemed. And when there appeared to be an opening to push things along, the Americans sometimes overreached.

One recalls cringing after the Malabar 2007 naval exercise when the senior US Navy admiral on the scene gushed that US and Indian defence relations had entered a 'new era' and implicitly would be going from strength to strength.

Afterwards, it seemed as if India put on the brakes. Maybe out of habit or out of fear of what China would think.

That was then. Over the last decade things have changed markedly.

The Quad is well known. Less well remembered is that while this loose security cooperation agreement between India, Japan, Australia and the US came along in 2007, it really came to fruition around 2017—and Prime Minister Narendra Modi is the only one of the four leaders who reinvigorated the Quad who is still in power. The Quad is still finding its way, but it is a real thing and not just a pipe dream.

A senior US defence official, speaking at the Pentagon last year, noted that the defence relationship between the US and India is developing in ways previously thought impossible. He commented on American and Indian forces conducting annual air and naval exercises.

But what is even more striking, he mentioned, is that twenty years ago the US sold no defence equipment to India. However, 'now, we're talking about co-producing and co-developing major systems together.'[1]

Indeed, the Indians and the Americans have signed an agreement for GE Aerospace to jointly produce military jet engines in India for use in Indian indigenous fighter aircraft. This sort of thing is not done lightly as jet engine technology—especially for military aircraft—is still one of America's 'crown jewels'.

The official was also quoted as saying: 'We now have working groups on everything ranging from cyberspace and critical technologies to maritime security, and India is leading in those forums together with the U.S. and like-minded partners.'[2]

That includes artificial intelligence, advanced sensor development, unmanned systems, quantum physics and undersea domain awareness, to name a few. These are sensitive technologies and indicate a degree of mutual confidence that long-time observers would not have foreseen even a decade ago.

Other breakthroughs include:

- India and the US signing a series of foundational defence agreements including, on 29 August 2016,[3] the Logistics Exchange Memorandum of Agreement (LEMOA). LEMOA is a facilitating agreement that establishes the mechanics and procedures for reciprocal provision of logistic support, supplies and services between the armed forces of India and the US.
- During the 2020 military crisis with China that took the lives of twenty Indian soldiers, the US provided key intelligence, hurried along critical supplies and then approved the lease of MQ-9B drones for deterrence by detection.[4]
- In 2021, Indian and US militaries signed a long-term fuel agreement between the U.S. Defense Department and India's Ministry of Defence. The agreement became operational on 1 June and enables reciprocal fuel sales and purchases, increased Indian military participation with US military exercises, and easier accounting and reporting of fuel transactions.
- The two countries signed a 2023 agreement that U.S. Navy ships will be repaired and serviced as a matter of course in several Indian shipyards. Talk about trust.
- India signed up for the Artemis accords on outer space exploration, and an Indian astronaut is training to visit the International Space Station in 2024.
- The two countries moving ahead to realise a shared mission of securing the Indian Ocean commons through India's recent participation in the Combined Maritime Force, and the Quad sponsored Indo-Pacific Partnership for Maritime Domain Awareness.

When you train together, co-develop and co-produce, there is also a political—and psychological—aspect to the activity that deepens a bilateral relationship. You start to see the other person differently.

And it is important to note that economics and commerce tie-in to defence—and there has been plenty of progress on this front in the last decade as well.

India is now seriously talked about—and being treated—as an economic and manufacturing alternative to the People's Republic of China (PRC), after the US government and even some leading business leaders having realised the dangers of getting into bed with the communist Chinese.

Remember 'Chindia'? How about 'Chimerica'?

Nobody talks much about these anymore, and the dangerous dependency—indeed addiction—to the PRC and the China market is lessening. The change is notable.

To see where we are, it is good to see where we have come from.

I remember India from the 1980s and recall that way back then we saw India as 'too much trouble'. It seemed anti-American and pro-Soviet. And some Indian officials and others gave plenty of reason to think so.

Like most stereotypes. It was basically true, or at least seemed that way.

As for India's economic prospects and attractiveness, it was seen more like an Eastern European, Soviet bloc economy that set up on the subcontinent.

And in the 'things that leave an impression category': I recall reading a story a few decades ago in the *International Herald*

Tribune or the like about legal cases in India that were multi-generational affairs.

Western business wasn't flocking to India for obvious reasons, despite the huge 'on paper' market. And it seemed they weren't exactly welcome anyway.

India scared us off—both militarily and commercially.

And it seemed it almost wasn't worth trying to be friends.

Meanwhile, China—communist and only a few years removed from the Cultural Revolution—made it easy for us and got all the attention.

India was just too hard.

And that applied to the military as well, or so it was said. Suggest within the US military doing more with the Indian military and you'd get ten reasons why it was impossible. Most having to do with the Indians being 'too hard'.

That didn't seem quite right to this writer.

It seemed that the uniformed Indian military was a different crowd, even if they seemed hampered by the fact that there was something at the Indian Ministry of Defence that could practically stop the earth from rotating on its axis. Some would say there still is, but the force is maybe less than it was.

In this writer's experience, Indians seldom seem to lack self-confidence. When it came to its military, this perhaps was not surprising in light of the nation's martial traditions, along with experience in Sri Lanka against the Tamil Tigers, counterinsurgency in Kashmir, and operations in tough conditions along the northern borders—squaring off against both the Pakistanis and the Chinese.

These are people who will fight.

Many of us also sympathised with India's fight against terrorism—no small part of it instigated by the Pakistan intelligence services. And occasionally—especially after years of Pakistani double-dealing during America's Afghan misadventure—we wished that history had turned out differently so that we'd prioritised India and someone else got Pakistan. I remember a Pakistani General muttering to himself around 1990, 'This country is self-destructing.' It's not like Pakistan has got better since then.

An Indian officer visited Marine Forces Pacific headquarters and commented that he would like to have 'the Marine Corps' ethos. That was nice, but given their experiences I'd thought at the time that we could do well with a little of theirs.

One was also impressed that unlike some other nations we were tied up with, they didn't even seem to want the Americans around—much less have us do the hard work. Just help them get the necessary hardware and they'd take care of the rest. That seems true even now when the defence relationship between India and America has greatly improved over the last decade.

Nor was there an Indian version of A.Q. Khan—backed up by a military and intelligence service—ensuring America's enemies got nuclear weapons.

SO WHAT HAS CHANGED?

The short answer: PRC seeks to dominate and control the entire Indo-Pacific region. And it has grown into a military and economic power with the potential ability to actually do so. And thus, posing a simultaneous threat to India and the US—and to Japan, Australia and all others who would try to remain sovereign as the PRC expands.

This would have catastrophic effects.

Serious planners and strategists look at the whole map—both the Pacific and the Indian Ocean regions together.

By doing so, one better understands the threat to India and the US individually—something Indians have known, and said, for a long time. Not long before Narendra Modi became the Prime Minister of India I was at a small meeting with several retired Indian flag officers and was pleased to hear them tell their American counterparts: 'We've been at war with the PRC since 1962. You Americans had better recognise that you are too.'

This shaped the welcome coming together in recent years to defend against Chinese expansion and indeed aggression.

It's worth taking a look at the nature of the aforementioned threat to each nation. Is it just hype?

EAST OF MALACCA: UNITED STATES—AND JAPAN, AND MAYBE AUSTRALIA

For decades, the US could take care of things in the Indo-Pacific by itself—as long as it avoided the temptation to go ashore and fight wars.

And there wasn't much for the Americans to take care of in the Indian Ocean region. Any problems there were, they were on land—and had more to do with moves such as the self-imposed, ill-advised effort to turn Afghanistan into a liberal democracy.

But since about a decade ago things started changing to the point even sceptics can't easily deny the danger. The might of the Chinese military is growing and it could give the US a bloody nose in a fight close to the Chinese mainland, and the reach of the People's Liberation Army (PLA) is expanding outwards.

India—Now More Than a Partner in Principle

Just as one data point, China has a much bigger navy than the U.S. Navy and the gap is widening. That's not surprising given that Chinese shipbuilding capacity is over two hundred times greater than America's.

Twenty years ago people—not least US military officers—laughed at the PLA being anything to worry about in their lifetimes. Not anymore.

China even has de facto control of the South China Sea—and has had it since the late 2010s. The People's Liberation Army Navy shadows U.S. Navy ships when they enter the South China Sea—and one won't envy a U.S. Navy destroyer skipper who finds himself with a dozen anti-ship missiles headed his way, if China one day 'pulls the trigger'.

Beijing is strong-arming the Philippines and has thrown down the gauntlet to the US, to see if the Americans will defend their treaty ally and risk a fight with the PRC.

Meanwhile, in a move of concern to all Indo-Pacific democracies, the PRC is tightening the noose on Taiwan.

China's goal is to dominate and control the entire region. And it has its sights set on driving the Americans out and back to Hawaii or beyond.

It is laying the infrastructure for eventual PLA operations in the entire Pacific by building ports in Latin America while building influence and access. The ports are 'commercial' for now, but one thing at a time.

And don't forget China's 'friends'—North Korea and Russia—that are always a distraction but will likely do more to divert American attention if and when the PRC makes its move.

The US military was the policeman—or at least the alpha male in the Western Pacific, east of Malacca—but it is no longer so. It can still defend itself and its friends but with considerable effort.

Wait few years, however, and it will be hard pressed.

Washington can no longer afford to have the Japanese sit in the corner while the Americans do the hard work. Those days are over. The work is getting harder and the Americans relatively less capable.

The U.S. Navy's 7th Fleet is not very big—it has maybe sixty surface combatants—and the Americans are occupied in other parts of the world, so not many more resources can be allocated to the Pacific.

Japan is an indispensable partner for basing US forces, but even more needed is a capable Japan Self-Defense Forces (JSDF) that can fight.

It's fair to say that without the Japanese, the Americans alone would not necessarily win an all-out fight with China—or even deter one.

But together, the odds improve for Japan and the US.

A word about the Australians: they are as game as they come. But the Australian Defense Force has always played a supporting role militarily to the US—and that will continue for the foreseeable future.

It's hard to call Australia a 'pillar' of regional defence. Maybe a 'buttress' but not a pillar—like India, America and Japan.

WEST OF MALACCA—INDIA

Earlier, India was the regional power, but looking seaward, it seemed most concerned about the Australians horning in on the region or even the Americans settling in too much.

However, now the Chinese are coming and are in the Indian Ocean in numbers and a level of presence that worries.

The Chinese presence will steadily expand. Beijing intends to do in the Indian Ocean (and Caribbean and elsewhere) what it is doing in the Pacific. That means building up infrastructure for the future operations of the PLA, including a deep-water report in Myanmar (while providing support to both the miliary regime and the insurgents simultaneously), along with port projects and access in Chittagong (Bangladesh), Hambamtota (Sri Lanka) and Gwadar (Pakistan).

Chinese political warfare is being conducted nearly everywhere—its most recent success being a security deal with Maldives—as is support for insurgents in Eastern India. And everything China does for Pakistan might fairly be considered support for terrorism.

And, of course, there is Chinese pressure on India's northern borders and via its proxy, Pakistan. And then there is China building a dam that would threaten major rivers flowing southwards from the Tibetan plateau into India and neighbouring countries.

NATURAL ALIGNMENT BUT NEEDS CONTINUED ATTENTION

Despite the justifiably optimistic tone at the beginning of this essay, there are still obstacles to India and the US coming together more deeply, not in small part because the two getting closer would pose a threat to major competing nodes of power.

That can take many forms. For example, there's a seemingly ideological angle to some US official attitudes towards India—or better said, Prime Minister Modi.

Consensual government, elections, a free press, a free enough economy, rule of law and the like seem not to matter so much.

Being woke and having 'authorised thoughts' as the Washington foreign policy crowd approves is more important—and 'authorised' by whom is a bit opaque.

The US is also opening two more consulates in India. This is nice but is more window-dressing than anything else.

How so? As of March 2024, the wait time for someone in Mumbai to get a student visa interview so they can study in America is around 540 days. The wait time in Shanghai for the same visa interview is only seven days.

This is as much evidence as needed that there's a slice in America's foreign policy class—including the Department of State—that views India askance.

One wonders how the Americans would feel about India or other key partner countries blowing hot or cold on the US depending on how they evaluate America's domestic politics and societal shortcomings, of which there are many.

Have you ever seen mobs of Indians in the US protesting—violently—and shutting down traffic in Manhattan? Or heard an Indian official call America 'the enemy'.

No need to answer.

India isn't the only country in this situation. Nowadays, the US tends to treat its friends this way. Especially if they aren't 'woke' enough.

Nonetheless, the US is not a monolith and many see India differently—PM Modi received a state visit last year and addressed the United States Congress. Few leaders do.

And most US politicians don't buy the tough on India—or tough on Modi line. Only seventy of 535 supported legislation targeting India for alleged human rights abuses.

However, that seventy did is irksome and one should remember that given the volatility in US politics—both from internal and external drivers—it's also potentially dangerous.

India does need to be mindful of US elite opinion. Delhi has been savaged for buying Russian oil and not being tough enough Putin's war in Ukraine. Which doesn't mean there is consistency in America's position on, for example, US sanctions waiver on and European business dealings with Russia. Inconsistency, indeed hypocrisy, is a permanent part of foreign relations.

And currently, as Israel is finding out, vocal sections of the US are seemingly being activated in new ways. Sometimes doing a few things you'd rather not do—and don't have to do—pays off in larger ways.

Also, India using Russia as leverage against the PRC is understandable, but it would be right to be careful. Such too-clever-by-half stratagems don't always succeed as intended. If Henry Kissinger was still around he still wouldn't admit it, but splitting off China from Russia wasn't the best move. Maybe it was worth trying, but to keep at it for another forty-five years was stupid.

LOOKING FORWARD: JAPAN'S HELP IN GLUING INDIA AND THE US TOGETHER

One way to provide ballast to the sometimes up and down US–India relationship is for Washington to regard the India–Japan relationship as at least 'complementary', if not directly supporting the US–India relationship.

And it's possible these days.

India's relations with Japan were always good, and they have deepened over the last decade. And the US ought to consider that as a good thing—strengthening the overall tie-up.

The Japan–India relationship is a very different relationship than ours, without a lot of baggage—and also the more recent 'woke' concerns.

Indeed, go to Yasukuni Shrine in Tokyo and you'll see the memorial to Justice Radhabinod Pal from the Tokyo War Crimes Trials. It's nicely kept and prominently displayed.

The late Prime Minister Shinzo Abe in particular saw India and Japan as having a special relationship. He personally got along very well with Prime Minister Modi and he had more of an affinity for the Indians than for the Americans. Though he was careful not to say that where too many people might hear.

That affinity translated into actions. Over the last six years, JSDF have trained with the Indians and deepened the relationship.

This works to America's advantage—as Indian forces help to improve JSDF capabilities—and also weaning Japan off its psychological overdependence on the Americans.

Japan also helps out with some of the technology and hardware requirements for Indian defence efforts to protect the Indian Ocean region in particular.

And there are no doubt things India would do more willingly with the Japanese than with the Americans. All the US has to do is encourage Japan to take the initiative and get out of the way.

Japan's huge (and strategic) investment and commercial presence in India—and in the Indian Ocean region—benefits the US's interests as much as anyone else's.

The more important thing is that India, Japan and the US see themselves as linked—and facing common challenges and even enemies—as the PRC's admissions, statements and behaviour indicate. They are also increasingly seeing each other as part of their own solutions.

Was this possible fifteen years ago? Maybe, maybe not. But the reality is that over the last decade things have moved farther and faster.

INDIA AS A GLOBAL ACTOR

India is now being properly recognised as a global actor—or least well beyond the Indian Ocean region—and one hopes that this will continue in the future as well. In a wide range of regions, more India would make a major difference.

The Pacific Islands are a case in point. The US has proven itself near incapable of having an effective on-the-ground presence throughout the area, and it is especially lagging in the commercial arena.

India can fill a huge gap here. Indian businesses in particular are confident and skilled enough to operate in difficult areas— and they have been doing so for decades and longer.

Prime Minister Modi's visit to Papua New Guinea in 2023 showed what's doable from both an official and commercial level. He offered tangible assistance that actually makes a difference in lives at the local level.

And in Southeast Asia there's a different dynamic for India. Once again, when India takes the lead and has successes it is mutually reinforcing for the US and Japan (and other free nations). Africa? Same thing, as seen during India's G20 presidency.

Indeed, it seems like Indian businesspeople and companies are the ones most able to operate in the far-flung regions—where the Chinese operate.

As for the Indian Ocean, India understands the politics and on-the-ground realties.

India always has, of course, but only in the last decade have we seen ourselves as part of a common effort. Indeed, 'political warfare' is a dirty word in Washington. India has been doing it for a few thousand years.

BRICS? India remains sort of an ally inside that dubious organisation.

Forty years ago, from the viewpoint of Washington, it seemed like India was marshalling the 'third world' or 'non-aligned world' for purposes that were contrary to US interest.

These days it seems like a nation holding the line for the democracies and bringing in other nations that would otherwise come under PRC influence and domination.

One is inclined to say, hallelujah.

NOT TRANSACTIONAL—WHAT TRULY TIES INDIANS AND AMERICAN TOGETHER

India is a serious participant as a pillar of free world. One could see stirrings from 2000 onwards, but only more clearly over the last decade.

American and Indian strategic interests align these days. And the last ten years have been good in this regard.

But there's maybe more to it than just strategic interest brought about by the PRC threat.

The following anecdote suggests a common element between America and India that doesn't apply to all our friends.

A bit of family lore: my father was in India and Ceylon with the OSS during the War. One day Mountbatten came to their headquarters in Ceylon for a meeting. My father sat across from Mountbatten at lunch and also spoke with him a bit after the meeting. Mountbatten ended up giving my dad the name of his tailor in Delhi who had made Lord Louis's bush jacket. (I've still got the jacket.)

Think about it: a twenty-nine-year-old guy who'd scraped through the Great Depression and would never eat Spanish Rice for the rest of his life after eating nothing but that for three weeks straight in 1932 was in a position to sit across from Mountbatten.

Only in America.

Or is it?

Of course, India has its problems when it comes to upward social mobility, but it's also a place where a fellow who gets his start selling tea on a railway platform can become prime minister.

And this says a lot about a country.

It has taken a while to find each other but as long as Americans and Indians believe in hope— hope for a better future as individuals, nations and for the world—we will get closer. And, hopefully, this last decade of transformation was just the beginning.

Grant Newsham is a retired US marine and author of *When China Attacks: A Warning to America*.

NOTES

1. David Vergun, 'U.S., India Rapidly Expand Their Military Cooperation', U.S., India Rapidly Expand Their Military Cooperation',

20 June 2023, https://www.defense.gov/News/News-Stories/Article/Article/3433245/us-india-rapidly-expand-their-military-cooperation/.
2. Ibid.
3. IDR News Network, 'India and the US Sign the Logistics Exchange Memorandum of Agreement (LEMOA)', *India Defence Review*, 30 August 2016, https://www.indiandefencereview.com/news/india-and-the-us-sign-the-logistics-exchange-memorandum-of-agreement-lemoa/
4. Vikram J. Singh, Jacob Stokes and Tamanna Salikuddin, 'India and China Come to Blows in the Himalayas', United States Institute of Peace, 4 June 2020, https://www.usip.org/publications/2020/06/india-and-china-come-blows-himalayas.

Dismantling a Legacy

AISHWARYA PANDIT

Legacy is a peculiar word. It is often used to discuss political dynasties, political parties, family-run businesses and even media entities across the world. Cambridge Dictionary defines legacy as 'money or property that you receive from someone after they die.' Social, political, spiritual and, most importantly, economic legacy is passed by our parents to us as inheritance. Then there is the legacy of the Colonial Raj, which we, the children of modern India, have to contend with even today—we are still living with the physical, social and cultural remnants of the Raj. Of all legacies, it is political legacy that we focus on, in this chapter.

Since the 1950s, critics of Indian democracy have often made predictions about its eventual demise or the fracturing of the social fabric of India. This cynicism is a legacy of the Colonial Raj and continues to haunt political and intellectual discussions even today. The British had the implicit belief that if they left, India would splinter into many halves. This cynicism remained a constant refrain of people of different hues even after Independence. Any attempt at embracing our cultural identity has critics up in arms. They portray it as the secular fabric being in danger of annihilation. However, it is not our secular fabric that is in danger but our cultural identity steeped in our collective pasts.

At the base of the Indian democracy lies its resilience, which was forged during the freedom struggle and remains its most defining feature. Narendra Damodardas Modi, the current prime minister of India, unlike his predecessors Jawaharlal Nehru, Indira Gandhi, Lal Bahadur Shastri, Rajiv Gandhi and P.V. Narsimha Rao, is not a product of Nehruvian consensus. Neither is he is an inheritor of legacy that represented many of his predecessors such as Lal Bahadur Shastri, Morarji Desai, Chandra Shekhar, P.V. Narasimha Rao or even Atal Bihar Vajpayee. With the exception of Vajpayee, all of them were a product of the 'Congress system' in one form or the other, whether directly or indirectly. This system, as defined by historian Rajni Kothari, represented a broad consensus that prevailed until the 1970s.[1] In contrast is PM Modi, a man not given to cynicism and one who doesn't believe in abandoning his identity. He has a strong sense of cultural pride, which draws heavily from India's civilisational past. But it is important to understand the background behind the transformation of the cultural, social and political fabric of the nation under PM Modi's leadership.

The 1990s can at best be described as a volatile decade, which witnessed frequent collapses of central and state governments, resulting in political instability. However, the economic liberalisation of 1991 was a pivotal moment that unshackled the economy and changed the course of history. The years between 2004 and 2014 were a mixed bag, and by the end of the decade people grew tired of policy paralysis and of the political class that was steeped in corruption. In contrast, while the period after 2014—or the Modi era—evokes strong reactions on either side of the political spectrum, few can deny the many changes introduced in this last decade that have had a lasting impact.

A quick research on global developments since 2014 led me to ten events with interesting revelations. In addition to the rise of ISIS, the disappearance of Malaysia Airlines flight 370 and the outbreak of Ebola, some websites listed 'Narendra Modi wins in India' as a noteworthy development of the period. Writing about the 2014–24 decade under PM Modi as he seeks a third term in office is a daunting task. Thinking of reference points for the decade or the persona of the prime minister is a complex task as comparisons are inevitable. During my research and interviews I thought about a term or description that would at best describe PM Modi—for, in India, there is a culture of prime ministers having popular nomenclatures that eventually find themselves as part of folklore. For instance, the political scientist Vinay Sitapati refers to former prime minister P.V. Narsimha Rao aptly as 'half lion'[2]; Sanjaya Baru has referred to Manmohan Singh as 'the accidental prime minister'; Indira Gandhi has been famously called Durga, a personification of the mother goddess; and Atal Bihari Vajpayee as a consensus PM. With Modi, I would like to make a departure, as reducing the man to one word would not describe him or his tenure effectively. This is because he constantly reinvents himself such that historians like myself find it difficult to slot him. Such has been the nature of his evolution from the chief minister of Gujarat to the Prime Minister of India that his transformation has been mapped on the covers of popular magazines like *India Today*. One cover aptly described him as 'the Modi machine', a reference to his ability to be in election mode constantly; another used the word 'Moditva', which is a slight modification of the term 'Hindutva'; a cover used the term 'game-changer' to describe him, and this is possibly the closest one can get to describing the almost two decades of Modi's state and national politics. On 8 May 2014, an article in *The Guardian* referred to Narendra Modi's election victory as another tryst with destiny. It argued that Modi's victory marks the end of a long era in which the structures of power were not very different from the ones that Britain used to rule over the subcontinent. The article was almost prophetic in its announcement that Modi was going to dismantle many legacies—colonial, political, socioeconomic and, most importantly, the cultural legacy of the earlier period. Now nearly a decade into his prime ministership and as he seeks a third term in the 2024 general elections, PM Modi has ushered in an India that warrants rediscovery.

Modi has turned the BJP into an electoral machine, leaving an imprint so deep that it rivals the scale of transformation achieved by his predecessor Jawaharlal Nehru. In the 1950s, Nehru commanded his party and the government with equal ease, especially after the 1952 elections when he became the undisputed leader of his party and the government. Congress emerged as an electoral machine under his daughter, Indira Gandhi, who began her first stint as the Prime Minister of India in 1966. You could disagree with Nehru, as many of his colleagues and historians like me do, even today. The case of PM Modi is no different. Some like to call him a disruptor; others see him as a rank outsider. However, neither his critics nor those who are in awe of him can deny that his years in the government have been transformational for the social, political and economic fabric of India. It is important to understand the transformational aspects of the Modi governments, as some argue that all prime ministers before him have brought significant changes since Independence.

Sanjay Baru sees the former prime minister P.V. Narasimha Rao as truly transformational. Rao had inherited a bad economic situation but went on to lead India's economic liberalisation. His decision to open the Indian economy is still seen as one of the most transformational feats achieved in independent India.[4] What made it even more significant was that PM Rao never commanded a complete control of his party, had a fractious relationship with the Congress president Sonia Gandhi and headed a minority government. Unlike his predecessor Indira Gandhi, Rao didn't have the advantage of the enduring legacy of being Nehru's offspring. He was not mentored by Nehru while in office, nor did he serve as the official host, which would have exposed him to the nuances of international diplomacy and delicate domestic issues much before occupying office as prime minister.[5] Indira Gandhi, on the other hand, was privy to the fact that her father subordinated the Congress party to the Congress government, and after the 1950 presidential election himself became the party president. This template was unique, an advantage that few prime ministers had. Some faced tough tasks as they headed unsteady coalitions in the 1990s. However, the commonality of all their tenures was their origins in the Congress system. They were all primary members of the Congress party early on in their careers and emerged as anti-establishment heroes, fighting the very system that had failed to realise their aspirations.

The case of Modi is markedly different. He is not, and has never been, a part of the Congress system so he doesn't share any kind of emotional appeal with it. Moreover, whether it is domestic issues or foreign policy, Modi has evolved his own doctrine, which is very different from that of his predecessors. The most significant aspect is his ability to evolve in response to every situation, which comes from his vast administrative experience from his early years as an RSS functionary who worked his way up the organisation and the BJP, and later as the chief minister of Gujarat. Neither has he allowed his ideological leanings to overshadow pragmatic considerations while dealing with powerful regional leaders and international heads of state. His foreign policy and global outreach to the Indian diaspora was an untapped area, which he harnessed extensively, to create more diasporic involvement not only in India but globally. None of his predecessors enjoyed this scale of engagement with the Indian diaspora, which has elevated India's position abroad and made every Indian interested in foreign policy—something that was earlier relegated to foreign policy experts and officials. Indians are, on the whole, conscious of how they are perceived globally as a community. Take the case of PM Modi's visits to Australia and the US in 2023 where the Indian diaspora was at the forefront of the reception he received.

On domestic issues, PM Modi has not been shy to highlight what he perceives as domestic and international 'blunders', stemming from the Congress system, which he believes favoured the status quo. Like US President Harry S. Truman, the architect of the Truman Doctrine, which ended an era of isolationism in US foreign policy post World War II, Modi has rejected the concept of non-alignment and propounded an 'India first' foreign policy where Indian strategic and economic interests are supreme and Indian foreign policy would service these needs. He saw that the non-committal stance adopted by India earlier vis-à-vis its position on global matters hindered her interests and reduced her to being a non-playing captain globally. Recently, despite criticism of remaining ambivalent in the light of the Israel–Palestine conflict, Modi has pursued the 'nation first' policy, putting India's interests ahead despite there being pressure to support or condemn one of the parties to the conflict. Modi prefers to walk the tight rope rather than giving into the pressure to react, an issue that brought down the Manmohan Singh government. The Modi government has rejected a Eurocentric or Western world-view on international affairs and is focused on improving the reception India gets in the world, especially the Global South. The conviction to take the controversial decision to purchase Russian oil, a decision that was dictated by domestic energy needs, while maintaining a delicate balance with the US has largely been the result of practical considerations rather than pandering to any lobby. These moves have largely been possible and acceptable due to the fact that, unlike Narasimha Rao and Manmohan Singh, Modi represents mass opinion. Rao and Singh had to contend with the fact that they were not mass leaders by any stretch of imagination and depended on their party for acceptability.[6] One of the lasting memories of Manmohan Singh's first term in office was that his government nearly fell because of the Left parties' decision to not support the nuclear deal that the prime minister viewed as necessary at the time for India's long-term energy needs. Manmohan Singh, like many before him, was exposed to the vagaries of coalition politics early on—something that Modi doesn't have to contend with. This has often invited the charge of critics that Modi is a dominant leader not given to consensus-building either with other political parties or within his own party. Modi has ensured that he is not the compromise choice of his party. This was not the case for Rao.

While Modi draws his strength from his party, he has also shared power with regional leaders within his party. There are several instances of this, including Shivraj Singh Chouhan, former chief minister of Madhya Pradesh; Vasundhara Raje Scindia, former chief minister of Rajasthan; and Yogi Adityanath, the current chief minister of Uttar Pradesh. When it comes to central leadership, Modi has shared power with Rajnath Singh, Amit Shah and Nitin Gadkari. In contrast, there was a lack of mass leaders after the death of Mukherjee and Upadhyay, who were still acquiring mass appeal before their untimely deaths, and before the rise of Vajpayee and Advani. The recent decision to make members of parliament and even ministers from the states of Madhya Pradesh, Chhattisgarh and Rajasthan contest state elections is largely dictated by this need to increase accountability of elected representatives, as well as to enthuse new blood into the party leadership. The comfort with which PM Modi deals with rumour-mongering about the future, with his possible successors being ready while he is in office, points to his being a secure leader. In this context, Modi is vastly different from Indira Gandhi, who was known to dismiss, replace and destroy any talk of successor or signs of succession.[7]

One of the fundamental problems that the Congress party has to contend with today is the lack of any serious regional leaders with a mass base. Congress leaders like H.N. Bahuguna were sidelined by the party in the 1980s, former chief minister Sheila Dikshit was sidelined after her term ended, former chief minister of Punjab Amarinder Singh was sidelined while in office and state congress leaders with a mass base are being shunted out the party periodically even today. As Ramachandra Guha writes in his book *Democracy and Dissenters*, in the years after Indira Gandhi became prime minister, she had little sustained interaction with senior Congressmen.[8] Here, I would like to make a necessary and important observation. Every time the election results were announced since 2014, the prime minister has always visited the central party headquarters (earlier on Ashoka Road and now on Deendayal Upadhyay Marg) to congratulate and interact with his karyakartas. His messaging is clear; he is speaking directly to his cadres who form the backbone of the party. Modi has communicated that the party comes first. He reinforces it every time he visits the party office, reminding the workers that no matter how complete and stupendous a victory you may achieve, no individual—not even him, despite being the prime minister—is higher than the party. This is the enduring legacy he will leave behind: strengthening not only the party but the belief that the party is supreme.

In his speech to party cadres after the election victory in 2019, he said,

> We the workers of BJP, our friends in NDA we dedicate the victory in the feet of the people.... Just like what our president [Amit Shah] said, the crores of BJP workers, their efforts and the purpose, I feel so proud that my party that I am a part of are full of generous people.... We have to accept the election results with humility. A government is formed with people's mandate we have to work with the spirit of inclusion.[9]

Modi had inherited a BJP with no clear vision; a party unable to recover from the debacle of 2009. The loss had demoralised cadres—and more so the RSS, which many believe decided to fully back the then chief minister of Gujarat, Narendra Modi. Vinay Sitapati argues in his book that prior to 2004, Vajpayee and Advani's reluctance to impose their party agenda was probably why almost no Hindutva causes made their way into law under the Janata government.[10] With Advani at the helm, the 1990s were seen as the golden era of the BJP, and the Rath Yatra for building the Ram Temple culminated in expanding the BJP's limited social base. Modi was a protégé of Advani and a young RSS functionary at the time. While the BJP vote share jumped from a mere 9 per cent and two seats in the 1984 general elections to 11 per cent and eighty-six seats five years later, and to 117 seats in 1991, a BJP government still seemed like a distant dream, if not impossible. One of the reasons for this was that, despite its tremendous success, the BJP remained confined to an upper-caste support base and failed to expand and reach out to lower castes and minorities. This led to the party being forced into coalitions with secularist state parties, thereby compromising its ideological foundations and succumbing to the pressures of coalition politics.

Sitapati argues that, even in 2004, BJP's manifesto document did not stress on Article 370 or the Ram Temple; rather it was titled 'An Agenda for Development, Good Governance and Peace'.[11] Moreover, as Swapan Dasgupta says, Advani was on tour for 'India Shining' whereas there was no clear planning and what many saw as the dilution of ideology.[12] So, Modi has walked a tight rope between balancing the institutional arm of the BJP with its electoral wing—a balance that Nehru struggled to establish within the Congress and which contributed to the decay of the organisation in the 1970s and 1980s. The BJP is also facing one of the biggest challenges today with the entry of outsiders who are seen with alarm by many within the BJP. The cadres need to be assured from time to time that they will be rewarded as, after all, it was they who suffered the most fighting the Congress on the streets in its heydays. The defection of leaders between parties has been a common practice since the time of Indira Gandhi and has continued ever since. Another challenge is that the cadre, for the first time, has seen such complete power, with the BJP and its allies being in power in more than sixteen states. This makes it imperative to insulate the cadres and leaders within the party from the problems associated with power. M.S. Golwalkar or Guruji, the charismatic Sarsanghchalak of the RSS, the ideological parent of the BJP, warned of the dangers of dilution of ideology and the challenge it would pose for the organisation. Modi, a pracharak himself, is conscious of these challenges, as the recent selection of old BJP hands as Rajya Sabha candidates from states suggests. The majority of Rajya Sabha candidates are party workers who have worked at the ground level for years. Multiple re-nominations for any individual come at the cost of opportunities for others.

Fighting the battle of perception had been a monumental task before the prime minister as the BJP was seen as an ideological party with little to offer to expand its base beyond urban voters in small towns and capital cities in India. This was a daunting task as leaders before him were tied up with a limited support base and had to contend with coalition partners, which nearly brought down governments. Modi's expansion of the BJP base beyond caste, community and religion will be his enduring legacy, as the pressures of national politics have been very different from that of being the chief minister of Gujarat. The party has relied on multiple surveys for getting feedback to keep the central party leadership informed and the prime minister is known to conduct regular meetings with his party leaders, members of parliament and cabinet ministers to assess the progress of implementation of his schemes or the work of the elected representatives on the ground. Non-performers have been replaced based on the feedback received from party workers and from ground-level surveys farmed out by the party to psephologists or agencies. Rather than insulate, the prime minister has built a solid feedback mechanism to allow free flow of information but has been equally careful to not compromise party discipline and unity, which he sees as the prime cause of problems in other larger parties such as the Congress. Moreover, Modi has also shown a readiness to campaign in areas where the party had a negligible presence before 2014 and is not daunted by the prospect of defeat or a lack of immediate big returns. Being a party organiser himself, he recognises that the build-up of the independent voter base of the BJP sans allies in areas such as Telangana, Tamil Nadu, the Northeast, Odisha and West Bengal is a long-term project. Despite strong leadership, it is the prime minister's credibility that translates into votes.

Critics, however, have been quick to point out that the BJP is emerging as a more centralised party or pursues a more centralised model of governance, similar to the Congress of the 1970s and 1980s, but there is a marked difference to be recognised. In her article in *The Print* in September 2021, Revathi Krishnan listed five things that a BJP leader needs to become chief minister, with grooming by the RSS and the 44–56 age group given prominence.[13] However, she emphasised that both Modi and Shah put a premium on leaders' loyalty to the BJP and their connection with the grass roots. Furthermore, she argued that people like Bhupendra Patel and Vijay Rupani, who started off as municipal corporators, and Devendra Fadnavis, who began as the youngest municipal corporator of Nagpur, as well as B.S. Yediyurappa, a leader with mass base in Karnataka brought in by Modi, illustrate this point. Moreover, the BJP under Modi has favoured more decisive mandates since the Mandalisation of Indian politics led to splintering of regional parties, creating unsteady coalitions. The outcomes of the 2014 and the 2019 general elections reflect that voters now favour a stronger government with more stability, as against the complexities of coalition governments that were the order of the day from 2004 to 2014. The BJP under Modi has been quick to harness this, using a combination of factors, such as the prime minister's personal appeal, extensive voter outreach, especially of first-time voters, welfarism and managing the caste calculus by partnering with smaller parties.

If one were to consider an international equivalent of PM Modi, who has ushered in an era characterised by style, charisma and substance, it would be the former president of the USA, John F. Kennedy. A disruptor in American politics, Kennedy was an excellent communicator, and it was during his campaign that the idea of televised TV debate entered into American politics. The Cuban Missile Crisis of 1962-63 was one of the grave international issues that had threatened to spill over into a full-scale nuclear war. Kennedy, despite domestic criticism, negotiated hard, forcing a Soviet retreat, which ended in the dismantling of nuclear war heads in Cuba that the Soviets had secretly installed to boost the position of Fidel Castro. Kennedy was the first Catholic US president and he unabashedly wore his belief system on his sleeve, which changed the way young Americans viewed American presidency. Despite his dynamic presidency being cut short by his assassination, Kennedy left an enduring legacy in American politics.

Modi, in certain respects, has been able to capture the imagination of Indians, much like Kennedy did for the Americans. Modi's entry on the scene coincided with the explosion of social media. This era was marked by a tense international situation exacerbated by the rise of the Islamic Caliphate in 2014, the Iranian nuclear programme and climate change crisis, a global pandemic in 2020, and the Russian invasion of Ukraine, among many other issues. It became very clear early on that the social media revolution ushered in by the digital revolution was fraught with unprecedented challenges. During Manmohan Singh's term, social media was at best peripheral to the mainstream media, but Modi used it extensively for citizen outreach in Gujarat, as pointed out by Andy Marino in his unofficial biography of Modi.[14] He used social media to communicate with voters of every age and region. This also pushed his party to use social media extensively, which also resulted in many of the debates on social media being led by the BJP.

The extensive use of social media to connect with voters, announce schemes and check their efficacy has ushered in greater accountability and a feedback system, which didn't exist before. This has changed the mode and manner of communication. In fact, Modi has also allowed social media to run free, conscious of the dangers it would pose for him in the long run. The mushrooming of YouTube channels has allowed different opinions to co-exist in what was earlier largely a preserve of a few—mainly legacy media channels. Many of these channels

Dismantling a Legacy 217

have been highly critical of the prime minister and his policies. However, much to the chagrin of his critics—alleging gagging of media—they are not only existing but thriving. Contrary to some opinions about its usage, social media has allowed many new entities to emerge, challenging established entities, ensuring equitable and quick delivery of news, and changing the medium of news, consumption patterns and also how elected representatives communicate with their voters. Modi has launched many of his schemes digitally, amplifying them using social media. The Vande Bharat trains were launched virtually and many election rallies, too, were held virtually during the pandemic—a phenomenon never seen before. In fact, all parties have taken advantage of the social media revolution to connect and engage with voters in new ways.

Marino further mentions in his biography that Modi's critics compare him with Margaret Thatcher, who was heavily criticised by the British Left but never let them get in the way of her beliefs.[15] As in the case of all heads of state, the scrutiny around the prime minister's actions is unmissable. His critics are mainly those affected by his brand and style of politics. For one, Modi has largely been a rank outsider, belonging to a backward community from a small town in Vadnagar in Gujarat, who has largely disrupted the style and narrative of Indian politics. Not only has he changed the narrative, he has dominated it in every frame. Marino points out that Modi stresses on the practical at the cost of the ideological.[16] Modi has demonstrated his resolve to gamble away personal prestige on many occasions, taking his decision directly to the voter to decide. Indira Gandhi took a similar gamble after the roaring success of the 1971 election and victory in the Bangladesh War. She used her mandate to suspend civil liberties and imprison Opposition leaders and anyone else who questioned her or her son Sanjay.

Modi fared differently for a variety of reasons. According to PR expert Dilip Cherian, he stood out because he was preceded by prime ministers like I.K. Gujral who was lacklustre, Narasimha Rao who was tactfully silent, and Manmohan Singh who was designed to be marginal. The Vajpayee era was studied but never attacked as Vajpayee was a calculable pacifist in everything he did and also romanticised because of his poet's charm. Moreover, what stood out for Modi was obviously the strength of his mandate in 2014 and 2019, as examples before him and his experience of Gujarat had shown that strong mandates would ensure strong governments. It helped him usher in a new India with ease, without having to give in to the restlessness of his cadres or the pressures to implement the BJP manifesto from Day 1. Article 370, the construction of the Ram Temple in Ayodhya and the issue of illegal immigration had been core issues of the Jana Sangh since the 1950s, but Modi preferred a legal recourse and had the patience to see them through. This is where he marks a departure from his predecessor Rajiv Gandhi who took his mandate of 400 plus seats as a blank cheque for sweeping changes, some of which had disastrous consequences. While the jury is still out on who got Babri Masjid unlocked in 1986, Rajiv Gandhi did deploy his mandate to overturn the Supreme Court judgment on the Shah Bano case in 1986, leading to a spate of resignations of his own ministers who condemned the pressure of the Islamic orthodoxy. There is no denying the fact that the Hindu sense of hurt and its past has been an ongoing battle since the colonial period, as Vasudha Dalmia has pointed out in her book *Hindu Pasts*.[17] But Narendra Modi has favoured a legal settlement of the issue, rather using extensive legislative powers as Rajiv Gandhi had done in the Shah Bano case.

Neerja Choudhary rightly refers to Rajiv Gandhi as a secular prime minister who undermined secularism as his overturning of the Supreme Court judgment in the Shah Bano case implicitly energised the Muslim orthodoxy that was unwilling to address issues such as the abolition of Triple Talaq.[18] On the other hand, despite the controversial nature of the decision and a heavy dose of sharp attacks on the decision to abolish Triple Talaq, which has already been banned in a dozen other Islamic countries, the Modi government went ahead and abolished it. It used legislative powers for a reformist impulse despite there being a real chance that the decision would be seen as a Hindutva onslaught on Islam. Triple Talaq, or the unilateral right of a man to divorce his wife under Islam, was seen as regressive and responsible for the economic degradation of scores of women in India. In the aftermath of the legislation, *The Wire,* in an article published on 9 January 2018, called it an act to demonise Muslim men and BJP's selective concern for Muslim women.[19] The article, however, did not discuss the issue of the economic degradation of scores of women who were subjected to the practice. While the decision to criminalise Muslim men has seen sections of lawyers, media and activist up in arms against the government,[20] the government has shown its deep resolve to counter the narrative, organising massive outreach programmes to explain the need for doing away with the practice legally.

Llyod Rudolph and Sussane Rudolph[21] have argued that the struggle between parliamentary sovereignty and judicial review became acute in the 1970s and 1980s, and this continues even today. Nehru and his like-minded colleagues believed that a viceregal-like strong centre was a necessary condition for realising substantive goals. Nehru's strongest statement on parliamentary sovereignty came during the constituent assembly debates when he said, 'no Supreme Court and no judiciary can stand in judgement over the sovereign will of the parliament representing the will of the entire community, ultimately the whole Constitution is a creature of the parliament.'[22] The BJP under Modi decided to abrogate Article 370 using parliament sovereignty and with a two-third majority vote that represented the collective will of the people of the country. This was one of the reasons why the Supreme Court dismissed an application challenging the decision. On 11 December 2023, a constitution bench upheld the President of India's decision to abrogate Article 370.

As the prime minister seeks a third term with a clearly outlined vision for the next five years, his overarching legacy will be that of transforming his party into an electoral machine, a party that can win elections. Having broken the perception of the BJP being a purely ideological party with no mass base, Modi is responsible for making the party and the RSS's ideology palatable to a larger audience, both within and outside the country. The party's ideology, which was seen as unsuited for the push and pulls of national and regional politics, had been a limiting factor to its growth so far. However, Modi has achieved the unthinkable by making the BJP hegemonic, commanding the narrative of elections and development, and ushering in a dynamism into the office of the prime minister that has few parallels across the world.

Aishwarya Pandit is Associate Professor at Jindal Global Law School.

NOTES

1. Rajni Kothari, 'The "Congress System" in India', *Asian Survey*, University of California Press, Vol. 4, No. 12 (December 1964), pp. 1161–73.
2. Vinay Sitapati, *Half Lion: How P.V. Narasimha Rao Transformed India*, Penguin, 2016.
3. Sanjaya Baru, *The Accidental Prime Minister*, Penguin, 2023.
4. Sanjaya Baru, *1991: How P.V. Narasimha Rao Made History*, Aleph Book Company, 2016, p. 5.
5. Neerja Chowdhary, *How Prime Ministers Decide*, Aleph Book Company, 2023, p. 17.
6. Baru, *1991*, pp. 255, 295.
7. Ramachandra Guha, *Democracy and Dissenters*, Penguin, 2016, p. 11.
8. Guha, *Democracy and Dissenters*.
9. Speech of PM Modi, *Business Insider*, 26 May 2019.
10. Vinay Sitapati, *Jugalbandi: The BJP Before Modi*, Penguin Viking, 2020, p. 286
11. Sitapati, *Jugalbandi*.
12. Sitapati, *Jugalbandi*, p. 287.
13. Revathi Krishnan, 'Five Boxes BJP Leaders Need to Tick to Become a Chief Minister in Modi-Shah Era', *The Print*, 17 September 2021, https://theprint.in/politics/five-boxes-bjp-leaders-need-to-tick-to-become-a-chief-minister-in-modi-shah-era/734794/.
14. Andy Marino, *Narendra Modi: A Political Biography*, HarperCollins, 2014.
15. Marino, *Narendra Modi*, p. xix.
16. Marino, *Narendra Modi*.
17. Vasudha Dalmia, *Hindu Pasts: Women, Religion and Histories*, Permanent Black, 2015.
18. Chowdhary, *How Prime Ministers Decide*.

19. Flavia Agnes, 'The Triple Talaq Bill and BJP's Selective Concern for Muslim Women', *The Wire*, 9 January 2018, https://thewire.in/gender/muslim-triple-talaq-bill.
20. Zeenat Saberin, 'India: Triple Talaq or Instant Divorce Now a Criminal Offence', *Al Jazeera*, 19 September 2018, https://www.aljazeera.com/news/2018/9/19/india-triple-talaq-or-instant-divorce-now-a-criminal-offence.
21. Llyod Rudolph and Susanne Hoeber Rudolph, *Explaining Indian Democracy: The Fifty-year Perspective*, Oxford University Press, 2008, pp. 183–90.
22. Rudolph and Rudolph, *Explaining Indian Democracy*, pp. 183–84.

Indian Re-emergence
The Foreign Policy Boom

CLEO PASKAL

It's in the eyes. Sure, you can see the change in India in bigger things—new metro lines, highways, moon missions—but for me, the most powerful glimpse of a transforming India is what you see when, as a non-Indian, you look into the eyes of Indians and see them looking back at you.

What do I see in their eyes? Confidence.

This is especially true for young Indians. If they are twenty, they have spent half their lives watching their country go through some of the world's biggest challenges—terrorism, attacks from China, a pandemic, America's withdrawal from Afghanistan, Russia's invasion of Ukraine and economic crises. At the same time, India took on complex, India-specific, nation-shaping issues like Article 370 and the Ram Mandir.

There have been ups and downs but, overall, young Indians have mostly known a period of economic growth, longer life expectancy, rising literacy and an increasingly globally important India.

They have seen a West that has seemingly acted capriciously (at best), with minimal ability to defend itself from even obvious dangers such as TikTok. Indeed, across a range of sectors, Western credibility has taken hit after hit. This includes the financial crisis of 2007-08 and the subsequent recessions (affecting the credibility about the stability and transparency of the US markets); the Afghan withdrawal (lack of strategic foresight); the handling of COVID-19 (corrupt academia); narratives around climate change (politicised energy policy); persistent derogatory and inaccurate coverage about India (biased media); polarisation in the West (shaky domestic integrity); harbouring of terrorists who want to harm India (strategic hypocrisy); extended wait times for the US visa (State Department's conflicted commitment to its relationship with India) and more.

Then, on the other side, they have seen a China that is militarising islands stolen from other countries, has imprisoned hundreds of thousands for their faith or political beliefs, has invaded its neighbours, including India, and continues to threaten to invade others, and is actively distorting the global economy through illegal trade practices.

And so, when I look into the eyes of, for instance, a young Indian researcher whom I'm meeting for the first time, what I see is someone who is proud of her country—imperfections and all—and who is keen to make it even better. She is also likely to have a healthy scepticism about anything I will say, given the track record of Westerners. She'll be polite, but I'll need to prove myself as someone worth listening to. And often, compared to the Indian experts she has access to, I can't.

It's great. And it's about time.

INDIA BEFORE THE RISE OF THE BJP

The change has been so organic that it is hard to remember what India was like just over a decade ago, before the elections of 2014. So, let's go back to the media archives from the period leading up to the vote.

One of the most burning issues of the times was corruption. In 2011, I wrote a piece for the *Huffington Post* titled 'World's #9 Most Powerful Person Now Accused of Corruption—Will She Fall?'[1]

Sonia Gandhi had just been named the world's ninth most powerful person by *Forbes* magazine, with the actual Prime Minister of India, Manmohan Singh, ranked only eighteenth. The *Forbes* article read: 'Gandhi remains the real power behind the nuclear-tipped throne [...] she has cemented her status as true heiress to the Nehru-Gandhi political dynasty.'[2]

However, as the *Huffington Post* piece detailed: 'The scandals are bursting on to the front pages fast and thick. Suresh Kalmadi, a Congress Party politician and the former head of the corruption-plagued Commonwealth Games, was arrested April 25. According to a report by the Indian Comptroller and Auditor General, the 2G spectrum scam alone, in which 2G licenses were sold off in a manner that was, to say the least, less than transparent, cost close to $40 billion in lost revenue. ... Even the Supreme Court is fed up, with Justice B. Sudarshan Reddy saying about the vast sums of Indian money being illegally hidden away in Liechtenstein Bank: *We are talking about the huge money. It is a plunder of the nation. It is a pure and simple theft of the national money. We are talking about mind-boggling crime.*'[3]

That level of corruption was having a debilitating effect both domestically and internationally. On 4 July 2011, a Supreme

Court of India order explained why vast flows of illegal money were a national security concern:

> The issue of unaccounted monies held by nationals, and other legal entities, in foreign banks, is of primordial importance to the welfare of the citizens. The quantum of such monies may be rough indicators of the weakness of the State, in terms of both crime prevention, and also of tax collection. Depending on the volume of such monies, and the number of incidents through which such monies are generated and secreted away, it may very well reveal the degree of 'softness of the State'. [...] If the State is soft to a large extent, especially in terms of the unholy nexus between the law makers, the law keepers, and the law breakers, the moral authority, and also the moral incentives, to exercise suitable control over the economy and the society would vanish. Large unaccounted monies are generally an indication of that.

While getting rid of all corruption in a country is nearly impossible, the scale involved shackled India's, and Indians', potential. It wasn't just the Supreme Court that had enough. In another article from 2011 for the *Huffington Post* I described how things were starting to change: 'Indians from all walks of life have been the real heroes of the modern anti-corruption movement in India. However, for a long time there was virtually no national-level civil society in India—most activity was regional, language or religion-based. Much of the media, which could have acted as a national unifier, is owned by some of the same large companies that have benefitted from the existing system. As a result, there was no real challenge to the arbitrary misuse of power.'[4]

But that was starting to change. On 14 October 2011, India's newly formed Action Committee Against Corruption in India (ACACI) held its first official meeting. It included long-term anti-corruption heavy hitters such as Professor R. Vaidyanathan from the Indian Institute of Management Bangalore, Dr Subramanian Swamy and Professor M.D. Nalapat.

At around the same time, Indians were noticing the 'Gujarat model' being pursued by the state's chief minister Narendra Modi, and wondering if that might work at a national level.[5]

We know what happened next.

(RE)EMERGING INDIA: THE IMPACT OF FOREIGN POLICY

India is very different now. Of course, corruption—in many guises and sometimes at quite serious scales—still exists in India (as elsewhere), but it no longer plagues the whole system like it once did, affecting everything from buying a train ticket to foreign policy. India had room to move, and moved it has.

As this book shows, there is a range of ways to look at the transformation of the last decade. I'll focus on India's now comparatively unfettered foreign relations, in the broadest sense.

Over the past ten years, India's foreign policy—shaped, as with all countries, by geography and national priorities—has grown into something unique and complex. And it continues to evolve quickly.

Look at just some elements of the defence relationship with the US. In 2014, if someone had said that India would:

- be designated by the US as a major defence partner (2016),
- sign a series of foundational American defence agreements (LEMOA, COMCASA, BECA),[6]
- become a leader in resurrecting the Quad along with the US, Japan and Australia,

they would have been ridiculed by the Washington, DC establishment for being 'too optimistic' about India. Not only did all this happen (and much, much, much more), United States' Pacific Command was renamed Indo-Pacific Command in 2018,[7] to highlight the importance of the region, and allies (to wit, India), in the region.

India also signed logistics agreements with its Quad partners Australia and Japan, and it has increasingly been working with other Pacific Ocean partners. This is a natural outgrowth of one of Prime Minister Narendra Modi's first foreign policy announcements, his 'Act East' policy. Ten years later, India is an increasingly important partner in the region. For example, India has backed the Philippines in its stand against China stealing its territory. It has conducted joint military exercises with the Philippines and sold it BrahMos missiles.

Other notable bilaterals include India's growing economic and security ties with Saudi Arabia,[8] the United Arab Emirates (UAE)[9] and even the quiet but real engagement between India and Taiwan that saw, in 2023, former chiefs of India's three military services visiting Taipei.[10]

Further, there have been innovative 'clusterings' that have resulted in, for example, the resurrection of the Quad and the creation of I2U2 (India, Israel, US, UAE).

India is also still a member of other (generally older) minilaterals/multilaterals such as BRICS (Brazil, Russia, India, China, South Africa) and Shanghai Cooperation Organisation (SCO), that may not be as 'like-minded', but the fact that India is staying in the room (and chatting in the hallways) also exemplifies India's unique position and complex approach. By sticking around these—at times near-hostile—environments,

India can learn, influence, find potential allies and identify potential threats.

(MIS)UNDERSTANDING INDIA

It is easy for countries that exist in less complex geopolitical geography to misunderstand India's multifaceted approach. Strategically, the US has considered itself almost as an island power. Given its overwhelming strength in comparison to the two countries that share its land borders (Canada and Mexico), Washington hasn't had to balance the same complexities as India, which has (at the least) two actively hostile neighbours. (As an aside, in the US, as a result of increasing reliance on compromised technology, the porous southern border and the confluence of malign state actors and international criminal organisations, a case can be made that America's traditional protection via geographic isolation is being systematically undermined from the inside and that US strategies can no longer assume there is a safety buffer of distance.)

Additionally, there has been a tendency by some policymakers and strategists in the US to invoke Lord Palmerston's 1848 statement that: 'We have no eternal allies, and we have no perpetual enemies. Our interests are eternal and perpetual, and those interests it is our duty to follow.'[11] And, in that context, they ask if India backs US interests.

To undermine US–India ties, some (particularly from the State Department school of thought) then bring up India's position on the Russian invasion of Ukraine (often inaccurately), and Delhi's ongoing relations with Tehran. The fact that India is fighting the same two existential threats as the US (the Chinese

Communist Party and extremism) is often overlooked by those looking to marginalise India—though not by those in the U.S. Department of Defense.

Even then, rarely do American strategists flip the construct on its head and ask if, from an Indian point of view, the US backs Indian interests. Leaving aside the relations between US and Pakistan, and the White House's seeming desire to 'normalise' relations with China, a simple examination of the method of the Afghan withdrawal—which left billions of dollars in weapons in the hands of those hostile to India—answers that question.

And yet, especially over the last ten years, India has patiently and persistently looked for areas to deepen cooperation with the US, including on defence. American strategists who want to throw the Indian baby out with the bathwater might want to read the rest of Palmerston's quote: 'When we find other countries that take a different view, and thwart us in the object we pursue, it is our duty to make allowance for the different manner in which they may follow out the same objects. It is our duty not to pass too harsh a judgment upon others, because they do not exactly see things in the same light as we see; and it is our duty not lightly to engage this country in the frightful responsibilities of war, because from time to time we may find this or that Power disinclined to concur with us in matters where their opinion and ours may fairly differ.'[12]

Of course, this approach wasn't invented by the British. And it is still limited. A more complete approach has become apparent in India in the last decade and is encapsulated by the doctrine of Vasudhaiva Kutumbakam—the world is one family—that guides Prime Minister Modi's foreign policy.

FRIENDS, INTERESTS OR FAMILY?

Here again, different perspectives have perhaps led to a misunderstanding of intent. To the West, where the common view of family is the nuclear family, 'Vasudhaiva Kutumbakam' can sound utopian.

However, in India, and in much of the rest of the world where sprawling, extended families are the norm, it makes sense. In much of the world, family is complex, sometimes difficult, always changing. There are births, deaths, marriages, divorces, siblings you trust, cousins who lie, fights, reunions and more.

But the bottom line is, you are stuck together, and you'd better try to make it work, for everyone's sake. If a rich brother lives next to a poor brother, the rich brother won't be secure until the poor brother is doing okay.

This is a different vision from the West's and also from China's. Perhaps not coincidentally, the Chinese Communist Party (CCP) waged war on the family internally, through the one-child policy. Traditional Chinese society was family-oriented, with extended families forming the security net of society. By destroying the extended family domestically, the CCP has fundamentally changed the culture, making individuals more dependent on other forms of security such as being in the good graces of the CCP.

Meanwhile, for those in the family-oriented and complex geopolitical neighbourhoods of Asia, Africa and Latin America, at an instinctive, even personal, level, India's 'Vasudhaiva Kutumbakam' vision resonates.

Leaders in many of those countries understood when, for example, India's first major response when Russia invaded Ukraine was to ensure that Indian students (and others who could follow India's path) made it home safely. They got it when India's quiet diplomacy turned the death sentence against its retired Navy officers in Qatar into a way to engage more closely with Doha (and bring the men home safely). And they show it by, like family, making compromises, understanding India's constraints and ensuring India's 2023 G20 leadership was a success. Do they sometimes find India difficult to deal with? Yes. Do they think, as with family, it's worth it in the long run? Increasingly, also yes.

It is not non-alignment—which defines itself by saying what it is not. It is, as foreign minister S. Jaishankar puts it, all alignment. Though perhaps it can also be described as realignment, around another way of seeing things and working together. If it persists, survives and thrives, it can change the world.

Of course, this poses a direct threat to the CCP, which wants to change the world in its own way—a way that, above all, benefits it. Therefore, as India's foreign influence has grown, so has the CCP's efforts to undermine it.

This has included Chinese-linked hacks of the Indian electrical grid,[13] attempts to block the United Nations' sanctioning of those who India considers terrorists, working towards 'elite capture' of India's neighbours to put social, political and economic pressure on India, spying on India, including from the sea and air,[14] using 'cognitive warfare' to try to affect India's internal politics[15] and waging proxy war against India using, among others, Indian Maoists and 'iron brother' Pakistan.

And, of course, there have been direct attacks by the People's Liberation Army on India in the Himalayas. In India's response to the 2020 Galwan attacks, we again see how India has transformed. The counter was swift and broad, including the banning of Chinese apps such as TikTok that were part of China's unrestricted warfare on India. The Indian military and its efforts were widely reported, the twenty fallen soldiers were publicly honoured and, when Nyima Tenzin of the previously secretive Special Frontier Force died shortly afterwards on patrol in Ladakh, BJP General Secretary Ram Madhav attended the public funeral.[16] Since then, there has also been a deep restructuring of the military, including changes in recruitment, which have the potential to transform India's strategic profile.

THE NEW INDIA

From a foreign policy perspective, the India of today is unrecognisable. As against the India of a decade ago, the nation is re-engaging with the world, standing up for itself and trying to find solutions to intractable problems. Most of what it does is done quietly—this isn't 'press release policy', but an attempt to be truly effective.

In the process, India is offering a pole of geostrategic stability and economic promise that many are finding attractive. The last decade showed that promise. From Africa to the Pacific Islands to the Philippines to Japan, a common refrain is, 'we want more India'. It is up to the next decade to deliver. It won't be easy. India's success over the past few years is making it a target of everything from disinformation campaigns to actual military attacks.

But more, including in the US and Europe, are realising that without a strong, stable India, the world is a much more dangerous place. And that India is India—and it will do things its own way. It may not be a friend or an immediate interest, but it can be family.

Things are far from perfect. But, looking into the casually confident eyes of the young researcher, or the small shopkeeper, or the vegetable salesman, or the doctor, or the teacher, it looks like there is no going back. They now know what India can be. And their eyes glint *Jai Hind*.

Cleo Paskal is Non-Resident Senior Fellow for the Indo-Pacific at the Foundation for Defense of Democracy, Washington, DC.

NOTES

1. Cleo Paskal, 'World's #9 Most Powerful Person Now Accused of Corruption—Will She Fall?', *HuffPost*, https://www.huffpost.com/entry/worlds-9-most-powerful-pe_b_853132.
2. PTI, 'Sonia, Tata in Forbes' Most Powerful People List', *Business Standard*, 21 January 2013, https://www.business-standard.com/article/economy-policy/sonia-tata-in-forbes-most-powerful-people-list-110110400119_1.html.
3. Cleo Paskal, 'World's #9 Most Powerful Person Now Accused of Corruption—Will She Fall?'.
4. Cleo Paskal, 'Weeding Out Corruption in India', *HuffPost*, https://www.huffpost.com/entry/corruption-in-india-2_b_1070114.
5. Uday Muhurkar, Kaushik Deka and Jayant Sriram, 'When Modi's "Gujarat Model" Inspired India', *India Today*, https://www.indiatoday.in/india-today-insight/story/from-the-archives-2014-when-modi-s-gujarat-model-inspired-india-1985266-2022-08-08.
6. Bureau of Political-Military Affairs, 'U.S. Security Cooperation with India', https://www.state.gov/u-s-security-cooperation-with-india/.
7. U.S. Indo-Pacific Command, 'Pacific Command Change Highlights Growing Importance of Indian Ocean Area', DoD News, 31 May 2018, https://www.pacom.mil/Media/News/

News-Article-View/Article/1537107/pacific-command-change-highlights-growing-importance-of-indian-ocean-area/.
8. 'India and Saudi Arabia Agree to Expand Economic and Security Ties After the G20 Summit', AP News, 11 September 2023, https://apnews.com/article/india-saudi-arabia-corridor-g20-9ecb469959ad9ab1a997b711db3dc902.
9. Anirudha Karindalam, 'How Bilateral Ties between India and UAE Have Grown Under PM Modi', *The Week*, 18 February 2024, https://www.theweek.in/theweek/cover/2024/02/16/bilateral-partnership-between-the-uae-and-india-has-grown-since-modi-became-prime-minister.html.
10. Pradip R. Sagar, 'Why Are Three Former India Service Chiefs Attending a Security Conference in Taipei?', *India Today*, 9 August 2023, https://www.indiatoday.in/india-today-insight/story/why-are-three-former-indian-service-chiefs-attending-a-security-conference-in-taipei-2418222-2023-08-08.
11. H.C. Deb, 'Treaty of Adrianople—Charges against Viscount Palmerston', Vol. 97, 1 March 1848, cc66-123, https://api.parliament.uk/historic-hansard/commons/1848/mar/01/treaty-of-adrianople-charges-against.
12. Ibid.
13. Insikt Group, 'Continued Targeting of Indian Power Grid Assets by Chinese State-sponsored Activity Group', Recorded Future, https://go.recordedfuture.com/hubfs/reports/ta-2022-0406.pdf.
14. Sachin Parashar, 'Another Jolt to Ties and Male Green-lights China Ship Visit', *The Times of India*, 24 January 2024, https://timesofindia.indiatimes.com/india/maldives-ignores-india-lets-chinese-spy-vessel-dock/articleshow/107093001.cms; The Wire Staff, 'Reports Suggest India Was Targeted by Chinese Balloon Too', *The Wire*, 9 February 2023, https://thewire.in/security/reports-suggest-india-was-targeted-by-chinese-balloon-too.
15. S.D. Pradhan, 'Is China Using Cognitive Warfare to Target Indian Political Parties?', *The Times of India*, 19 December 2022, https://

timesofindia.indiatimes.com/blogs/ChanakyaCode/is-china-using-cognitive-warfare-to-target-indian-political-parties/.
16. Suhasini Haidar, 'With Public Funeral for Tibetan Soldier, Delhi Sends a Signal to Beijing', *The Hindu*, 7 September 2020, https://www.thehindu.com/news/national/ram-madhav-in-tibetan-soldiers-funeral-a-strong-signal-to-beijing/article61709367.ece.

The Redeemer's Rite
How Narendra Modi Has Redefined Power

S. PRASANNARAJAN

On a wintry morning in Ayodhya, dressed in crisp off-white and carrying the golden crown, he walked confidently towards the destination he had vowed to reach one day, undeterred by any obstacles that stood in his way. His strides were as solemn as the air was thick with devotion. In the next few minutes of India's most televised homecoming of a god who had been displaced by a disputed history but never abandoned by aggrieved Hindus, he presided over a ceremony that no other head of government in a secular state has done in the past.

On 22 January 2024, in Ayodhya, Uttar Pradesh, Narendra Modi fulfilled his promise as he led the consecration of Ram in a grand temple. The world's most popular politician in a liberal democracy redefined national freedom in terms of cultural inheritance and civilisational memory, and in doing so, he achieved a rare feat in the history of political power in this country: in the restoration of a much-beloved god to his birthplace, he has ordained himself as the redeemer of Hindu nationalism, which, in his own words, is not a repudiation of modernity but a reminder of its cultural content.

It was a moment of religious and cultural rupture.

Nationalism has always been a contentious sentiment in the evolutionary story of independent India, maybe as much as it was a kinetic force in India's struggle for independence. If nation with a capital 'N' was the idea under occupation before 1947, after independence, it was this same idea that needed guidance from the original nation-builders with a deeper understanding of it. India was not different in this lofty mission of dutiful liberators seen in most postcolonial societies. The only difference—and it was a big one—was that India defied the trajectory of most of the newly freed colonies where the liberators took the surest path to tyranny. In the book of the original nation-builders, what the modernisation project of free India needed was a restriction of primordial impulses and an enforced adherence to officially sanctified secularism. It is this progressive view of India that made the idea of the nation and the public attitudes of religion anti-modern. The New Indian, scientifically tempered and secularly programmed, like the New Man of socialism in another era, was meant to be modernity's ideal advertiser. Was it a hollow golem?

In the summer of 2014, when Narendra Modi became prime minister, it was not the end of perhaps the longest campaign in Indian politics—a campaign that erupted from the embers of Gujarat 2002. He was unarguably India's most popular chief minister, but he made himself inevitable to the state in three consecutive elections not as a politician with a provincial agenda but as a passionate interpreter of the nation, which, in his stump speeches, was slave to an establishment that distrusted India's cultural ancestry, its civilisational memory. Power in 2014 intensified his campaign for rebuilding the nation. And it was going to be a long journey. Redeemers don't want the foreword to their saga to be written in haste.

The India story of the Modi decade, from 2014 to 2024, turned that worn-out word every politician with revolutionary aspiration overuses into a political intimacy in the world's most impatient democracy. 'Change', for once, became a lived experience. One politician's struggle—and his conversation with the future—would become a nation's reassessment of its very being. The nation was no longer a restricted pride; and a public expression of religion was not a subversion of the secular ideal. India, as a nation state, shed its inhibitions. It was a higher sense of the nation that allowed Modi to interpret power not as a privilege but as an emotional engagement with the cultural identity of the land. He brought to the arena the question that has mobilised, divided and united nations through centuries: *who are we?* If a Hindu adjective to nationalism looks organic and inevitable today, it is because he, as the rebuilder of the nation, doesn't see the cultural impulses of a people as a threat to modernity. After all, the back stories of the world's most developed societies have an overwhelming religious content, though 'Christendom' has already normalised its indebtedness to the Book. India's nationalist text with a religious flavour has just begun. Modi simply wants to emphasise the obvious. Secularism, he implies, is not a repudiation but an integration of traditions. His message is this: nationalism with a religious accent is not a project in fear, as those who are still trapped in the jargon of majoritarianism would love to cry out; it is the kind of cultural synthesisation that makes secularism meaningful.

Modi's battlefield, as a lone warrior with a larger waiting period for acceptability in India's middle class than most of his contemporaries in their struggle for power, has never been confined to the electoral space. Once in power, the other constituency got equally important for him: the Great Indian Mindspace. He is not a proselytiser or an indoctrinator. He is a storyteller. Stories change nations. He told them as motivational pieces, and the frisson was generated by the seamless blending of aspiration, dreams and patriotism, and the style varied from avuncular intimacy to prophetic grandeur to conversational casualness. And the India in his telling is not a fairyland—a familiar place in the fantasy of nationalist-autocrats—but a place rooted in hard realism. Its full realisation, he tells you, is the ultimate realisation of nationhood itself. *Mann ki Baat*, his storytelling session with India in which the listener becomes a part of the story, is the best episodic expression of a country that has ever emerged from a politician. The great communicator may be a media construct that is too eager to turn every windbag on the stump into a Cicero, but certain politicians have had an easy access to the popular mind; for instance, storytellers such as Churchill, Reagan and Thatcher. They make political communication an art of alternative reality—beyond the wretchedness of the present lies a perfection worthy of us. As one of the most effective communicators in politics today, Modi makes the idea of the nation a shared enchantment among the millions who see in him their own unrealised possibility. That's a sure recipe for a bestseller.

Still, even if the past propels his mission for the future, and even if tradition adds content to his modernisation agenda, the tomorrow he intends to build doesn't draw its raw material from a perfumed history. The Modi of the marketplace makes the best use of technology to make India as egalitarian as possible. That is why the digital destiny is not just a trendy mantra but an acceptance of the inevitable. He is not a revolutionary in the marketplace, and he has never intended to be a panegyrist of capital, and that is one reason for the disappointment of those who anticipated an Indian version of Reagan or Thatcher in him. As a gradualist reformer, he knew that India was in too unequal a place to withstand ruthless reforms. The state still has a role to play, and the role need not be of socialist vintage, not a nanny state but a state that provides the best context to the individual's most daring text. Modi gave his own nationalist spin to Deng Xiaoping's famous aphorism: it's glorious to be rich. The so-called start-up nation is a fine indicator of how the state doesn't restrain the individual but frees him. The pinstriped Davos man can be spotted with a dash of the tricolour on his lapel. A true nationalist in the marketplace can afford only one ideology: freedom.

And it is this ideology of freedom that underpins his internationalism. India has come a long way from its leadership of 'Third Worldism'—though as a mindset it may not have been fully eradicated from the establishment—and its relic, the Non-Aligned Movement, continues to get New Delhi's patronage. Still, that is not the India that has got a seat at the global high table. In the India of the new Wise Man from the East, anti-Americanism is redundant, and national interest is not subordinated to a foreign policy built on borrowed ideology. Modi's India doesn't belong to a bloc; it belongs to alliances and attitudes sustained by freedom, politically as well as economically. As a pragmatic globalist, Modi has achieved that rare feat of remaining a trusted friend to big-power antagonists, without devaluing his country's international morality; Ukraine is a good example of this. With regard to China, India may have suffered from an inferiority complex for long, despite the advantages of democracy. It was as if an intimidated New Delhi made a diplomatic virtue out of its stoicism even as Beijing continued with its provocations along the border. Not anymore. Once again, this belated display of confidence in the dividends of freedom allows Modi's India to strike a fine balance between national interest and international responsibility. Today, India's global ambition matches its influence. No other prime minister after Nehru has excelled in the art of internationalism with such panache.

In the end, no politician in a democracy as unforgiving as India can play out a script of individual audacity and nationalist ambition without one quality: authenticity. Look around and you will realise that what those leaders desperate for postponing political mortality lack is the same quality. Authenticity comes from old-fashioned virtues a people disillusioned with the political class seek from a new leader on a mission: credibility, integrity and honesty. Modi is not a 'professional' politician. He is a politician for whom politics is a permanent struggle of the most dutiful, and that too in one of the most deified nations. It is this devotion to the nation that adds a spiritual content to his idea of power. He has never been tentative about his relationship with power, which, in his book, is the most effective instrument for change, culturally as well as economically. He has turned power into the highest form of spiritual contentment, in which the personal blends with the national. It is this terrifying clarity of purpose that makes Modi authentic. He continues to remind

India that, through every word uttered with such rhetorical flamboyance, his pursuit of power is a necessary condition for national renewal.

Authenticity is rewarded by trust. In a country where power and corruption coexisted in harmony for so long, principled governance has become an enforced norm. In the pre-Modi India, privilege and patronage, or entitlement and entrenchment, alone ensured the persistence of political power. Modi gave power a spartan intensity, never letting himself be distracted. There was nothing at stake but the nation, which could be redeemed only by the one who held power with detachment and clarity in equal measure—and for a vast majority of Indians, he was the one. The most popular politician in a democracy is powered by a massive wealth of trust. The more he grows in power the more those who trust him feel empowered. In a country where elections are won and lost by the poor, and where every social engineering, every salvation ideology has failed to create a revolutionary, an ordinary man, an outsider in power, announces that what his nation needs is not a phoney revolution but a cultural transformation. They trust him for that.

In Ayodhya, in the afterglow of Ram's consecration, he said, with his customary rhythmic flourish, 'Ram is flow; Ram is effect.'[1] He was invoking the god to emphasise the great cultural continuum, and as prime minister, he implied that he was within his 'constitutional' right to do so because even secular India's Constitution invoked Ram. So, in Ayodhya, it was consecration as national reassertion: 'We have to lay the foundation of the India of the next thousand years.'[2] In the flow of the nation, such a mission stretching into the distant future can only be stated by a man who sees power as a sacred text. When Narendra Modi plays the national redeemer, he makes sure that god stands witness to the occasion.

S. Prasannarajan is the Editor of *Open* magazine.

NOTES

1. 'Narendra Modi's Ayodhya Speech: Ram Is Not Fire, Ram Is Energy. Ram Is Not a Dispute, Ram Is a Solution. Ram Is Not Just Ours, Ram Belongs to Everyone', *The Indian Express*, 23 January 2024, https://indianexpress.com/article/opinion/columns/ayodhya-ram-mandir-inauguration-lord-ram-narendra-modi-ram-setu-ramlalla-9122567/.
2. Ibid.

America and India

Brothers in Democracy, Only Cousins in Geopolitics

DON RITTER

A secure and prosperous future for India is tied to fellow democracies America and the 'West' winning two shooting wars, one in Europe, Ukraine, and the other in the Middle East, Israel. Another conflict faced by the West is heating up over Taiwan. In all these arenas, the West is faced with a budding axis of powers involving Russia, Iran and China, with each bringing their own unique strengths to the group. Add a nuclear-armed and belligerent North Korea as junior partner and the axis becomes even more threatening. China, already a world military power, is even further empowered by this axis.

CHINA STAYS IN THE REAR BUT IS THE AXIS LEADER

India's most immediate interest is not only keeping China from dominating Asia and Africa but increasing their already strong sway over Europe and even North America. China's vast and expanding purchases of Russian and Iranian oil and gas is the sole reason those countries can continue to wage war.[1] China's exports of manufactured products, including dual use technologies and trans-shipped products via third countries, help sustain Russia's and Iran's domestic economies. China would be a great beneficiary if both Russia and Iran prevail, a circumstance that would weaken the axis's greatest adversary, America, not only when it comes to defending Taiwan but globally as well.

If the axis prevails in those wars, China wins and, by definition, India is diminished. Turns out, Kyiv and Tel Aviv are not that far from Delhi. And then again, if China takes Taiwan, a whole other story unfolds in Asia for India.

Thus, even while India is tied closely via energy trade with Russia and Iran, countering the power of an autocratic Russia–Iran–China axis is beneficial to India. A Russia held at bay—or even defeated in Ukraine—will still supply energy to India while China's global reach, especially their military influence over India, will be diminished. If Iran and proxies are defeated, it will strengthen America and thus diminish China, a positive outcome for India.

A wild card for India is the future capacity of the US to stand up for democracy in the world. There are troubling signs ahead. After 9/11, the US fought two wars far from its shores, in Iraq and Afghanistan. The former was riddled with poor judgements but with a somewhat longer tenure might have left a stronger, distinctly Iraqi government. But between domestic American politics turned against America's presence in Iraq and Iran's build-up of their Shiite militias, with all their political and military influence inside Iraq, America's intervention to remove Saddam Hussein, in the end, vastly empowered the mullahs in Iran. A terrible setback for America and the West resulted.

And then, there's the war over Afghanistan.

America's toppling of the Taliban government in Afghanistan led to the creation of an emerging democratic order where India was an essential, indeed leading, partner with the US and NATO. But continued terrorist attacks by the Pakistan-controlled Taliban meant ongoing conflict, year after year. While bipartisan support in the US for the Islamic Republic of Afghanistan was strong till the end, both President Trump and President Biden, particularly the latter, rejected stalemate and deserted Afghanistan. The reality was, Pakistan could not be defeated, they could only be kept at bay, meaning stalemate was the only alternative to surrender. The global impact of that surrender to Islamic terrorists and their Pakistani mentors and suppliers has thus far been incalculable. The surrender, indeed, betrayal of loyal Afghan allies was done in the most incompetent and heartless fashion. Many knowledgeable observers believe that the gratuitous surrender of Afghanistan led Putin to invade Ukraine and Hamas (read Iran) to invade Israel. This author believes that to be 100 per cent true.[2]

What is crucial for India, the second-largest supporter after the US of the then emerging democratic Afghanistan, is that Pakistan has emerged victorious and achieved what its military and intelligence services had always coveted—'strategic depth' in their competition with rival India and virtual control over Afghanistan.

Pakistan's Inter-Services Intelligence (ISI) had given birth to the Taliban in the mid-1990s during the time of Prime Minister Benazir Bhutto. With civil war raging next door, the Taliban were a way for Pakistan to influence events and put a stop to neighbouring political and, importantly, economic chaos in Afghanistan during those times, well before the US removed the Taliban from power. America, in 2001, after the Taliban refused to hand over the Al-Qaeda mastermind of 9/11, Osama bin Laden, toppled the Taliban with the support of both Tajik, Hazara and Pashtun Afghans.

The 2001 removal of the Taliban had nearly unanimous support from a wide spectrum of the Afghan people. Over the next twenty years, Afghanistan, with strong support from the US and the West, despite a bloody Pakistan-promoted Taliban insurgency (read terrorist war), built a new nation, based on nascent but evolving democratic institutions and a market economy with substantial potential. One can only wonder at what the achievements of this new nation would have been without the constant military pressure coming out of Pakistan.

With Pakistan's triumph in August of 2021 and the removal of US forces, also removed was this example of a budding democracy on its long western frontier showing steady economic, political and social success. Such success in Muslim Afghanistan was seen as a threat to the way a still unstable Pakistan is constituted, most particularly as a danger to the role of the Pakistani military. Taliban proxies, led by the Haqqani network, could fight on indefinitely, given the safe haven and material support they enjoyed from Pakistan. For Pakistan, it was a worthy investment to keep a free Afghanistan and its allies on their back foot.

The Taliban are in the process of solidifying their control, stabilising their economy and seeking recognition abroad while taking in large quantities of 'humanitarian' aid from the United Nations, meaning largely and ironically, from the US. There may even be a degree of direct but covert support to the Taliban from the US as incentive for the Taliban to better control ISIS in

Afghanistan. All this while the Taliban are joined at the hip with Al-Qaeda.

The danger looming in the future for India is whether Pakistan, in league with this nation of terrorists, will seek to engage and destabilise India, first in an insurgency over Kashmir, or elsewhere. Also important for India, once again, is the reliability of America as India's friend in the event of major terrorist activity against India, especially if that activity has the fingerprints of Pakistan all over it.

THE EMERGENCE OF A BIPARTISAN ANTI-WAR COALITION AND THE FUTURE OF AMERICAN ENGAGEMENT IN THE REGION

America's current leadership is fearful of speaking hard truths—whether in Ukraine or the Middle East, or even in the Indo-Pacific—and this incapacity at the top is fuelling a new anti-war strain in American politics at home and perceived weakness by adversaries and fence-sitters abroad. The isolationist Right and the progressive Left are both proposing the equivalent of submitting to adversaries in the current two 'shooting wars'. The Right seeks to leave Ukraine to its own devices vs the Russia–Iran–China axis and the Left is opposed to a complete Israeli victory over the Hamas, Iran–Russia–China axis, which would mean a continuation of the Iran/Hamas threat to Israel and the US.

India must be assiduously aware of isolationist tendencies in the US today.

On one side, led to a large extent by an oft-quoted American on Russian Television (RT), ex-talk-show host Tucker Carlson and his Republican colleagues on the hard Right, America is experiencing a movement chillingly reminiscent of the original isolationist 'America Firsters' of the late 1930s.³ Those isolationists were silenced only after Pearl Harbor and Hitler's subsequent declaration of war against the US four days later. Such a scenario to wake up the isolationists seems far-fetched today.

Allowing an increasingly fascist Russia to defeat America's ally, Ukraine, essentially our proxy, would lead to an autocratic Russia's domination of Europe. It would be a major victory for the axis and a disaster for America, Europe and Israel in the Middle East. It would surely not be in the best interests of democratic India because of Russia's near-existential relationship with China.

On the other side of the political spectrum, the progressive Left, the base of the Democratic Party these days, is supporting the Palestinian cause while failing to acknowledge the atrocities of Hamas, a proxy of America's enemy and axis partner, Iran. Progressive American demonstrators against Israel are allied with students and Muslim-American groups of all origins, particularly young people from the Middle East and South Asia who are studying in the US. Their demonstrations appear to be well-organised and funded. By the axis perhaps? Certainly via massive global disinformation campaigns conducted by Russia and China.⁴ Demonstrators are disrupting movement in our major cities and pushing hard for the Biden administration to pressurise and deter Israel in its war against axis Iran's proxy, Hamas. The situation is even worse in the UK.

The defeat of Israel by virtue of a Hamas still standing would be a victory for Islamic extremism all over the world and that, of course, includes India.

Such demonstrations in Europe by large numbers of unassimilated Muslims and Muslim students aligned with Progressives seek to limit Israel's effort to put an end to Hamas and pacify Gaza. This is also true in America where the party of the present administration covets the Muslim vote in a closely contested presidential race.

The Ayatollahs and the Iranian Revolutionary Guard Corps (IRGC) are the brains, bank and arms depot for its octopus-like military and political proxy forces in the Middle East. Iran funds Hamas, Hezbollah, the Houthis, etc.

As a result of axis collaboration, thousands of Iranian-made drones, now being manufactured in Russia, are wreaking havoc over Ukraine. Iran's drones are killing our (actually) Ukrainian proxies on behalf of Russia. Axis junior partner, North Korea's seemingly endless supply of missiles and, particularly, artillery shells are being used by Russia to attack Ukrainian targets and kill Ukrainians. North Korea empowers China.

And perhaps soon we'll be seeing more sophisticated Iranian of North Korean-produced ballistic missiles not only over Ukraine but Israel too. Iranian missiles, given to their Iranian-trained and led Houthis proxies, are currently attacking global shipping in the Red Sea and Israel as well. America's response to date has been 'proportional' and the Houthis continue their attacks, yet undeterred.

ISRAEL: AMERICA'S ANCHOR IN THE MIDDLE EAST AND INDIA'S LONG-STANDING FRIEND

Israel has been America's permanent foothold in the Middle East for three quarters of a century. Israelis are a well-armed, economically strong, freedom-loving people who hold values similar to democratic nations. Israel is the free-world's best forward operating base (FOB) in that part of the world. Having abandoned (a legacy of the present Administration) major

FOBs in Afghanistan—Shindand, virtually on the Iranian border and Bagram, a short flight to a strategic region of China—the geostrategic impact of the loss of these bases is perhaps greatest for India.

Israel's war is America's and the free-world's war as it boils down to a war against radical Islam, be it Sunni or Shia, aligned with axis partners. Israel must prevail decisively, which means the elimination of terrorist Hamas as a military and political force in Gaza or the West Bank. The same is true for Ukraine prevailing over axis partner, Russia. Yet, both those outcomes are being vigorously impeded by the progressive American Left and the isolationist Right, respectively.

UKRAINE AND ISRAEL ARE FIGHTING AXIS TYRANNIES

In Ukraine, make no mistake, Ukrainians fighting and dying in their struggle against Putin's aggression means that Americans and other Europeans won't have to. America's and Europe's defence dollars invested in Ukraine are a deterrence as America and NATO, at some point, need not directly fight an axis-backed Russia with designs on changing the map of the European continent. Russia's support for Hamas is strong, and not just via Iran, as presented in a thorough Middle East Institute (MEI) analysis in November 2023.[5] It should be sobering to all as it provides further evidence of an axis aligned in a war against Israel, America and democratic values worldwide.

America finances Ukraine's defence of their homeland so that the homelands of crucial NATO allies are not threatened with attack (read Estonia, Lithuania and Latvia, small nations, all of whom share borders with Russia). Poland shares a 250 mile border with Putin satellite, Belarus, a country that served as the launch pad for Putin's invasion of Ukraine. In the event of a Putin victory in Ukraine, far more American troops than now would have to be deployed to a potential European battle zone. Those Americans could become directly embroiled in a war with Russia if NATO's Article 5 were to be activated. At that point, America and the West, needing to invest far greater resources in Europe, would have to diminish their capacity to engage in the Indo-Pacific, thus strengthening the hand of China. Not a good look for India.

ASSESSING THE IMPACT OF AMBIVALENCE

If Americans are concerned about expenditures in the Ukraine and Israel wars right now, we need to consider what we might have to spend above and beyond our present support, should Russia achieve dominance in Europe and Islamists and axis partner Iran triumph over Israel in the Middle East.

A setback, read a perceived surrender to Putin in Ukraine, would not only be an historic defeat on the European continent but also a major defeat in the Free World's larger war with the Russia–Iran–China axis. Likewise, the survival of Islamic extremist and axis proxy Hamas as a political and military force would not only be a major defeat for America and her allies in the Middle East but be seen as a blow to American leadership worldwide.

China is watching the outcomes in Ukraine and the Middle East closely as it ponders how best to take Taiwan. Iran benefits if axis partner Russia succeeds in Ukraine and vice versa if Iran succeeds in the Middle East.[6] Again, *it's one war*. Historically, the axis has a strong communist connection to Russia and China, beginning with the KGB inventing Palestinian terrorism in the region in the 1960s.[7] Interesting that Hamas's governing body has a 'Politburo', a creation of communist Russia. The axis is following Lenin's words, 'You probe with bayonets, if you find mush, you push. If you find steel, you withdraw.'

Presently, India is appropriately staying out of the wars in Ukraine and the Middle East as it seeks to build its economy and its own military capacity. India needs to counter an aggressive China, and a Pakistan that's ever more dependent on China, economically and otherwise. India's military has started to wean itself away from its traditional arms supplier, Russia, but still deeply dependent on its Russian-built military equipment and Russian energy. Thus, democratic India is engaged in a delicate dance with axis partners Iran and Russia over energy purchases and arms supplies, respectively, while axis partner China finances the wars of both those autocratic allies.

Over time, Indian democracy is threatened by axis autocracy, particularly a China that uses a weaker Russia as its 'gas station' and raw materials depot. The axis's embrace of powerful Islamic extremist elements also does not bode well for a democratic, largely Hindu nation. A big problem for the democratic world is that America seems to be losing its taste for global leadership, militarily, and has started energy-disarming, while China pushes its global reach everywhere it can.

Rather than investing in defence and deterrence, America and the West are pouring trillions of dollars into green energy that has registered zero impact on climate thus far and is unlikely to change the trajectory of global temperature and climate. Human-caused climate change is also a very debatable scientific presumption backed up by significant scientific research, despite what climate alarmists believe.

Most importantly perhaps, given the role of money as a deciding feature of the human landscape, the West has created a vast environmental–industrial–media–academic complex where enormous taxpayer- or deficit-funded government subsidies are driving investment away from fossil fuels and into production in green energy. That focus on green, while downgrading fossil fuel production and investment across the board, has the potential to deindustrialise the West while providing little or no impact on the climate. The process has already started in Western Europe as its industry moves to more fossil fuel/energy-friendly countries and America, absurdly, is modelling its own transition to 'green' after Europe's. This while the rest of the world craves fossil fuel energy to feed their people and develop and run their industries, economies and militaries.[8]

Green energy may well turn out to be the biggest self-inflicted blunder the West has ever made as energy is the lifeblood of modern societies and giving it up so cavalierly, so ideologically, is committing a form of national suicide.[9] It is imperative that India does NOT follow in the West's footsteps.

Author's climate change aside: *'Virtue signal' if you so wish, India. Take all the free money the West might throw at you, India. Build solar and wind capacity but only where it makes economic sense, India. Finally, stay true to scientific, economic and national security reality, India, and resist mightily the political pressures to conform with the West's (in reality, unsubstantiated) climate change ideology.*

Meanwhile, the autocracies end up producing oil, gas and coal for the whole world, not only growing their wealth but enhancing their influence, authority and military power in the process.

China is by far the leading example of vast consumption of fossil fuels regardless of what climate change proponents are advocating.[10] India, greatly dependent on coal and other imported fossil fuels would emasculate itself by following a green energy agenda.

In the nuclear age, major powers avoid direct confrontation and fight their wars via proxies. These are real wars, nonetheless, and have similar consequential global outcomes to the full-on wars of the past. Currently, there has been no effective communication within the West that there is a real ongoing war with the Russia–Iran–China axis, a war that will define the legacies of present and successor global leadership and the nations they represent. What will be India's role?

The good news is that through policies of Peace Through Strength, America and its allies can reverse the current weakening of the West vs the axis. India should do all in its power to follow those same policies, of Peace Through Strength, in league with the West or not, and by example encourage the democratic world to follow suit.[11] Given its size, human resources and its growing strength economically and militarily, there is definitely a leadership role in the world, indeed a necessary one, for India to play as it navigates future global uncertainties.

Don Ritter served fourteen years in Congress on the Energy & Commerce and Science & Technology Committees, was Ranking Member on the Congressional Helsinki Commission, founding Co-Chair of the Baltic States-Ukraine Caucus, founding Co-Chairman of the Congressional Task on Afghanistan. He was a National Academy of Science Exchange Fellow in the USSR during the Vietnam War and speaks fluent Russian. He is Trustee Emeritus of the Victims of Communism Memorial Foundation, Trustee and President & CEO Emeritus of the Afghan American Chamber of Commerce. Dr Ritter presently publishes on the issue of world power and how it relates to fossil fuels and climate change. He holds a doctorate in science from MIT.

NOTES

1. Muyu Xu, 'Explainer: Iran's Expanding Oil Trade with Top Buyer China', *Reuters*, 10 November 2023, https://www.reuters.com/markets/commodities/irans-expanding-oil-trade-with-top-buyer-china-2023-11-10/.
2. Don Ritter, 'Total Withdrawal from Afghanistan: Two Years Later', *The Sunday Guardian*, 24 September 2023, https://sundayguardianlive.com/investigation/total-withdrawal-from-afghanistan-two-years-later.
3. Mary Ilyushina, 'Tucker Carlson finds a new booster: Russian TV', *The Washington Post*, 25 September 2023, https://www.washingtonpost.com/world/2023/09/25/tucker-carlson-takes-dubbing-debut-russia-show/.
4. Steven Lee Myers and Sheera Frenkel, 'In a Worldwide War of Words, Russia, China and Iran Back Hamas', *The New York Times*, 3 November 2023, https://www.nytimes.com/2023/11/03/technology/israel-hamas-information-war.html.
5. Jonathan M. Winer, Essential Questions about the Russia–Hamas Link: The Evidence and Its Implications', Middle East Institute, 28 November 2023, https://www.mei.edu/publications/essential-questions-about-russia-hamas-link-evidence-and-its-implications.
6. Simon Watkins, 'Russia And Iran Finalize 20-Year Deal That Will Change The Middle East Forever', Oilprice.come, 22 January 2024, https://oilprice.com/Energy/Energy-General/Russia-And-Iran-Finalize-20-Year-Deal-That-Will-Change-The-Middle-East-Forever.html.

7. Ion Mihai Pacepa, 'The KGB Man', *Wall Street Journal*, 22 September 2023, https://www.wsj.com/articles/SB106419296113226300.
8. Mark P. Mills, 'The Energy to Prevent and Prosecute Wars', *City Journal*, 12 March 2024, https://www.city-journal.org/article/the-energy-to-prevent-and-prosecute-wars.
9. https://www.post-gazette.com/opinion/guest-columns/2023/12/29/cop28-climate-change-china-india-coal-oil/stories/202312290014.
10. Don Ritter, 'China Scorns Biden's Climate Agenda', *The National Interest*, 28 October 2023, https://nationalinterest.org/feature/china-scorns-biden%E2%80%99s-climate-agenda-207087.
11. Corban Teague and Daniel Twining, 'How the U.S. Can Deter and Defeat the Axis of Autocracy', *National Review*, 23 January 2024, https://www.nationalreview.com/2024/01/how-the-u-s-can-deter-and-defeat-the-axis-of-autocracy/.

Vasudhaiva Kutumbakam
India and the World

SAMIR SARAN

Perhaps the greatest legacy of the Western philosophical tradition is the idea of 'dichotomy', a legacy which finds its most distilled expression in the teachings of Manicheanism. A major world religion and philosophical force in the first centuries of the Common Era, Manicheanism spoke of a strictly dualistic world-view, with the fundamental struggle between good and evil at the very core of its cosmology. Owing to the proliferation of this strand of thought, at the cost of other Oriental traditions (including the Indic tradition), it has almost become a natural tendency of the human mind across much of the world to think in terms of opposites. That quintessential contrast between good and evil continues to animate some of the deepest narratives undergirding contemporary societies. Subjective vs objective, explicit vs implicit, external vs internal: the human psyche is shaped by these divisions.

    This legacy is both a gift and a curse. A proclivity for taxonomy lends itself to structured thought, which can be highly productive. Yet, too often, contradictions coerce our thinking into either side of the divide. Too often, the insidious dichotomy of us vs them—you are either one of us or one of them—transforms the world into a battlefield. The service of the self must now necessarily be at the expense of the other. The world is now conceptualised as a zero-sum game. This is the curse of Manichean duality.

One cogent example of this false dichotomy is the rupture between the national and the international. On the one hand, policies that benefit the nation are seen as inimical to internationalism and are accordingly labelled protectionist, conservative, insular and exclusive. On the other hand, states that contribute to global causes are perceived by their citizens as undermining national interests. In such a divisive milieu, how can collectives serve both the immediate and the beyond?

The most potent antidote to this dilemma is the philosophical tradition of 'Advaita Vedanta'. The notion of Advaita, literally translating to non-duality and thus representing the very negation of Manicheanism, collapses all dichotomies by emphasising the unity of all that is real. This powerful notion is distilled in the phrase 'Vasudhaiva Kutumbakam' ('the world is one family'), which stands as a testament to the inherent unity of humankind and the planet we call Earth. Through the practice of this principle, in the past decade, India has shown the world that there is no dichotomy or contradiction between nationalism and internationalism.

By adopting 'Vasudhaiva Kutumbakam' as the theme of India's G20 presidency, the country espoused to the world the deep-seated belief that a nation's ability to serve the planet and wider humankind is only bolstered when it helps its own citizens first. That within the service of the local lies a solution for the universal. That nationalist policymaking can coexist with and, indeed, complement internationalist thinking. That harmonising the local with the global is an imperative in the twenty-first century world. The regional and the global together comprise the constituency that must be addressed by global governance and its institutions.

A RADICAL NEW NATIONALISM

In our times, 'elitist' cosmopolitanism and 'parochial' nationalism are in an ostensibly irreconcilable conflict. By dismissing either of the two as pejoratives or as undesirable, we risk forgetting lessons of history.

In the twentieth century, nationalism and the evocation of national consciousness were crucial to freedom struggles in nations across the world, not least in India. The quest for political self-determination and independence from colonial rule flowed from this ethic. On the other hand, the battle against the depletion of the ozone layer, the creation of global trading arrangements that facilitated the growth of developing economies, the investment into entities such as the Bretton Woods Institutions, the United Nations and the World Trade Organization—these endeavours were undertaken through internationalist thought processes, which in turn were largely motivated by national interests and ambitions. The reality of the past century puts paid to any notion of a confrontation between the two.

For India, this is a moment of deeper reflection. Today, the nation is seventy-six years free and has overthrown the shackles of foreign rule. It may seem that the need for nationalist thinking is past. Think again! Political self-determination and self-rule are but one step in exiting the colonial era. The second and more important step is the creation of an identity, one that is truly independent of the coloniser, determined by the self, consistent and culturally contextual. It requires shedding the identity that has been groomed by the colonial elite and tamed to adhere to the assessments, attitudes and values of the coloniser. In other words, the decolonisation of political geography must be followed by the decolonisation of identity, approach and ethic.

How to decolonise the mind? This question has engaged the brightest minds in the discipline of post-colonialism since the pathbreaking Francophone Afro-Caribbean political philosopher Frantz Fanon observed in 1952 that centuries of colonial subjugation and cultural infantilisation have served to shatter and splinter the self-image of the colonised, leaving them with an inferiority complex correlated to the superiority complex in the coloniser.[1] Putting it succinctly, in 1957, French-Tunisian theorist Albert Memmi theorised that the period of colonisation does not end with the mere cessation of physical subjugation; there is still the need to decolonise the mind.[2] Gayatri Chakravorty Spivak takes this argument forward by (re)introducing the vocabulary of the 'subaltern' into the discipline.[3] This rich intellectual heritage has been carried on by the likes of Nobel laureate Amartya Sen, who argues that the native's viewing of themselves and their cultures through the coloniser's prism of prejudice is one of the most dehumanising legacies of the colonial period.[4]

The world has yet to reckon with the challenge and reality of breaking free from the tyranny of colonial thinking. In the case of India, while the political project of self-rule was achieved in 1947, the social project of decolonisation was not. In many ways, the colonial elite was replaced by a native elite—trained, educated, and incubated in the institutions and in the image of the colonisers. And the aspiration of the masses remained one of assimilation to a colonial ideal.

Scrutinising the project of Indian independence reveals yet another reality: the processes of the freedom struggle largely remained an elitist affair, distant from vast sections of society. This continued into post-Independence India, with the majority consigned to the right to vote once every five years, without being allowed the agency to express their disapproval and disagreement at any other point of time.

The past decade has been different. It has been instrumental in allowing India to break out of this past and move on from its colonial hangover. New India's emergence has been on the back of unprecedented mass participation—loud and argumentative—on the role, identity, spirit and ethic of the larger project of nation-building. Beyond all the cacophony and the noise, what sustains India today is the polyphonic national consensus, which is always dynamic and evolving, contested and debated.

Through all of this, we have finally begun to forge a truly Indian path. As the title of this volume identifies, the past ten years have seen an Indian Renaissance, with the revival of Indian ideas, modes of philosophical thinking and ways of being. Indigenous knowledge and native customs are being brought into the foreground and coupled with modern learning and scientific sensibilities. Indian modernity is being shaped by our heritage.

We are inculcating confidence in our culture—our languages, dress and food. We are throwing off the shackles of Western cultural hegemony to use Gramsci's turn of phrase. The project of 'Atmanirbhar Bharat' is a plan of economic development; it is also an endeavour to build national self-confidence, both at home and abroad. And regardless, any project that serves one-sixth of all humanity is bound to be a global endeavour.

We are asking ourselves basic questions. Why must Indian ideation be limited by an alien grammar? If academic papers can be written in a European language, spoken by a mere handful of people compared to the population of India, why can't they be written in our native tongues? Why must Indian attire be diminished with the pejorative 'ethnic' when its strength in numbers and the period of its use privilege it against Western modes of dress? Why must Indian formal attire, rooted in a storied legacy that is more than 6,000 years old, be seen as inferior to the Western suit, born on a small island off the western coast of Europe less than 400 years ago?

A NEW (INTER)NATIONALIST PARADIGM

India has worked to collapse the dichotomy between the national and the international. Its efforts at home to inoculate against Western cultural hegemony have resonated with nations across the world. Fortunately, the hegemony achieved and consolidated by a select few is finally loosening its grip. The models—of thought, language, dress, food, even dominant schools of economics and politics—propagated by the hegemon are now being scrutinised.

Because the truth is out: yesterday's world order lies in ruins. Self-appointed guardians of the international order and established multilateral frameworks are either unequipped to respond or unable to deliver. The multilateral status quo was codified in the post-War twentieth century and last reformed at the height of the Cold War. Originally designed for the narrow goal of maintaining peace, these frameworks are not adequately equipped to deal with the interconnected and octopoid problems of the twenty-first century—an existential climate crisis, disruptive technological innovation, global supply chain vulnerability, a pandemic of polarisation, threats to global health, all in addition to the time-old issue of war and peace.

On top of this, three interconnected trends are visible today. First, it is true that globalisation has benefited many, creating unprecedented wealth and prosperity. Yet, the processes at play have been uneven and patchy. It has served a billion people well, but the other seven still seek its benefits. For the latter, the promise of globalisation has yet to be kept, betraying the Global South's aspirations of a better, more equitable world. Second, the nations most invested in these global frameworks, the architects of globalisation as we know it, appear to have divested from its perpetuation and upkeep. The fact is that these very nations are today its most egregious violators. And finally, the legitimacy of the institutions governing globalisation lies in tatters. Reform alone will not be enough: what we need is re-formation. Re-formation of management boards to be more inclusive and more dynamic with respect to geographies, demographics and economies.

In short, globalisation needs new protagonists and a new script.

Look around. A new world is dawning. The world as we know it is changing, and global leadership is changing in tandem. New actors are stepping into the global arena with new models of leadership. India is finally taking its rightful seat at the table.

India has emerged as the new global voice that internationalism sorely needs, providing a fresh template for what twenty-first-century (inter)nationalism should look like. Indian foreign policy has made a conscious effort to collapse the dichotomy. Through its G20 presidency, the country strove to do just this by foregrounding the concerns of the Global South. The inclusion of the African Union—a salve and necessary corrective to the elitist admission of the European Union into the grouping—was a step towards building an inclusive and equitable world order. This Indian conviction is also reflected in the creation of the Voice of Global South Summit, a platform to deliberate on the concerns and priorities of the people left behind by yesterday's globalisation, exchange ideas and solutions, and foster a sense of purpose in building unity and consensus.

There was no incongruence in hosting the G20 Summit and the Voice of the Global South Summit within a span of weeks, each bringing its own contribution to what the world at large sought. As a matter of fact, there were synergies to this approach. The Voice of the Global South added heft and purpose to the G20, legitimising the demands for sustainable development that was at the heart of India's G20 presidency. And the democratisation of the entire process, by taking it to the people and making it participatory by design, bridged the gap between global governance and the globally governed. India's approach to the G20 may be a harbinger of Indian foreign policy in the days ahead.

NATIONALISM AND INTERNATIONALISM

India is certainly among the leaders ushering in an era of fairer re-globalisation. It is a key international actor that has embraced the idea of bearing responsibility for shaping global governance for the future. The nation is bringing the patience of an ancient civilisation, the aspirations of a young population, and the momentum of 1.6 billion people to a project most vital to humankind in the twenty-first century. This is the spirit of 'Vasudhaiva Kutumbakam': our paths are collective, and everyone must be brought together on this journey.

In sum, nationalism vs internationalism is a false binary. India is a testament to that truth. Whether as a global first responder, a pharmacy to the world, a fountainhead of talent and innovation, a crucial link in the global supply chain or an exporter of digital public infrastructure, India could only serve the world more fully after making strides at home.

The one cannot exist without the other. The dialectic of the two is singularly responsible for offering a kaleidoscope of perspectives from different corners of the world. It ensures that homogeneity—of path, pathway and approach—never undermines heterogeneity and diversity, the two values that humankind must celebrate above all else.

Samir Saran is President, Observer Research Foundation (ORF).

NOTES

1. Frantz Fanon, *Black Skin, White Masks*, translated by Charles Lam Markmann, Paladin, London, 1970.
2. Albert Memmi, *The Colonizer and the Colonized*, translated by Howard Greenfeld, Profile Books, London, 2021.
3. Gayatri Chakravorty Spivak, 'Can the Subaltern Speak?', in

Cary Nelson and Lawrence Grossberg (eds), *Marxism and the Interpretation of Culture,* Macmillan, London, 1988.
4. Amartya Sen, *The Idea of Justice,* Penguin, Delhi, 2009.

The Disruptor vs the Inheritors

PRIYA SAHGAL

The rules of engagement were set down by Prime Minister Narendra Modi during the 2014 Lok Sabha campaign, as he wove the narrative of the humble chaiwala taking on the pedigreed dynast. This was even before he reached New Delhi. He pitched himself as the 'outsider' who was battling the 'establishment', a sort of David vs the UPA's Goliath. The mood of the nation, fed by various corruption scandals involving the government of the day, swung towards this champion of change. Here was a non-dynast, someone who had worked his way up the ladder, a kaamdar not a naamdar. Plus, he didn't have a bloodline waiting in the wings for the spoils of office. He was clearly the game-changer, the anathema of everything Congress. The 2014 election was won by the 'idea of Modi' and all that he represented; the 2019 election was won on the 'reality of Modi' and all that he delivered. And 2024 will be contested on the 'belief in Modi' and all that the people believe he can do.

The Modi era is clearly here to stay, and Indian politics has never seen this before. However, the makeover did not happen in the blink of the Lord's eye. A very systematic dismantling of the old was done to usher in the new. And in doing so, Modi followed one basic truth: permanent change only comes when you raze the existing entities to the ground and replace them with new ones. All other changes are cosmetic. Accordingly, Modi began the process of undoing the Congress way of life by attacking its very foundations.

First, the 'other' had to be named and shamed. The presiding cultural czars, left-leaning liberals, Ivy League-educated socialites and various sponsors of the Gandhi–Nehru ecosystem were labelled the elites of Lutyens' Delhi. The categorisation was not just geographical, it was also stratospherical. Apart from occupying spacious government bungalows, the Lutyens' elite also represented a way of life that took its cues from the West rather than from within India. It was with great glee that Modi told the media that he had come to power despite the Lutyens' Delhi elite and the Khan Market gang. He was not wrong.

History books are being rewritten and new statues being built. The strategy is fairly simple: eradicate anything that reeks of the Colonial Raj or that commemorates the Muslim marauders who destroyed our temples. And eclipse any markers that glorify the Nehru–Gandhis.

The Nehru Memorial Museum and Library Society has since been renamed and reworked as the more egalitarian Prime Ministers' Museum and Library Society. Subhas Chandra Bose's statue now stands proudly under the canopy at India Gate, which was once occupied by a marble statue of King George V. Chhatrapati Shivaji now has more chapters in history textbooks than Aurangzeb. And Sardar Patel is now getting way more plaudits than Jawaharlal Nehru. To cut a long story short, it is a narrative where Modi's Bharat is pitched against Nehru's India—one that finds its nationalism within its borders against the 'inter-nationalism' of the other. It is ironic that it was Rahul Gandhi who had earlier pitched this narrative of India vs Bharat when he first began his Discovery of India tours. That divide still exists only in the Modi era, but it is Bharat that is at the centre stage while India is being shoved to the left.

What should worry the Congress leadership more than the symbolism is the actuality of it all. The response that these moves have got from the public at large has shaken the regime at its core. What Modi has done is tapped into layers of resentment that were not so much against Nehru per se, but against projecting him to the extent of excluding all the others who had been part of the freedom struggle. There was resentment at the fact that the same set of people occupied seats of power in Lutyens' Delhi—decade after decade—passing on whatever mantle they had to their children without giving anyone else an entry point. There was resentment at the fact that while Marxist and left-leaning governments were being overthrown all over the globe, India was still hostage to comrades who barely ruled over one and half of our states. There was resentment at the fact that minority communities were being appeased at the cost of the majority whether it was Haj subsidies or the fact that the Ram Janmabhoomi did not have a temple to house the Lord's idol. There was resentment at the fact that the people of Jammu and Kashmir had a special law in place that gave locals certain rights over 'outsiders' who were also Indians. There was resentment at the fact that Western philosophers and religious texts were quoted more often than Chanakya, Vivekananda and the Gita.

There was resentment that the Congress didn't even know existed but Modi was quick to tap into as he weaved a narrative of change and promised to usher in the Amrit Kaal, or the Golden Age. This Golden Age has a newly minted soul that comes with a cabinet stamp of approval. Two days after the Ram Janmabhoomi Temple inauguration on 22 January 2024, the Union Cabinet adopted a resolution stating that while 'the body of the country attained independence' in 1947, the 'Pran Pratishtha of its soul was done on 22 January 2024'.

Every text has a context and to fully comprehend Modi's narrative one has to juxtapose it with the alternative worldview. With the Congress seats reduced to double digits—and falling—in the 2014 and 2019 elections, it is clear that the old order doesn't have too many takers. What can they offer to the voters to woo them away from Modi's promised Amrit Kaal? The Congress under Rahul Gandhi has toyed with its version of a softer, gentler Hinduism but that failed to take off. Now, after the inauguration of the temple at Ayodhya, it will be even more difficult to outperform Modi's image as the Hindu Hriday Samrat.

Perhaps realising this, Rahul has also ventured into the politics of caste, reviving the old Mandal vs Kamandal debate. However, it is regional parties like the Samajwadi Party (SP) and the Rashtriya Janata Dal (RJD) that make for more credible champions for the OBCs than the Congress. As expected, the Congress did not find too many takers for its promise of a caste survey in the Madhya Pradesh, Rajasthan and Chhattisgarh Assembly polls in December 2023.

If you recall, it were the allegations of corruption that were the last nail in the UPA's coffin. The aam aurat lost faith in the Dr Manmohan Singh government as a series of alleged scams hit the headlines, beginning with the *Volcker Report* (2005), the Commonwealth Games scam (2010), the allocation of 2G spectrum and coal blocks (2008), the Indian Premier League Kochi franchise controversy (2010), the Adarsh Housing Society scam (2011) and the Railways appointment scandal (2013). Most of these remained as allegations, with jail terms for only A. Raja and Kanimozhi for the 2G scam and Suresh Kalmadi for the Commonwealth Games scandal. Yet, the minute each of these allegations came to light, the then UPA Chairperson Sonia Gandhi demanded that those accused submit their resignations. As a result, Natwar Singh, D. Raja, Kanimozhi, Shashi Tharoor, Pawan Bansal and Ashwani Kumar lost their cabinet berths while Maharashtra chief minister Ashok Chavan had to step down. The irony is that most of these allegations never even made it to the courts as the investigators could not find anything to back the allegations. As for those that did, most were given a clean chit by the courts like in the 2G case.

But by then the damage was done. The Opposition was quick to label the UPA's second term as 'the most corrupt regime'. Their charge stuck as it was backed by the optics—the spate of resignations and the trial by media. Add to the fact that by its second term the UPA government had lost steam and failed to implement any big idea or reform that had characterised its earlier stint. That's the problem, if you don't have a charismatic leadership then you need to deliver on governance. But the UPA 2 was so overwhelmed battling charges of corruption that it lost control over everything else.

This is one lesson learnt well by Modi's BJP. Control the narrative. Accordingly, it will never admit to any scandal or be the face of bad news. Soon after Modi took office, the Vyapam scam involving Shivraj Singh Chauhan, the then Madhya Pradesh chief minister, hit the headlines in 2015. But despite pressure from the Opposition, no resignation was sought and the allegations soon faded away as the media moved on to another story. This template was set during the first few months of the Modi regime as were the optics that there are no (admitted) scams under Modi's watch. As a former cabinet minister from the Congress once commented, 'We all were victims of a heightened sense of Christian morality.' If Sonia Gandhi had not demanded resignations at the whiff of a scandal and waited for law to take its own course, would the UPA have been so scam-tainted in the public imagination? There is politics, and then there is realpolitik.

It is not that the Opposition has not tried to pin something on the PM. During the 2019 elections, the Congress tried to question the government over the 2016 Rafale deal with France. But there were few takers for Rahul Gandhi's cry of *chowkidar chor hai*—the guard is a thief—that he raised against the PM. That is Modi's biggest asset. His credibility. No matter what the Opposition may claim, the public at large trusts the PM implicitly. Even during the ill-conceived demonetisation or with the no-notice lockdown that led to the long march of the migrants, there were no recriminations. U*nki neeyat theek hai*— his intentions are honourable—was the dominant reaction. This and the fact that Modi has no family living with him in the prime minister's house, to benefit from any alleged 'corruption'. And so, the same people who stood in long lines to get access to their own money and trudged for days without food or water to get back to their families still voted for Modi in the elections that followed.

Does this mean that we are soon heading for an Opposition-mukt Bharat, an Opposition-free Bharat? It would be pertinent to recall that the BJP got only 37.4 per cent of the vote share in 2019, while the Congress got 19.5 per cent. Around 62.6 per cent of India did not vote for the BJP. That is a huge chunk that the Opposition can reach out to. But first it needs a credible narrative to counter the idea of Modi, because that is fast becoming the BJP's sole USP. With elections getting more and more presidential in nature, the pressure is all the more on the Opposition to find a face to counter the current PM. And clearly Rahul Gandhi doesn't quite cut it. Then who?

The optimists within the Opposition hark back to the 1977 elections where a strong leader like Indira Gandhi was defeated by a faceless coalition. The vote at the time was not in favour of the Janata alliance, as it was against the Congress. This was a vote against a leader who had gone from strong to dictatorial and imposed Emergency. The Congress was defeated not by Morarji Desai but by Indira Gandhi. Does the same apply to Narendra Modi? He himself stated very famously in a television interview on the eve of the 2019 elections, 'I am the issue.' He was the issue then, and the same works for the 2024 Lok Sabha polls. The Ram Janmabhoomi temple will not be the issue; neither will be the caste census or the economy or anything else. The vote will be for or against Modi. And the way things stand, he hasn't yet crossed over to the dark side. In the public's imagination, the PM is seen as strong, not dictatorial. (As an aside, it is interesting that when we compare Modi to former prime ministers, the one that comes to mind is not the BJP's Atal Bihari Vajpayee but Congress's Indira Gandhi. In fact, Vajpayee was more in the Nehruvian mode, but that's a conversation for another day.)

Then should the Opposition just pack up, or do a Nitish Kumar and fold into the BJP? Even if there is no predominant face, there is still a fight out there. Moreover, the BJP is yet to conquer the south. The Opposition's task is two-fold. First, identify the issues to be raised. (Steer clear of Hindutva—you cannot defeat the BJP on its home turf. However, what the Congress does need is a consistent Ayodhya policy. It needs to figure out if it is still apologising for the Babri Masjid demolition or celebrating the construction of the Ram Temple. Thanks to the courts it can do both, but it has to get the articulation right. Temple hopping in between visits to random masjids doesn't quite cut it.) And the second must have is consistent and credible messaging. It has to take back the narrative from the BJP.

That's easier said than done. Look at the way Modi controls the headlines. Take, for instance, August 2023 when the INDIA bloc got together with much fanfare and optimism. It had coined just the right name to counter BJP's jingo nationalism, and the mood at the alliance's meeting in Mumbai was fairly euphoric. They were talking seat-sharing and going to pick a convenor. The media was giving them adequate play. Then suddenly Modi dropped a bombshell by announcing a session of the parliament in mid-September. Not only did this distract the media but the entire meeting got hijacked as the Opposition began discussing simultaneous polls and early elections. For the next fortnight, the entire country debated 'One Nation, One Election', only to have the Women's Reservation Bill on the table when the new parliament met. As for the Opposition, the move to appoint a convenor got pushed back by six months. It was only in January 2024 that Congress president Mallikarjun Kharge was appointed INDIA bloc convenor.

Another example of how Modi outplayed the Opposition is the demand for a caste survey. The minute the Opposition raised this demand, pitching the Mandal vs the BJP's Kamandal plank, the PM came up with his own four caste formula—women, youth, poor and the annadatas, the farmers. But, as a safety net he also poached the INDIA bloc's caste mascot, Janata Dal (United) [JD(U)] leader and Bihar chief minister Nitish Kumar, who had initiated the demand for the caste survey. While the INDIA bloc was busy underplaying Nitish Kumar's loss, the news came that another ally Jayant Chaudhary, a Rashtriya Lok Dal (RLD) leader, had tied up with the BJP.

Not only is the BJP reaching out to the Opposition allies, it is also poaching Congress icons that the party has ignored. Take the Bharat Ratna for former PM P.V. Narasimha Rao, a Congress leader who has been since ignored by his own party. The Congress, which should have celebrated the achievement that it was under Narasimha Rao that India ushered in the era of liberalisation and game-changing economic reforms, has only focused on the shame that it was during his regime that the Babri Masjid was demolished.

With Modi's BJP, expect the unexpected. Over the last decade, cabinet reshuffles are being done without the media having a clue as to who is being sworn in. The concerned ministers don't know themselves till the very last minute. This was not the case during the UPA where the converse was true, with cabinet ministers lobbying with 'journalists with access'. Today, access is given only on a need-to-know basis. Communication in the Modi government is only one way: it is pretty much one man's *'mann ki baat'*. 'Godi media' is an aspirational terminology, for the PM is not wooing the media; it is some within the media who are auditioning for the role.

It is this juggernaut that the Opposition has to stonewall if it wants to win back the mandate. Incidentally, even before the 2024 elections were announced, the PM raised the game, claiming in parliament that the BJP will win over 370 seats. (It is not just a psephological statement but also a psychological one, reminding the voters of the abrogation of Article 370.) He may or may not get this figure—for let's not forget that the BJP got nowhere near the target of 200 seats set by Amit Shah, cabinet minister for Home Affairs, in the 2021 West Bengal elections. But the bar has been set. Any conversation around the polls will revolve around the 370 mark for the BJP, while the Congress is still struggling to get the public to believe it can make it past double digits. The BJP has its optics ready, with the Ram Janmabhoomi Temple in the backdrop, and the PM with his *'Modi ki guarantee'* in the foreground. As for its campaign strategy—that's easy to access: the username is BJP, but the password is Modi. Can the Congress hack it?

Priya Sahgal is a senior journalist. She is the Editorial Director of NewsX news channel and the author *The Contenders*.

The Catalyst

KARTIKEYA SHARMA

For centuries, Indians have worshipped goddesses in their many avatars, and women in India have been revered and celebrated as powerful political and social figures who ushered in revolutionary changes. *Vande Mataram*, India's national song, imagines Durga as the mother with ten weapons of war.[1] Likewise, the concept of Bharat Mata, which focuses on the mother as the embodiment of the Indian nation, has existed for centuries. However, the concept of women power must not be merely symbolic; it must translate into the empowerment of women through their social, political and economic upliftment. Whether it was the celebrating of the birth centenary of the lesser-known Naga freedom fighter Rani Gaidinliu in August 2015 or the decision to establish a central university in Nagaland in her name, Prime Minister Narendra Modi's vision for women has been to move beyond mere tokenism and symbolism, which characterised the approach of previous governments.[2] Since Independence, while they have had the power to vote, power eluded women for a variety of reasons. Financially independent women were a rarity in the 1950s and 1960s. The primary role of women in traditional Indian society was bearing and rearing children. This approach was largely based on the Victorian notions of chastity and morality, which relegated women to the domestic space outside the purview of the public. The British favoured this approach to keep on their side the orthodox elements, who had a stake in maintaining the status quo. Prime Minister Modi has contributed to disrupting this status quo.

Historically, the narrative around women voters was problematic. They were perceived as passive participants in the electoral process and they would simply follow their husband's voting preferences. However, over the years, the role of women voters in India has undergone a significant transformation. Under PM Modi's leadership, there has been a noticeable shift in how women are perceived—from being seen solely as voters, they are now recognised as individuals with agency and political influence.

In the landscape of global politics, few figures have garnered as much attention as Narendra Modi, the fourteenth Prime Minister of India. Since assuming office in 2014, PM Modi has been synonymous with bold initiatives, and he is known for his unwavering determination to transform India. Central to his agenda is the empowerment of women, recognising their pivotal role in nation-building. He aims to ensure their participation in every sphere of society.

As Narendra Modi said, 'Women are a reflection of ethics, loyalty, decisiveness, and leadership and represent that. That is why our Vedas and tradition have given a call that women should be able and capable of giving direction to the nation.'[3] PM Modi understood that change could not be achieved only through the legislative or the judicial processes, as experience shows that these channels restrict the choices for women and delay necessary reforms. He realised that change could be achieved only through a change in mindsets. One of his first initiatives, the Swachh Bharat Abhiyan and the construction of toilets was aimed at restoring the privacy and dignity of women. Through a combination of targeted programmes, legislative reforms and cultural initiatives, he sought to dismantle barriers and create opportunities for women to thrive. His work in this realm reflects a nuanced understanding of the challenges facing women in India and a commitment to fostering an environment where they can unleash their full potential. It is dictated by an understanding that women voters are a constituency in their own right. This is why PM Modi has chosen to communicate with women voters directly.

Throughout India's political history, the journey of the empowerment of women and their recognition as autonomous individuals has been a complex one, often influenced by the approaches of its leaders, political parties and, of course, prime ministers.

India's first prime minister Jawaharlal Nehru recognised the importance of women as significant voters but often failed to prioritise their rights and agency. Despite Nehru's progressive rhetoric and commitment to social justice, his administration failed to prioritise women's rights as a central tenet of India's democratic project. While Nehru advocated for women's education and participation in the workforce, these initiatives were often overshadowed by broader nation-building agendas. In 1938, a newsletter published by Nehru, titled *Gaidallo Ranee*, recounted his visit to Naga Hills and the folklore and fighting spirit of Gaidinliu Rani.[4] He was more supportive of her because she represented his vision of the unity of India as opposed to the Naga leader A.Z. Phizo.[5] However, while espousing these causes, much remained to be done for the cause of the Nagas and of women leaders like Rani Gaidinliu. The absence of comprehensive policies aimed at addressing gender disparities and empowering women reflects Nehru's limited engagement with the complexities of gender inequality in India. Nehru had a paternalistic approach to the citizens, often viewing them as entities who needed a civilisational push, so he was less inclined to challenge the traditional power structures and advocate for substantive gender equality. Moreover, the composition of the parliament for the first two decades after India became an independent nation was primarily landed interests, zamindars and traditional elements of society who preferred a status quo. While the Government of India Act, 1935 reserved forty-four seats for women in provincial legislatures, only twenty-four women were elected to the parliament in 1952. The perpetuation of male-dominated political institutions and decision-making processes further limited women's access to political power.

Prime Minister Indira Gandhi remains a contentious yet powerful figure in India's political history. Renowned for her strong leadership amidst tumultuous times, her tenure was marked by significant strides in various policy domains. However, a critical examination of her approach towards women's empowerment reveals a paradox: while she championed initiatives like the establishment of the National Commission for Women, her focus often seemed to prioritise rhetoric over recognising women as autonomous individuals. Although she herself earned the nomenclature of Durga after the 1971 Bangladesh Liberation War, Indira Gandhi failed to create other Durgas in the social and political space who could be agents of social change. The social revolution, a precursor to the economic revolution, was wanting in the 1970s and 1980s. Throughout her tenure, Gandhi strategically leveraged women's votes to bolster her political base. Initiatives targeting women, such as the introduction of family planning programmes, the Equal Renumeration Bill, 1976 and the National Commission for Women, were undoubtedly significant. Yet, they were also instrumental in securing political allegiance rather than driven solely by a commitment to women's rights.

Gandhi's Garibi Hatao campaign, launched with optimism and promising poverty eradication, fell short in addressing the specific concerns of youth and women, ultimately failing to resonate with these demographics. While the campaign aimed to uplift the impoverished masses, it lacked a nuanced approach tailored to address the unique challenges faced by women and the youth. It wasn't just the lack of a social change that posed a challenge to women but also a lack of representation in parliament and assemblies, unequal sex ratio, lack of sanitation facilities and complete ignorance of menstrual hygiene. The government also moved towards removing the binaries that existed between the public and private, which were counter-intuitive to the proposed plan of women empowerment. Issues such as the availability of affordable sanitary napkins were considered a women's problem. Therefore, despite their availability being central to women's health, successive governments did not prioritise it.

Despite being a pioneering female leader in a male-dominated political landscape, Gandhi struggled to implement policies that directly tackled the issues of gender inequality and women's access to education and employment opportunities. Similarly, the youth, comprising a significant portion of the population, felt sidelined as her campaign primarily focused on broader economic reforms rather than addressing their specific needs and aspirations. Consequently, the failure to adequately address youth- and women-centric issues led to a lack of appeal among these demographics for the Garibi Hatao campaign, highlighting the importance of inclusivity and targeted policymaking in addressing societal challenges. Gandhi's approach to women's empowerment reflected a dichotomy.

Indira Gandhi was succeeded by her son, Rajiv, who, despite his modern outlook and initiatives for technological advancement, faced challenges in fully connecting with the youth and women during his tenure as prime minister. Rajiv Gandhi had what his predecessors didn't—the mandate of 400 plus seats, a mandate to usher in revolutionary changes. But as Vinay Sitapati argues, Rajiv Gandhi squandered his mandate for narrow and limited advantages.[6]

While Rajiv's reforms, such as the Panchayati Raj system, aimed to promote women's participation in grassroots governance and empowerment, the benefits of these initiatives did not adequately reach or resonate with the youth and women, who often faced socioeconomic barriers to accessing and benefitting from such advancements. Rajiv Gandhi's failure to effectively communicate the relevance of these reforms to these demographics further widened the gap between his vision and their expectations. Additionally, his leadership style and approach may have contributed to the disconnect. One key factor contributing to this disconnect was the Shah Bano case, in which Rajiv Gandhi's government overturned the Supreme Court's decision to grant alimony to a divorced Muslim woman, bowing to pressure from conservative Muslim groups. This decision was perceived as a setback for women's rights and equality, tarnishing Rajiv's image among women who expected him to champion progressive ideals.

After his assassination, political instability ushered in by coalition governments took the focus away from women-centric issues. For instance, the Bill for 33 per cent reservation of seats for women brought up during the tenure of successive governments could not be passed due to lack of political will and the desire for preserving the status quo.

In contrast to his predecessors, some of the initiatives taken by PM Modi have managed to dispel the notion that only women can advocate reforms for women. PM Modi has emerged as an ambassador for women's rights and a champion of the cause of women's increased representation in all spheres.

PM Modi's approach to women's empowerment is characterised by a multifaceted strategy aimed at fostering gender equality and socioeconomic inclusion. Since assuming office, he has launched several initiatives focusing on women's welfare, education and economic participation. He has actively engaged with women and youth through various platforms, including social media, public events and interactive forums. His radio programme *Mann ki Baat* often features stories of women achievers and addresses issues relevant to the youth. Modi's interactions with women and youth extend beyond the rhetoric, as he has consistently sought their input and feedback on policies and programmes through the initiatives of his government. By directly engaging with these demographics, PM Modi has demonstrated a commitment to understanding their concerns and aspirations. Through initiatives like Beti

Bachao, Beti Padhao, Yojana Sukanya Samriddhi, Pradhan Mantri Ujjwala Yojana, Pradhan Mantri Matru Vandana Yojana and Lakhpati Didi Yojana, the Modi government has effectively addressed various aspects of women's empowerment, ranging from education and healthcare to financial independence and skill development. The Beti Bachao, Beti Padhao programme, for instance, has played a pivotal role in increasing awareness about the importance of the girl child and has contributed to improving the literacy rate among girls, especially in states such as Haryana, which are notorious for their unequal sex ratio. Similarly, schemes like Sukanya Samriddhi Yojana and Pradhan Mantri Matru Vandana Yojana have provided financial security to women, thereby alleviating their concerns and empowering them economically. Furthermore, initiatives such as Pradhan Mantri Ujjwala Yojana have directly impacted the health and quality of life of rural women by providing them with clean cooking fuel and programmes like Lakhpati Didi Yojana have equipped women with the necessary skills and resources to become financially independent and enter the business world. These schemes have not only provided women with access to finance and ownership rights but have also challenged traditional gender norms and empowered women to participate in entrepreneurship and politics actively.

Under the leadership of PM Modi, the National Democratic Alliance (NDA) government introduced the historic Muslim Women (Protection of Rights on Marriage) Act, 2019, which criminalised the practice of Triple Talaq, marking a significant milestone in ensuring gender equality and justice for Muslim women. His stance against Triple Talaq, which resonated deeply with millions of Indian women who have suffered its injustices, remained strong. Moreover, the prime minister has carefully dismantled the concept of tokenism on the issue of representation of women as his government's initiatives have been well-thought-out and with an intent to have a lasting impact on the ground. In contrast, in 1986, a year after the Supreme Court mandated that Muslim husbands who gave talaq must provide monthly maintenance to their wives, a decision opposed by Muslim hardliners, Rajiv Gandhi's government reversed the decision through new legislation, prioritising political considerations over the welfare of marginalised communities. Despite opposition labelling the BJP as anti-Muslim, PM Modi's inclusive approach ensures justice and empowerment for all segments of society, including Muslim women, dispelling such perceptions and other accusations. Earlier governments and political leaders abandoned reforms, as they felt that labelling and narrow community considerations would affect their vote bank if reforms were too revolutionary and out of tune with the ideas of the conservative Islamist orthodoxy. This empowered the orthodoxy but delayed reforms for women, who were seen as passive rather than active players in society. The introduction of the Nari Shakti Vandan Adhiniyam (Women's Reservation) Bill in 2023 further underscores Modi government's commitment to gender equality and women's empowerment. His speech in the Lok Sabha while introducing the Bill was telling. He said, 'While the inauguration of the new parliament makes today a historic day, it's the inauguration of the new Nari Shakti Vandan Adhiniyam Bill which makes it even more meaningful. Whenever the new parliament will be discussed, this Bill will also be discussed. Triple Talaq Bill also went through many ups and downs and many women had to wait for justice for a long time. Even when the courts had granted them the rights, their haq or rights eluded them. It is the 17th Lok Sabha which has freed women from triple talaq that has contributed to women empowerment.'[7]

Prime Minister Modi's tenure has indeed been marked by his proactive approach to addressing issues concerning youth, reflecting his visionary leadership. One notable initiative is the Skill India campaign, launched in 2015, aimed at equipping millions of young Indians with the skills necessary to succeed in the modern workforce. Under this programme, numerous skill-development initiatives, including vocational training and apprenticeship programmes, have been implemented, benefitting millions of youth across the country. The prime minister's approach to the youth is informed by the fact that we have the biggest population of young people in the country and this population demographic can be converted into an asset. The New Education Policy was defined to shake up the education system and make it more driven by the demands of the workforce, where education would include practical training with the latest educational tools. Understanding that school-going children must be acquainted with technology, a need was felt to equip the tardy school infrastructure in the towns and villages as well as teacher training programmes towards this end. Rather than considering the youth as something outside the mainstream discourse, PM Modi has brought them right to the centre of the discourse about the nation.

Additionally, the Startup India initiative, inaugurated in 2016, seeks to foster entrepreneurship among the youth by providing them with access to funding, mentorship and regulatory support, thereby nurturing a culture of innovation and enterprise. These initiatives highlight PM Modi's recognition of the pivotal role that the youth will play in driving India's economic growth and development. These initiatives targeted at the youth were encouraged to push them towards entrepreneurship and move away from a culture where majority of Indians saw government jobs as the only form of employment. By empowering them with the tools and opportunities needed to thrive in the twenty-first century, the Modi government has demonstrated its commitment to harness India's demographic dividend for the future. PM Modi's strategic use of technology and social media platforms has revolutionised the way he connects with the youth of India. Through initiatives like *Mann ki Baat* and *Pariksha pe Charcha*, Modi has adopted a conversational and relatable tone, addressing the everyday concerns of young people in a manner that makes him come across as approachable. In all of these initiatives, PM Modi has been a catalyst, leading from the front.

These interactive platforms not only foster a sense of intimacy and belonging but have also managed to break down barriers between the leader and the citizen, presenting PM Modi as a mentor figure who understands the challenges faced by young Indians. Additionally, his engagement with social media influencers and prominent youth icons further amplify his reach and relevance among the younger demographic. Collaborations with influencers for initiatives like Swachh Bharat Abhiyan and women's entrepreneurship have added a relatable touch to government programmes. His interactions with youth icons like cricketer Virat Kohli, the CEO of Humans of Bombay Karishma Mehta, YouTuber Ankit Baiyanpuria and his *Pariksha pe Charcha* series with school children showcased his willingness to engage with youth culture. Furthermore, the prime minister launched the Fit India movement that underscored his recognition of the vitality of youth and his commitment to promoting a healthy lifestyle among them. As India transitioned into a digital era, PM Modi's embrace of technology resonated with a generation born with smartphones in their hands, positioning him as a leader who not only understood their needs but also empowered them to shape their futures. The prime minister's online persona serves as a captivating case study in digital leadership, drawing young Indians towards him while striving to translate this online engagement into tangible improvements in their lives. However, being equally concerned with the dangers of social media for the youth, PM Modi uses his social media appeal and following to warn the youth about the dangers posed by online tools such as deep fakes that represent the dark side of the social media revolution. The BJP drive at the grassroots to encourage the youth to vote in large numbers has largely been replicated by many parties, including the Congress, which launched a membership drive for young people to come and join the Congress party and engage with its programmes. This has allowed for a change in the mindset that politics needs to be based on the representation of youth and women and not the preserve of old men. PM Modi has emerged as a brand ambassador by connecting with the youth directly rather than farming out to his party. This is a significant shift from how the country's political class has worked in the past.

As all the initiatives taken by his government reveal, PM Modi has spearheaded a transformative agenda for the upliftment and empowerment of women and youth in India, marking a significant departure from the approaches of his predecessors. Moreover, the prime minister's engagement with women and youth extends beyond the rhetoric, as evidenced by his proactive use of social media and interactive platforms to solicit feedback and address the concerns of these groups directly. By leveraging technology, engaging with influencers and championing legislative reforms, PM Modi has moved beyond tokenism and rhetoric, the hallmark of Indian politics for many decades.

Kartikeya Sharma is Member of Parliament, Rajya Sabha.

NOTES

1. Artokong Longkumer, *The Great Indian Experiment: Hindutva and the Northeast,* Stanford University Press, 2020, p. 221.
2. Ibid., Chapter 6.
3. Narendra Modi, 'Progress of Women Gives Strength to Empowerment of the Nation', NarendraModi.in, 8 March 2022, https://www.narendramodi.in/text-of-pm-s-address-at-a-seminar-on-international-women-s-day-in-kutch-560541.
4. Longkumer, *The Great Indian Experiment,* pp. 196–7.
5. Ibid.
6. Vinay Sitapati, interview with Priya Sahgal on ideas, 24–25 August 2023.
7. Speech given in Parliament, translated from the Hindi by the author.

India's Transformation from 2014 to 2024

PENNY STREET

My earliest memory of India was when my Qantas flight from Sydney to London landed in Bombay in the early 1970s. It was a steamy, hot evening and I remember a crowded transit lounge with very few seats, a pitted concrete floor, punkahs going flat out and a Pepsi vending machine that didn't work. The several hours spent in transit due to various delays was not a particularly auspicious start to what would turn into a lifelong love affair with the great subcontinent.

It was many years later that I returned with my husband to attend a legal conference in Bombay, which by then had come to be called Mumbai. My work with museums in Australia and other parts of Asia had drawn me into the wonderful Prince of Wales Museum, a short walk from my hotel. The scale of this museum's collections and the range of exhibits and galleries meant that I spent two full days wandering through this treasure trove of artefacts, antiquities and paintings. I was hooked.

Established in Sydney in 1988, my company Narrowcasters provides multilingual audio guide services to museums and visited sites. We are storytellers, and we tell the story of a site in many different languages. By the time we arrived in India, Narrowcasters already had operations in New Zealand, Singapore and Malaysia as well as sites in Thailand, Laos and other parts of Southeast Asia. India became a natural extension of my business, and in 2001 we established Narrowcasters India with our office in Delhi.

The Prince of Wales Museum, now called the Chhatrapati Shivaji Maharaj Vastu Sangrahalaya, became our first site in India. From the very beginning, what set this market apart from every other Narrowcasters market was the depth and strength of its culture and the strong national pride in its heritage. I was, however, surprised at the relatively low domestic tourist numbers compared to foreign tourists, but this gradually started to change. Over the last ten years, following the rise of India's middle class, I have seen a significant increase in domestic tourism.

In 2002, we launched Narrowcasters's second site in India, at the magnificent medieval Mehrangarh Fort in Jodhpur. This experience gave me an appreciation for the sheer number of World Heritage Sites in India and the massive challenge faced by the government in conserving and maintaining them. India's ancient temples and exquisitely carved monuments made for a UNESCO Shangri-La that few countries, if any, can match.

One of the novel ways that the Indian government has maintained heritage sites has been to introduce the Adopt a Heritage programme. This initiative encourages public–private partnerships for the development and maintenance of heritage sites. In addition, the Clean India campaign has been successful in improving sanitation and cleanliness around tourist attractions, thus enhancing visitors' experience. Another imaginative way that the government is encouraging tourism in rural areas is by introducing homestay programmes. This, along with other rural tourism projects such as Airbnbs and artisanal workshops, offers travellers unique and authentic experiences while at the same time supporting local livelihoods. Involving communities in tourism activities provides a greater sense of ownership and stewardship towards the preservation of cultural heritage.

The Incredible India! campaign, launched first in 2002, was given further momentum after 2014. The campaign aimed to promote India as a vibrant tourist destination globally, highlighting its diverse cultural, historical and natural attractions. From around 2014 onwards, India's Department of Tourism introduced the Swadesh Darshan and the Prasad schemes. They targeted the tourist infrastructure, particularly around pilgrimage sites, and enhanced the visitor experience in various ways, including introducing theme-based tourist circuits.

Over the years my marketing activities around India have left me with a rich tapestry of wonderful memories that will never be forgotten. I've ridden camels in the Thar Desert and negotiated with a large and curious tortoise that wandered into my hotel room and took a most proprietorial approach to my suitcase; I've battled to send an urgent text message from my old Nokia while riding in an unsprung taxi over bumpy back roads near Hampi, not to forget the many fruitless attempts to find internet in rural districts back in the early 2000s—all these and many other events will remain etched in my memories forever.

One of the striking features of travelling around India is the warmth of the hospitality allied with a great sense of fun. This tends to defuse tensions experienced by foreign tourists who arrived with a whole set of expectations. As has often been noted by many people throughout the ages, the main game in India is not the destination. It is the journey itself. Finding the unexpected lies around every corner in India, and as a traveller it is what gives India its charm, challenges, allure and—it must be said—its fair share of frustrations.

Another initiative which, as a regular traveller to India, I very much appreciate has been the introduction of e-visa facilities and simplified visa regulations which has made it easier for international travellers to visit India.

In addition to mainstream tourism, there has been a focus on promoting niche tourism segments, of which India has an abundance. These include adventure tourism, wildlife tourism, eco-tourism, wellness tourism, rural tourism and tourism for those seeking spiritual enlightenment. This diversification has attracted a broader spectrum of tourists with varied interests from all corners of the globe.

More recently, India's medical tourism has emerged. India has become a preferred destination for medical treatments and procedures due to its world-class healthcare infrastructure, skilled medical professionals and cost-effective services. Medical tourists come to India for treatments ranging from cosmetic surgery and organ transplants to cardiac care and alternative therapies.

Culinary tourism and film tourism are emerging as other strong areas of growth. India's cuisine is famously diverse and the spices that are an integral part of it have been in demand for centuries. Culinary tourism involves exploring local food markets, participating in cooking classes and indulging in regional delicacies like dosa, biryani and kebabs across different states and cities.

Bollywood's vibrant film industry attracts film enthusiasts from around the world. Fans can visit film studios, attend movie screenings and explore filming locations in cities like Mumbai, Kolkata and Chennai, broadening the base of world cinema and its cultural impact.

Another area which has a significant impact on tourism in India is sports. Indian Premier League (IPL) cricket matches draw huge crowds not only from within the hosting cities but also from across the country and even internationally. Cricket fans flock to the host cities to witness their favourite teams and players in action, leading to a surge in tourism during the IPL season.

Big matches regularly give a huge boost to tourism revenue. Additionally, the IPL has contributed to the development of sports tourism in India, with fans travelling specifically to attend matches and explore the culture and attractions of the host cities. Furthermore, the IPL has helped showcase various Indian cities as vibrant destinations with world-class facilities, thereby boosting their tourism profiles. Cities like Mumbai, Chennai, Kolkata, Bengaluru and Hyderabad, which host IPL teams, witness a significant influx of tourists during the tournament.

Overall, the IPL acts as a catalyst for tourism in India, driving economic growth, promoting local businesses, and enhancing the country's image as a premier sports and leisure destination. Although India's appetite for engagement in a range of other sports is still developing, it is surely only a matter of time before India hosts Olympic Games.

With the rise of digital platforms and social media, digital tourism plays a significant role in promoting Indian destinations, sharing travel experiences and facilitating travel planning and bookings. Websites, mobile apps and virtual reality tours offer immersive experiences and personalised recommendations to travellers. Narrowcasters has had decades of experience in providing tourists with great stories through a range of technologies, about whichever site they happen to be visiting. We strongly believe that when visitors take an audio tour they should be careful to recognise the difference between simply receiving basic information and listening to a wonderfully engaging and evocative story, told through oral histories, interviews, music and other production techniques. The two experiences could not be more different.

In recent years, the digital revolution has been a defining feature of India's economic transformation. With a burgeoning start-up ecosystem and increasing internet penetration, technology-driven innovations have disrupted traditional industries and created new growth opportunities.

Initiatives like Digital India have been introduced to bridge the digital divide, promote e-governance and enhance digital infrastructure in rural and urban areas. The rise of fintech companies, e-commerce platforms and digital payment systems has revolutionised the way business is conducted, making transactions more efficient and transparent.

Festivals are historically a big part of Indian life. India has become an essential stop on the global literary festival tour. The expansion of these events now provides platforms for authors, poets, journalists and other literary figures to engage with audiences and discuss various aspects of literature, culture and society.

There are several well-established literary festivals taking place in India, which include the Jaipur Literature Festival,

Kolkata Literary Meet, Bangalore Literature Festival and Tata Literature Live! held in Mumbai, among others. These events attract not only renowned Indian authors but also international literary figures, fostering a diverse and vibrant literary environment.

The growth of these global literary phenomena can be attributed to various factors, including the astonishing growth of India's educated middle class, the rising interest in literature, the desire for intellectual and cultural engagement, and the increasing support from sponsors and the government. Additionally, the accessibility of these festivals through online platforms has also played a role in reaching a broader audience.

India stands as a global hub for spiritual and religious tourism. The country's spiritual landscape is adorned with temples, mosques, churches and other sacred sites, attracting millions of pilgrims from around the world. One of the key aspects of India's spiritual tourism is its deep-rooted connection to ancient traditions and philosophies. The country is the birthplace of major religions such as Hinduism, Buddhism, Jainism and Sikhism. Each of these religions has left an indelible mark on India's landscape, with temples, stupas and gurdwaras dotting the country.

Varanasi, situated on the banks of River Ganges, is one of the oldest continuously inhabited cities in the world and a significant pilgrimage site for the Hindus. The ghats along the Ganges are thronged by devotees seeking spiritual cleansing through ritualistic bathing and prayer. The city is also known for its numerous temples and cultural events, making it a hub for those seeking a deeper understanding of Hindu spirituality.

Similarly, Bodh Gaya in Bihar holds immense importance in Buddhism as the place where Siddhartha Gautama attained enlightenment under the Bodhi tree. Pilgrims from around the world visit the Mahabodhi Temple complex to pay homage to the Buddha and experience the serene ambience that pervades the area.

India's spiritual tourism is not confined to a single religion, as the country is renowned for its religious diversity. Ajmer Sharif in Rajasthan is a revered Sufi shrine attracting devotees of Islam. The annual Urs festival at the shrine is a vibrant celebration of unity and spiritual fervour, drawing people from various faiths. In Amritsar, the Golden Temple, the holiest shrine of the Sikhs, beckons millions of visitors each year. The temple's pristine surroundings and the community kitchen serving free meals to all visitors exemplify the Sikh principles of equality, selfless service and devotion.

Over the last ten years, the government has initiated campaigns to promote religious tourism, showcasing India's spiritual heritage on the global stage. International tourists are increasingly drawn to India's religious diversity, participating in festivals, rituals and cultural events.

Despite the challenges posed by the global pandemic in the early 2020s, the resilience of religious tourism in India remained evident as travel restrictions eased. The renewed interest in spiritual practices and holistic well-being has contributed to the sustained growth of religious tourism, marking the years from 2014 to 2024 as a transformative period for India's sacred destinations.

It has often been said that India possesses more soft power in one small kilometre of its land than most countries in the world combined. And when examining its heritage and culture alone, it's hard to disagree.

Over the years my business has taken me to nearly every corner of India and as is often the case, you see things more clearly than that of a local person. It has, therefore, been something of a mystery to me that many of India's inventions and discoveries—particularly those that emerged from the Indus Valley civilisation thousands of years ago—have not been fully appreciated by other civilisations.

I have often asked myself, why I never learnt that India invented the use of the decimal point in connection with zero in its mathematics. And why we were never taught about its early plumbing and irrigation systems, its astronomy and astrology as well as being familiar with Sanskrit, the oldest written language in the world that is still in use. We were taught so much about the early Greek and Roman civilisations, and rightly so, but almost nothing about other ancient civilisations such as what emerged from the Indus Valley. Indians were early traders, and much of what they traded to other civilisations was passed down through the ages as the innovations of others.

In many Southeast Asian countries there seems to be a reluctance to credit India as being the origin of so much of its own culture. From language, dance, music, textiles, religion and spices, India traded all these things across the rivers, roads and seas to the known world.

Very soon, Narrowcasters hopes to introduce a dazzling Immersive Lumiere show, to right this record. We will be depicting the inventions and discoveries that emerged from India from as far back as the Harappan people who thrived in the Indus Valley region thousands of years ago. So many of these discoveries and inventions that we today, around the world, take for granted.

In 1954, the great Indian academic A.L. Basham published his book *The Wonder That Was India*. It left a lasting impression on me, reinforcing that India is indeed a wonder, and a wonder that, in my view, does not receive the full credit that is its due.

Over the last ten years, India's economic transformation has been characterised by both enormous opportunities and huge challenges. The country experienced robust GDP growth rates, averaging around 7 per cent annually, making it one of the fastest-growing major economies globally. However, the growth has been uneven across sectors and regions, with disparities in income distribution persisting.

Infrastructure gaps remain, many facilities are inadequate, and bureaucratic hurdles continue to hinder the growth of the sector. Balancing tourism development with heritage conservation remains a delicate task, requiring a nuanced approach.

However, if any country in the world can address these issues, it is India. India's can-do approach, her enormous reserves of resourcefulness and creative fertility, not to mention her strong work ethic, make the country unique among the world's developing economies.

The overall karmic spirit, along with cultural treasures and chaotic cities, makes for an irresistible experience for anyone visiting the country. India's magnetism has drawn visitors from around the world for centuries and judging by its annual tourist numbers, they will only continue to increase.

As India continues its journey towards becoming a global cultural tourism hub, there is immense potential for growth and innovation. Embracing sustainable practices, fostering community partnerships and leveraging digital platforms will be key drivers of success. By showcasing its diverse cultural heritage to the world, India can position itself as a premier destination for cultural travellers.

I have every confidence that in the not-too-distant future India will be the dazzling star in the firmament, surpassing all countries in the years ahead.

Penny Street is Founder and Managing Director, Narrowcasters Private Limited, a Sydney-based audio guide company to cultural heritage across South Asia and Australia.

The Decade of Progress for US–India Relations

RAYMOND E. VICKERY, JR

When Prime Minister Narendra Modi took office in 2014, he was the inheritor of progress in US–India relations that had begun in 1991 with the opening of the Indian economy and the fall of the Soviet Union. However, the last ten years have seen the relationship soar to heights only dimly glimpsed at the beginning of the US–India rapprochement and certainly undreamed of at the time of Indian independence.

The flowering of the relationship over the last ten years is a measure both of Modi's diplomatic abilities and the strong bipartisan support for US–India cooperation on both sides. During his tenure, Modi has dealt with three US presidents. Barack Obama was the first US president to visit India twice during his tenure and was the Republic Day chief guest at the invitation of Modi. Donald Trump participated in mass rallies with Modi both in Ahmedabad and Houston. Joe Biden has been all-in on India with a spectacular Modi visit to Washington and a starring bilateral engagement with Modi at the G20 in New Delhi. Democrat or Republican, the US–India relationship has been on an upward trajectory for the past ten years.

With US–India relations now at an all-time high, the question is whether this relationship will grow into an alliance useful in building peace and prosperity throughout the world, or whether it will be focused on narrower interpretations of transactional self-interest. Consideration of this question requires an examination of three pillars of the relationship: (i) values, (ii) economics and (iii) strategic interests.

The issue of values is often dismissed by realpolitik analysts of international relations, but in democracies such as the US and India, where relations are determined by more than the will of an authoritarian, common values affect the will of a nation to cooperate with, or come to the aid of, another. Even though basic democratic values are under pressure both in the US and India, the fact that both countries look to elections, legislatures and courts to decide questions of power inclines both countries to view each other as 'natural partners'. In his 2023 speech to the US Congress, Modi emphasised on India being the 'mother of democracy' and cited the fact that the US and India are democracies 'augers well for the future of democracy'. As an example of values affecting support for the relationship, the influential Indian American community and Modi have looked to commonalities in values in their successful interactions in New York City and Houston during Modi's visits to the US, and the community has had a significant impact on US–India relations.

Values alone are insufficient to account for the upward trend in US–India relations. From Indian Independence until the early 1990s, the US and India were, in the words of the author Dennis Kux, 'estranged democracies'. The countries shared many democratic values but little cooperation. In part, what changed was the movement of India away from the command economy or Licence Raj to the use of markets and opening to international trade and investment.

The progress made in economic engagement, including the related fields of the movement of persons, educational and health cooperation, and cultural interchange, has been significant over the last ten years. As examples, in 2013, US–India trade was about USD 95 billion and cumulative two-way direct investment about USD 38 billion. Recently, trade ministers of both countries estimated the trade in goods and services to have surpassed USD 200 billion in 2023. Two-way investment stock was about USD 80 billion. In other words, over the last ten years, trade and investment between the US and India have about doubled. Although the US–India trade and investment figures are dwarfed by US–China trade and investment numbers, this is changing, with the US apparently overtaking China as India's number one trade partner in 2023.

Common concerns about China have had the most visible effect in furthering the US–India strategic relationship. India and the US are increasingly alarmed by expansionist moves by China in the South China Sea, the Indian Ocean and along the Indian border and have acted accordingly to strengthen their defence ties. Naval exercises have been enlarged and deepened, with Exercise Malabar focusing particularly on the Strait of Malacca, a chokepoint entrance to the Indian Ocean from the Pacific, and Exercise Sea Dragon focusing on joint anti-submarine warfare. On land, high-altitude military exercises are obviously pointed towards the India–China Himalayan border, where China claims an entire Indian state as well as other areas. India now conducts more military exercises and personnel exchanges with the US than any other country.

Less and less is heard from India about 'strategic autonomy' and 'non-alignment' when it comes to China. The question is what commitments make India safer and more secure. The Quadrilateral, composed of the US, India, Japan and Australia, is not a formal defence alliance. Nevertheless, the commitments made by these four countries have seen the Quad grow over the past decade from a mere discussion forum to include programmes that are an obvious counterweight to China.

Defence trade and technology transfer between the US and India have increased markedly as India moves away from an overdependence on Russia. In 2013, Russia accounted for about 75 per cent of arms imports and the US only 7 per cent. For the 2018–22 period, reliance on Russia had dropped to 45 per cent and the US share increased to 11 per cent, displaced as India's second-largest arms supplier only by US NATO partner France, which had a 29 per cent market share due to the outsized influence of the Rafale fighter jet deal. More importantly, the US and India have agreed to an unprecedented proposal to jointly produce in India the General Electric F414 jet engine and launched a Defense Acceleration Ecosystem (INDUS-X) to expand and accelerate defence technology transfer and defence industrial cooperation.

Most remarkable of all strategic progress over the past ten years is the recent Indian deployment to the Red Sea, in cooperation with the US and other naval powers, of guided missile destroyers and reconnaissance aircraft. This Indian naval force is already credited with helping three ships attacked by Houthi rebels and a fourth that was endangered by an attack that the US blamed on Iran. This cooperative action shows progress in moving from defence preparation to actual cooperative action to promote stability and freedom of the seas.

Thus, US–India relations have progressed markedly across the board over the past ten years. This past decade has set the stage for an even stronger partnership in the future. However, this will occur only if both countries have views of their national self-interests as including the US–India actions that build peace, prosperity and freedom throughout the world. The US and India have come a long way from viewing their national interests as only including what happens within or in protection of their borders. Underlying the progress in US–India relations have been commitments to common democratic values. This extraordinary progress will continue as long as the US and India remain committed to their expansive views of national interests and democratic values.

Raymond E. Vickery, Jr is Senior Associate, Center for Strategic and International Studies; Senior Advisor, Albright Stonebridge Group; and former US Assistant Secretary of Commerce, Trade Development.

Modi—Taking the BJP from Strength to Strength

PANKAJ VOHRA

On the eve of the 2024 parliamentary polls, one can categorically state that the ascendancy of the Bharatiya Janata Party (BJP), particularly in the last ten years, has been phenomenal. This is solely because it is driven by Prime Minister Narendra Modi, who has emerged as not only a cult figure but a strong leader with a massive following of his own.

The BJP's unprecedented performance under Modi is unique, especially because its seats have come mostly from north India, and one can only imagine what would happen if the party is able to make deep inroads into the south, where, barring Karnataka, it is yet to make its mark.

Modi has propelled the BJP into a fighting force so robust and powerful, both organisationally and financially, that it is, in the electoral arena, virtually unbeatable. The rise of the BJP coincides with the decline of the Congress, which is truly the only pan-India party but has lost its way in the past decade, primarily because of weak leadership and the inability of its high command to recognise ground-level realities.

Modi is to the BJP what Indira Gandhi was to the Congress. Interestingly, the current prime minister has made digs at many of his predecessors, but seldom criticised Indira Gandhi, perhaps realising that despite being gone for almost forty years, she continues to be a popular figure for a large number of Indians.

If one has to delve into the history of the BJP since its Jana Sangh days, it is evident that the saffron brigade has come a long way. Therefore, to understand Modi and his contribution to the growth story of the BJP, it is important to visit the past. When the party was founded by Shyama Prasad Mukherjee and Balraj Madhok, it had a clear objective. It was the party that wanted to protect Hindus while simultaneously spreading its ideology amongst the masses. Mukherjee passed away prematurely, and Madhok encountered multiple difficulties during his tenure leading the Jana Sangh, where he served as its primary ideologue.

Atal Bihari Vajpayee, who later became the prime minister, was drafted into the party to assist Mukherjee, as Mukherjee's command over the Hindi language was not very strong and he needed a sharp interpreter to effectively convey his message to the people, especially in the north Indian states. The Jana Sangh had to struggle hard, and Vajpayee—despite being in the Opposition—was identified by the then prime minister, Jawaharlal Nehru, as a promising young man. He eventually became one of the better-known faces of the party since he would actively participate in the parliamentary debates.

Vajpayee had a Nehru fixation, one that lasted till his very end and which many of his colleagues did not approve of. Madhok, in particular, was a strong critic of Nehru, and the story that was often discussed in the Central Hall was regarding the frequent disagreements between Vajpayee and Madhok. In 1961, when

Madhok won the by-election from New Delhi—necessitated by the elevation of the sitting MP, Sucheta Kriplani, to the post of the chief minister of Uttar Pradesh—he made some disparaging remarks about Nehru. Vajpayee confronted him in Central Hall, but Madhok held his ground regarding his opinion and language. When Vajpayee had departed from the scene, Acharya Kriplani, who was also a staunch critic of Nehru, branded Vajpayee as the prime minister's sycophant.

The Jana Sangh had started deepening its roots in several parts of the country. Delhi became its nucleus, as its population included a large number of refugees from Punjab, who had been rendered homeless due to the Partition. These refugees could never agree to endorse the Congress as they held the party's leaders responsible for their plight. Not only had they been displaced, many of them had lost family members in the Hindu–Muslim riots that broke out.

In Delhi, Vijay Kumar Malhotra, now in his nineties and perhaps the senior-most member of the Sangh Parivar in terms of electoral politics, contested and won in the municipal polls. The Jana Sangh became the rallying point of the refugees, and to begin with, it had elements from both the Hindu Mahasabha and the Rashtriya Swayamsevak Sangh (RSS).

It is significant to note that the Jana Sangh was headed by luminaries such as Moily Chander Sharma, Vasantrao Oak and others, and not all of them agreed with Vajpayee's views on Nehru. Many of them even left for this reason.

Madhok stood strongly by his ideological beliefs and in 1967, the Jana Sangh, under his overall command, won six out of seven Lok Sabha seats from Delhi. It did exceedingly well in some other places too, such as Rajasthan and Madhya Pradesh. And with

Deen Dayal Upadhyaya taking over the reins, it appeared that the party was heading towards a bright future. In February 1968, Upadhyaya died under mysterious circumstances, and Vajpayee and Nanaji Deshmukh asked Madhok to resign from the party to make way for a brahmin from north India.

Madhok declined to quit, and after a spat with the two leaders, he accused them of being involved in the plot to kill Upadhyaya. However, this did not stop Vajpayee from taking over. With this started the Vajpayee era.

It is important to point out that in the first fifteen years of its existence, the Jana Sangh had ten presidents. In the next thirty years, including the period after the BJP was founded in 1980, the party had only two—Vajpayee and Lal Krishan Advani. With the sole exception of Murali Manohar Joshi, who was inspired by M.S. Golwalkar and Deen Dayal Upadhyaya, there were their acolytes who held the august office.

This is where Modi should be brought back into the context. He was also a die-hard RSS volunteer, and for him, the objective was to take his party ahead without trying to emulate any other national leader. Modi was a small-time activist when Vajpayee and Advani were at their peak, but for him, the inspiration came from the Sangh and not from any of the Congress leaders. Vajpayee saw in himself a replica of Pandit Nehru, while for Advani, Sardar Patel was his ideal. Both, despite being in the RSS in their early years, were not as committed to the ideology, and often deviated from the basic principles to suit their political march ahead.

Formed in 1980, the BJP had a difficult path ahead. It had to leave the Janata Party after the Socialists raised the dual membership issue, and in the 1980 elections, which Vajpayee won with a slender margin from New Delhi, the RSS had backed the Congress. The BJP lost Delhi, its stronghold, to the Congress in the February 1983 local polls, and in 1984, following the ghastly assassination of Indira Gandhi by her two security guards, the RSS stood behind the grand old party. The Congress won over 400 seats in 1984, a feat accomplished because it was a tribute of the nation to an assassinated prime minister. The BJP ended up winning only two seats, Ashok Patel from Mehsana in Gujarat and Janga Reddy from undivided Andhra Pradesh.

Vajpayee had failed to take the BJP forward and when Advani took command, he set certain goals that were consistent with the core issues connected with Hindutva politics. The BJP started carving out its own identity, different from what the Jana Sangh had been, though most of the characters in the game were the same.

The Bofors scandal helped the party to use the organisation network to dent the image of the Congress and of the then prime minister Rajiv Gandhi. The exits of Vishwanath Pratap Singh, Arif Mohammad Khan and Arun Nehru from Congress assisted in changing the narrative, and the Opposition unity seemed possible, with the top-ranking leaders reaching an agreement on friendly fights and a common front, to take on Congress.

The 1989 Lok Sabha elections saw the end of the Rajiv Gandhi dispensation and, in the next one and a half years, first under Advani and then Joshi, the BJP consolidated its position. The declaration of the implementation of the Mandal Commission affected the unity of the Opposition and the BJP pulled the plug, which led to the fall of the V.P. Singh government. The Chandra Shekhar regime was short-lived, and the BJP queered its religious pitch to emerge with impressive figures in 1991.

Shortly before he handed over the reins of the party at the Jaipur Plenary session, Advani made a pitch for the presidential form of government, a matter that was overshadowed by the Gulf War and the introduction of satellite television on an international scale. As this scenario was unfolding, Modi was watching from close quarters and, in all probability, assimilating varied things of which Advani had been a proponent. At that point, it appeared that Advani, among the second-ranking leaders, was promoting Pramod Mahajan, who had accompanied him on his Rath Yatra from Somnath to Ayodhya. The Ram Mandir issue, brought into prominence primarily to neutralise the effects of the Mandal Commission, had become the BJP's war cry.

Joshi's presidency brought out differences of approach between his predecessors and him, and due to his proximity to the RSS and its ideology, the Sangh encouraged him to take out the Ekta Yatra from Kanyakumari to Kashmir to highlight national unity.

For Modi, this was the biggest opportunity to be known nationally. As the companion to the BJP president, he was able to spread his network. He had a distinct advantage; he learnt the tricks from the trade simultaneously from Joshi and Advani. Modi had a ringside view of power politics, and he seems to have extended the lessons he learnt then to the last ten years as India's PM.

Modi was inspired by Advani largely because of the calculated and systematic manner in which he had been positioning himself, while transforming the BJP into a national force. As against the politics of Vajpayee, which positioned him as a moderate, Advani had created a hawkish and hardliner image, which suited Modi.

Looking back at the ten years of Modi, he seemed to have imbibed in his personality more of the early Advani than any other BJP leader. Advani was image-conscious and had requisitioned the services of top journalists and intellectuals to show him the way. He was inspired by Ayn Rand's *Fountainhead* and based his image makeover on some of the elements of this tome of a book.

From Advani, Modi also acquired the advantages of projecting himself as a politician who had time for every other task despite being actively involved in politics. Advani had made it a point to visit cinema halls to watch films, to exhibit himself as an ordinary human being. Similarly, Modi found a mechanism of his own to project himself to the people.

Somewhere in his subconscious, Modi was looking for a bigger canvas and he knew that to get there he needed to be seen as a strong and decisive leader. Like every politician, he planned his next moves keeping in mind his ultimate objective while concurrently working on his image and tactics. When Jana Krishnamoorthy was the BJP president, Modi approached him to replace Keshubhai Patel as the chief minister since Patel was unable to consolidate the BJP's position. Having worked all his life in the organisation, Modi was well conversant with its ways and methods, and he used his skills to further his ambitions.

At that point of time, Narendra Modi and Uma Bharti were the only two leaders of the post-Vajpayee and Advani generation with mass appeal. Bharti didn't make it due to internal politics and was out of reckoning, leaving Modi as the sole charismatic younger leader.

Some other events occurred and it would be significant to recall how the late Pramod Mahajan had viewed the future scenario. In 2006, Mahajan was asked in the presence of Sudhanshu Mittal, his close associate, whether he would be a contender for prime ministership in 2009 since the BJP had lost power in 2004.

Mahajan had this uncanny ability to foresee the future, and he didn't hesitate to say that in 2009, Advani would be the face of the BJP. However, he hastened to add that in 2014, he would certainly be in the fray, and his competition for BJP's nomination would be with Modi. However, destiny willed otherwise, and Mahajan was shot dead by his younger brother.

Thus, Modi remained the singular and sole aspirant. What worked for him was that Advani fell out of favour with the RSS following his visit to Jinnah's mausoleum in 2005, and his attempts to transform his image from a hawk to a dove boomeranged. Therefore, Modi emerged as the sole hardliner and a right-wing hawk, whose acceptability for his pursuance of Hindutva politics had expanded beyond that of any other leader prior to him from the BJP and the Sangh Parivar.

Being an organisation man, Modi had to reckon with some difficult choices. There were two doctrines propounded by two different RSS chiefs. One was to transform society in order to gain power and the other was to grab power and use it as an instrument to transform society. Modi used both these approaches to his advantage and, in no time, became the favourite of the Sangh followers.

When Modi arrived on the national political scene, he had successfully conducted many experiments to make the BJP into an invincible force. He was a leader who was admired by the party activists and, after being made the BJP's face for prime ministership in 2014, he had galvanised his supporters in a manner never witnessed before.

Modi effectively used the media, thanks to Arun Jaitley, and leveraged the thriving social media landscape to create a narrative and debunk the Congress. If during the peak of Vajpayee and Advani's popularity, the BJP struggled to cross the 182 mark, it was under Modi's leadership for the first time that the saffron brigade secured a majority on its own.

The BJP as a party became all the more formidable, and Modi ensured that it underwent an image makeover, thus putting an end to the chapter that had Vajpayee, Advani and Joshi in its discourse. The new-look BJP was Modi's creation, and he its mascot. New faces and newcomers with exceptional organisational ability came to the forefront, and the earlier dispensation in the party was replaced by Amit Shah and a handful of Modi's most trusted men and women. It spelt the end of the Advani-era politicians.

However, what needs to be underscored here is that while the BJP expanded both its base and influence nationally, its fortunes got hinged to those of Modi. The prime minister transformed the BJP's campaigns to those of presidential types where he was always the central figure.

The noticeable change was that while the BJP's supporters and vote bank stood with the party and voted for its candidates, the entire effort was supplemented by Modi's own following, which added at least 10 per cent more votes to that of his organisation. In other words, Modi became a cult figure, and his ability to change the narrative (or control it) was more pronounced than that of his party, which was glad to play the second fiddle.

It may be supreme irony, but for Modi's followers, as they are referred to by the media, he is the BJP and the BJP is Modi, reminiscent of the era when 'India is Indira and Indira is India' was the dominant theme. Many political analysts wonder how the RSS has come to terms with this transformation, since the credo for the Sangh has always been 'country first, the organisation next, and the individual last'.

The long-term implications for the BJP and the Sangh would only be known in the post-Modi scenario. But as things stand today, the strong BJP organisation, which serves the prime minister for his political objectives, has his brand embossed all over.

Modi is an exceptionally perceptive and astute politician and strategist and does nothing that is off the course. He has his hand on the pulse of the people, and his schemes and programmes are designed to rake in political dividends. The BJP is completely dependent on him, and his personality has an overwhelming presence, so far as national politics goes. The BJP is the nucleus around which the political narrative revolves, and like it was once the Congress vs the rest, it is now the BJP vs the rest, with the rest being reduced to very small players.

This is an era of Narendra Modi, totally dominated and controlled by him. The BJP and Sangh are among his multiple instruments. As a politician, he is sharp and ruthless, and as the prime minister, he knows how to control or reset the agenda. He is a towering political figure around whom his party revolves. Modi has carved out his name in history and by ensuring that the Ram Temple was built during his tenure, he has become synonymous with the sentiments of the common Hindus. He has also been able to fulfil other promises in the BJP manifesto, like the abrogation of Article 370, and could, perhaps, bring in a Uniform Civil Code if he gets his third term, which at present appears certain.

To sum it up, Modi's distinctiveness is the outcome of his keen observance of the emerging political situations, which contributed to his evolution as a shrewd and perceptive leader. His campaign style is presidential, and he possibly worked on it in his subconscious when Advani had made a pitch for the presidential form of government. In the democratic set-up, which is based on the Westminster model, Modi has been able to introduce an element of the presidential form, in a government where he is the head, as the prime minister.

His strength lies in the fact that, unlike Vajpayee and Advani, he did not have any Congress leaders as his role models and thus has etched out his own place amongst the top leaders from the Sangh stable. His political nurturing took place purely in the Sangh nursery, and since he was never a member of parliament, he did not carry any baggage that could prove to be an obstacle. Vajpayee and Advani knew many political leaders, cutting across party lines, and on several occasions, their judgement would be influenced and swayed by their personal rapport and relations. Modi did not have to abide by any niceties and was absolutely focused on the party and his personal agenda. Therefore, he was able to achieve much more, taking the party's tally to unprecedented heights. For his followers, Modi is a living legend.

While his status as the big star politician at this juncture is indisputable, what needs to be seen is how he shall be remembered in history. For the BJP, the post-Modi scenario could be uncertain since the party, as well as the Sangh, is at present totally dependent on his charisma, to carry it past the finish line. What needs to be clearly understood is that for an organisation to move forward, there has to be some inherent resilience and strength, which shall be tested on the scale of time. Only the future will tell.

Pankaj Vohra is a senior journalist and columnist with *The Sunday Guardian*.

India Under Transformation

TAGUCHI YOJI

My first assignment to India was from 2007 to 2012, when I was posted in Coimbatore to set up a new company that provides electric discharge machines to die and mould industries in India. During this time, I was given the opportunity to understand many differences between India and the other countries and be taught by many Indians about the uniqueness of Indian business and various aspects of similarity with Japanese culture as well. In 2019, I got my second opportunity to be stationed in India as chairman and managing director of Mitsubishi Corporation India. I would like to share some of my observations on how India has transformed based on my eleven years of working here.

When I first started working in India in 2007, I realised that there were several operational and business challenges, including the quality of physical infrastructure as well as complex regulations and procedures. In the 2000s, given the double-digit speed of China's GDP growth rate at that time and considering the demographic scale of the Indian market, a rapid development of India on similar lines with other Asian economies was expected. But the pace of growth and expansion of the market was slow. This was partially due to slow progress in the tough internal and external reforms that were needed to realise the full potential of the market.

When I returned to India on my second assignment in 2019, I felt that India had come a long way. Today, I see a significant improvement in the overall business environment, especially in the last ten years. The strong determination and sense of urgency shown through Prime Minister Narendra Modi's leadership to develop, reform and move India forward towards a new globally competitive economy is one of the big changes I notice.

FOCUS ON PHYSICAL AND DIGITAL INFRASTRUCTURE

India is a large country with a complex federal structure. Back in the days, one of the first challenges for a foreign manufacturer entering India was setting up a logistics and supply chain network within the federal regulations and complex tax structures. In addition to this, there were issues of planning for uncertainties in delivery times, high transportation costs and interfacing with local authorities. A significant amount of time had to be spent on resolving these issues rather than focusing on the business. These challenges increased even more if the operations involved importing or exporting.

However, there has been a remarkable improvement in the decade. The upgraded and new national highways, implementation of the goods and services tax (GST) system and the digitalisation of procedures have brought in change and eased many of the challenges mentioned above. By increasing the capital expenditure as a percentage of annual national budget from 12 per cent in 2013 to 24 per cent in 2024,[1] Modi's government has given high priority to the much-needed infrastructure development, especially in terms of improving nationwide connectivity.

The impact of widening of highways and the addition of over 50,000 km of new highways in last decade[2] can be very much felt on the ground. Now I am able to reduce my business travel time by almost half. For instance, New Delhi to Neemrana in Rajasthan, which used to take me 4–5 hours previously can now can be covered in 2.5 hours. Moreover, with the doubling of airports and improved airport facilities, air travel across India has now become much more convenient and smoother. These are important considerations for foreign investors while doing business in India.

The new taxation system of GST introduced in 2017 has also helped significantly reduce the logistical challenges including compliances, transportation time and costs, and cross-state distribution hurdles. The digitisation of tax and customs compliances is also improving operational efficiencies. This progress is evident in India's World Bank Logistic Performance Index, which has improved from the forty-fourth place in 2018 to the thirty-eighth place in 2023.

Quality and cost competitiveness in logistics are important metrics for foreign investors, and I feel there is still scope for improvement. This is critical especially if India wants to attract foreign companies to move their supply chains, and for Indian exports to compete globally. I am encouraged to see that the government continues to accelerate investment in related infrastructure. Introduction of new initiatives like the 2021 National Master Plan for Multi-modal Connectivity and the National Logistics Policy 2022 targeting to reduce logistics costs by half and improve performance to match the global standards show the high priority given to this improvement area by the current government. Foreign investors such as myself are eagerly hoping to see the implementation of these new measures and the progress towards achieving the intended targets.

IMPROVEMENTS IN INVESTMENT ENVIRONMENT

Despite the huge market potential of India, ease of doing business here has been the common concern among foreign investors. However, in the last decade, proactive and continuous efforts by the government in enhancing industrial infrastructure, as well as simplification and digitalisation of operating procedures, is gradually but surely improving the ease of doing business in India. This is also showing up on the World Bank's Ease of Doing Business ranking, which, for India, has moved from the 142nd place in 2014 to sixty-third place in 2022. Although this ranking was discontinued by the World Bank in 2022, I believe India would be ranked around the fortieth position now, considering factors such as reduction in the corporate tax rate, easing of tax compliance, and reforms in the credit and power sectors.

The bad loans crisis in the non-banking financial sector and its impact used to be a concern for us. But, with the introduction of banking sector reforms in 2016, non-performing loans of banks were reduced from around 11 per cent in 2017 to 3 per cent in 2023, and I am relieved to see the Indian banking system getting healthier. On the external front, doubling the foreign exchange reserves from USD 300 billion in 2014 to USD 600 billion is a notable indicator of good performance under Modi's administration.

These measures and a stable pro-business political regime have resulted not only in increased foreign direct investment (FDI) flow into India, but it is also helping the Indian economy to shift from a medium growth rate to becoming one of the fastest-growing economies in the world, with a remarkable rise from the eleventh position to becoming the world's fifth largest economy in just a decade. The increasing global interest in India and investor confidence in Modi's government is also translating into attracting foreign capital flows into the stock market. The market capitalisation reached USD 4 trillion in December 2023, making it the fourth largest in the world after the US, China and Japan. Annual FDI inflows into India have also seen continuous increase and almost doubled from USD 36 billion in 2013-14 to USD 71 billion in 2022-23.[3]

Investment from Japan has also increased from ¥ 282 billion in 2014 to ¥ 641 in 2022, and the number of Japanese establishments across India have gone up from 2,503 in 2013 to 4,091 in 2022.[4] According to the Japan Bank of International Cooperation (JBIC) survey of Japanese manufacturing enterprises conducted in 2023, the proportion of Japanese companies with business plans in India has jumped from around 35 per cent in 2021 to 45.8 per cent in 2023. This same survey also found that India was the most promising country for overseas business for Japanese firms, followed by Vietnam and China.[5]

While the strength of Japanese companies is in high-end manufacturing, the Indian manufacturing sector has not evolved much and so far we have not been able to fully bring our manufacturing expertise and high-end technology to India. However, with the Production Linked Incentive (PLI) scheme launched in 2020, as part of the 'Make in India' initiative, we are finally seeing some shift, and it has kickstarted growth in industrial manufacturing sector of India.

We are already seeing the initial success in the electronics manufacturing sector, which has grown at a rapid pace. With Apple's iPhone production in India increasing from USD 2.2 billion in 2021-22 to USD 12 billion in 2023-24,[6] electronics exports are the now the fastest-growing among India's major export commodities and the fifth-largest export commodity. This was unimaginable to us even five years ago. Though it would take some time to see the full effects of the PLI scheme across all sectors, this success in developing local smartphone supply chains will provide a model and inspiration for development in other areas of high-tech manufacturing from precision components to semiconductors.

The Indian government has well realised that successfully emerging as a global manufacturing hub is critical to achieving India's economic growth targets and strategic strength in geopolitics. It is, thus, acting at a speed and urgency not usual for India in the past. The time taken from policymaking to implementation on the ground has also dramatically shortened. We can see this in the speed with which new-generation businesses like green hydrogen, electric mobility and semiconductors were conceived and the investment materialised.

This proactive drive under Modi's political leadership is catching the attention of foreign investors, and we are already seeing several leading companies from across the world actively considering how to make India a global manufacturing hub. For Japanese companies whose main strength lies in manufacturing, I believe that these sectors as new growth avenues would bring large investment opportunities for us.

RISING GLOBAL STATUS AND CONFIDENCE

In the last decade, there has been a major transformation in India's approach to engaging with the wider world. We are seeing the emergence of an India that is more assertive and self-confident on the global stage, positioning itself with an independent global identity. The highly successful G20 presidency, emergence as the leading voice of the Global South and the achievements of the Chandrayan-3 lunar mission has further boosted this status. India is also blessed with plenty of outstanding and thoughtful leaders, such as the G20 Sherpa Amitabh Kant, B20 Chair Chandrasekaran and CII Chair Dinesh, who are playing a critical role in the advancing of a new global India.

This evolving geopolitics is also providing tailwinds for India's growth. Prime Minister Modi is engaging in extensive economic diplomacy while aligning foreign policy with the economic interests of India. India has rightly started leveraging its geopolitical status and strong bilateral partnerships to attract global supply chains to expand into India and help strengthen domestic high-end manufacturing capabilities.

The US–India iCET (Initiative on Critical and Emerging Technology) partnership, signed in May 2022 to expand bilateral strategic technology partnership, is a good example. Similarly, in July 2023, India and Japan signed a semiconductor supply chain partnership to cooperate on opportunities in the semiconductor supply chain and leverage complementary strengths. With these developments, I am eagerly anticipating the growth of the high-tech manufacturing sector in India.

While India could build world-class expertise in software, it also has a unique edge in agile development and frugal innovation as proven in the capabilities to mass manufacture affordable vaccines, building highly effective public digital infrastructure, and more. These combined strengths of India are now expanding into areas such as green energy, space technologies, AI and biopharma and becoming globally influential.

This rise of India as an important power on the global stage is also reflecting on the business community in India. These days I notice a sense of confidence and eagerness among the leadership of not only large conglomerates but also mid-size companies to open up to global markets and take on the challenge of innovating and expanding into emerging technology-intensive sectors.

The sign of a changing India is even evident in the youth and in vibrant entrepreneurship. India now boasts of one of the largest start-up ecosystems in the world and ranks as the fourth-most popular destination for global venture capital, with the third-largest number of unicorns in the world. This achievement is largely attributed to the proactive encouragement and support provided to the start-up community by the Modi government in terms of funding and incubation. As a result, we can see the youth of India increasingly contributing to and driving the innovation economy. Particularly in new and emerging business segments such as space technology, AI and clean technologies, I believe that the entrepreneurial spirit of young Indians will lead India's emergence in these fields.

AREAS FOR FURTHER IMPROVEMENT

Doing business in India is becoming steadily easier, and the investment environment is improving. However, to fully harness India's large and growing economic market potential, there are still some challenges that need action to improve the perceptions of global investors.

One of this is the efficiency of legal system. Though India has a mature and independent judicial system, the inefficiencies in the functioning of courts and the resulting delays have long been a concern for foreign investors. No significant improvements in this regard have been observed so far. The Supreme Court is functional, but there are many hardships to get there. There are some cases in which my company has also been struggling for decades to get a resolution. This is unimaginable in Japan. I hope that these challenges will be addressed and improved by the government in the coming years.

The world has surely started moving towards India, and many rightly believe that the next decade will be India's decade. I pray for India's further development and wish success for its emergence as the leading economic power in the coming decade, progressively moving towards a new and modern India as per the vision for 2047 set by PM Modi.

Taguchi Yoji is Chairman and Managing Director of Mitsubishi Corporation.

NOTES

1. IndiaBudget.gov.in, *Expenditure Budget Vol. I, 2014–2015*, Part I: General, https://www.indiabudget.gov.in/budget2014-2015/ub2014-15/eb/stat01.pdf.
2. Ministry of Road Transport and Highways, Government of India, *Year End Review 2023*, https://pib.gov.in/PressReleaseIframePage.aspx?PRID=1993425.
3. Japanese Bank for International Cooperation, FY2023 *JBIC Survey (35th) Report on Overseas Business Operations by Japanese*

Manufacturing Companies, Press Release, https://www.jbic.go.jp/en/information/press/press-2023/press_00148.html.
4. Embassy of Japan to India, *Japanese Business Establishments in India, 2022*, Press Release, https://www.in.emb-japan.go.jp/files/100353089.pdf.
5. Shomik Sen Bhattacharjee, 'Apple Plans Ambitious iPhone Production Ramp Up In India, Targets $12B Value by 2023–24', Yahoo Finance, https://finance.yahoo.com/news/apple-plans-ambitious-iphone-production-082108791.html.
6. Ministry of Commerce and Industry, Department of Commerce, 'Quick Estimates for Selected Major Commodities for December 2023', https://commerce.gov.in/wp-content/uploads/2024/01/Quick-Estimates-December-2023.pdf.

www.ingramcontent.com/pod-product-compliance
Lightning Source LLC
LaVergne TN
LVHW020430070526
838199LV00025B/590/J